AF231679

The Length of the Shackles

Denis Collin

THE LENGTH OF THE SHACKLES
On Freedom in the 21st Century

Max Milo Editions, Paris, 2023
www.maxmilo.com
ISBN : 978-2-31501-150-6

Introduction

The Wolf and the Dog
by Jean de La Fontaine

A Wolf had only bones and skin,
So many Dogs were on guard.
This Wolf meets a Dog as powerful as beautiful,
Bold, polite, who had inadvertently gone astray.
Attack it, quarter it,
Sire Loup would have done it gladly;
But the battle had to be fought,
And the Mastiff was big
To stand up boldly for yourself.
The Wolf therefore approaches it humbly,
Entering the subject, and complimenting him
On his stoutness, which he admires.
"It will be up to you, beautiful Sire,
To be as fat as I am," said the dog.
Leave the woods, you'll do well:
Your kind are miserable there,
Dorks, nerds, and poor devils,
Whose condition is to starve.
For what? Nothing assured; no frank lippage;
Everything at the point of the sword.

Follow me, you will have a much better fate."

The Wolf said: "What will I have to do?

- Almost nothing, says the Dog: giving chase to people

Carrying sticks and beggars;

To flatter those of the house, to please his Master:

In return for which your salary

Will force reliefs in all ways :

Chicken bones, pigeon bones,

Not to mention many a caress."

The Wolf is already forging a bliss

Who makes him cry with tenderness.

Along the way, he saw the Peeled Dog Pass.

What's that?" he said. - Nothing," he said. - What? Nothing? - Not much.

- But still? - The necklace I'm attached to

From what you see is perhaps the cause.

- Attached? said the Wolf: you do not run

Where do you want? - Not always, but what does it matter?

- It matters so well, that of all your meals

I don't want to in any way,

And would not want even at this price a treasure."

That said, Master Wolf runs away, and runs again.

Are we still able to hear Jean de La Fontaine? The astonishment and the real gagging of the wolf, "you do not run then / Where you want?", will perhaps astonish the immense majority of our contemporaries. Or if it doesn't surprise them, it's because they don't know how to read this brilliant author anymore, victim of his success. The word "freedom" and its derivatives such as "liberal" have perhaps never been used so much, and yet we have become accustomed to wearing a necklace, "Nothing [...] - Little. [...] The collar I am tied to. Are there still, and for how long, wolves to notice our peeled collar? It seems that even the rebels have become accustomed to negotiating the length of their chains.

We pretend to wonder about the legislative inflation, in France as well as at the European level. We should not. We want prohibitions and obligations in all fields. We have already criticized this "exterminating angelism" (Alain-Gérard Slama), this State that wants our good in spite of us, that wants to deprive us of the pleasure of spitting out our smoking bronchial tubes when we get up, or that claims to regulate the vocabulary and the use of insults and other picturesque bird names. But this is only the surface of things. And the critics of "political correctness" are often quick to call for police intervention and a return to "law and order. To the "political correctness" of the moderns, they oppose the political correctness of the ancients. That's all there is to it.

Every metropolis is under surveillance. The obsession with security has invaded every pore of society, abolished the very notion of privacy, and made possible what the liberals of past centuries would only have imagined with horror. So-called anti-terrorist legislation follows one another and tears apart *habeas corpus*.

As Proudhon said,

> "To be governed is to be guarded, inspected, spied upon, directed, legislated, regulated, parked, indoctrinated, preached, controlled, esteemed, appreciated, censored, commanded, by beings who have neither title, nor science, nor virtue...
>
> "To be governed is to be at every transaction, at every movement, noted, registered, counted, priced, stamped, rated, assessed, patented, licensed, admonished, prevented, reformed, corrected.
>
> "It is under the pretext of public utility and in the name of the general interest to be put to contribution, exercised, ransomed, exploited, monopolized, concussionned, pressured, mystified, stolen ; then, at the slightest complaint, at the first word of complaint, repressed, amended, vilified, vexed, hunted down, hounded, stunned, disarmed, garroted, imprisoned, shot, machine-gunned, judged, condemned, deported, sacrificed, sold, betrayed, and to top it all off, played with, fooled, outraged, dishonored.

It is no better with classical political freedom: democracy is reduced to a staging of the comedy of power: deprived of real stakes, for lack of serious political differences, the electoral contest is reduced to a choice between two versions of the single thought, a kind of beauty contest without the slightest beauty, or rather a rigged sports show in which the athletes all wear jerseys in the colors of the big brands. Confirmation of Max Stirner's imprecations[2] : any State, whether monarchical or republican, has no other aim than "to bind, limit, subordinate the individual, to subject him to the general thing" and if some States are strong enough to tolerate some free activities of individuals, it is only "the tolerance of the insignificant and the inoffensive[3].

Nothing new under the sun, one might say. Traditional societies had little regard for freedom of thought, freedom of expression and public liberties; it will also be recalled that constitutional governments in Europe and America have always applied their own principles only sparingly, never shying away from emergency laws, police surveillance and the provocation that goes with it. This is true. But domination now benefits from the violent irruption of information and communication technologies and biotechnologies. Biometrics is on the march. Yesterday we were subjects of a sovereign political power. We are marked like cattle, with electronic chips and not rings in our ears like cows, but the difference here is not important: it is for our own good! The political power is a good shepherd who takes care of his flock and wants to protect it from wolves and black sheep. An invaluable metaphor of the shepherd. But in the end, the flock is always led to the slaughterhouse.

---

1. PROUDHON (P.-J.), *Idée générale de la révolution au XIXᵉ siècle*, Garnier Frères, 1851, p. 341.
2. STIRNER (M.), *The One and His Property*, p. 254.
3. STIRNER (M.), *op. cit.* p. 253.

Almost nothing new except, and this is essential, the ongoing involution of a movement that comes from far away (probably from the first communes in the Middle Ages) and that turns freedom against freedom.

Freedom is an idea, detestable says Valery:

> "Liberty: it is one of those detestable words which have more value than meaning; which sing more than they speak; which ask more than they answer; of those words which have done all the jobs, and whose memory is smeared with Theology, Metaphysics, Morality and Politics; words very good for controversy, dialectic, eloquence; as suitable for illusory analyses and infinite subtleties as for the ends of sentences which unleash thunder[4]."

Philosophical quarrels about freedom seem vain, they are quarrels of words which necessarily arise when one takes a word out of its "natural element". But if there is not a precise meaning of freedom in general, if there is not a concept of freedom, there are perfectly defined uses of this term, specified concepts and not only as Valéry seems to say "in the dynamics and the theory of mechanisms". But in all these uses, the idea of freedom seems progressively emptied of its meaning. Whether it is a question of political freedom, of the rights and immunities of individuals, or of freedom in its most metaphysical sense (freedom as free will or as the power to act), our century no longer leaves much room for it, although we make immoderate use of the word... the better to bury the thing.

However, we must be careful not to consider this process in too one-sided a manner. The counter-utopias of the twentieth century have said everything that needs to be said about the threats posed by scientific progress as well as the delusions of the "social engineers" who propose to model a "new man". But what is perfectly licit in literature cannot be suitable for a philosophical reflection. One must consider this erasure of liberties from a "dialectical" point of view: it is not only the result of the concerted and liberticidal action of a handful of dominants; it is also a product of the liberal and progressive claims of the preceding centuries and it produces

---

4. VALÉRY (Paul), "Fluctuations sur la liberté", in *Œuvres II*, La Pléiade, Gallimard, p. 951.

its own contradictions. There is, of course, no "law of history" that would make the "*soft* totalitarianism" of our time the obligatory passage to a new era (or area!) of the blossoming of freedom. It is only a question of perceiving that, however desperate our situation may be at times, it conceals possibilities that can only be actualized if we know how to see and understand them. Just one example: the new forms of management - with the introduction in the 1980s of the methods of Toyotism, which undoubtedly marked a new stage in what Marx called "the real domination of capital" - in particular through the pulverization of the work collective and the expropriation of workers' knowledge. But we must understand, at the same time, that these new methods were only able to impose themselves because wage earners massively rejected the Fordist organization of work and wanted to increase their power over the production process. Toyotism is not just about "just-in-time", but includes procedures for integrating workers into the very process to which they are subject, through "quality circles", for example. The new forms of exploitation proceed from the old, not linearly, but dialectically. Even in unrecognizable forms, the hold that labor has exerted on workers still manifests that man seeks to realize his "generic being," to use an expression from Marx's *1844 Manuscripts*.

What I propose here is an analysis of the various uses of the word "freedom", of the different concepts that can be made of it, and a state of affairs at the beginning of the 21st century, before we move on to the "post-human" and it is too late to realize it.

We will start with freedom in the sense of political freedom by asking ourselves what is really happening with the triumphant democracy of our time.

While liberals think they are protecting individual freedom against the "despotism of freedom" by reducing freedom to what Isaiah Berlin calls "negative freedom", it will be seen that these individual freedoms, these freedoms not to be prevented from acting, are gradually being torn apart.

We will then see that the system of work in our time, far from increasing human freedom, is fully in line with the mechanisms of perfecting domination.

Modern philosophers have long believed that man could free himself from the tyranny of needs by developing production and by making the "man rich in needs" the model of civilized man. The "consumer society" reverses this hope by pushing to its most extreme consequences the "fetishism of the commodity".

More generally, it will be necessary to question freedom as a "metaphysical" subject: in what sense can we still consider freedom as the spiritual essence of man at a time when biotechnologies open up the possibility of a radical transformation of human nature?

To conclude, we will ask ourselves what use we can still make of the old liberal and republican freedoms and in what way they can be articulated on the multiform resistances that are manifesting themselves against the transformation of humans into predictable and rationalizable beings according to the rules of market rationality. What are the conditions of a true human liberation? What is a free human life? These political questions, but also and above all ethical ones, must be asked if we want to keep a meaning to the word "freedom".

Chapter I
Democracy, oligarchy, elites and control of the masses

Freedom is first and foremost political. To be free is to be alternately governed and governed, as Aristotle already said. The oldest claim of the plebs is to claim the right to have a say in the actions of those who govern. From Athens to republican Rome, from the Italian city-states to the English revolution, to American independence and the proclamation of the Republic in France, there seems to be a thread that peoples and generations hold tightly together. The differences between the slave republics of Athens and Rome, the republics of artisans, bourgeois and aristocrats of northern Italy and the modern republics of the late eighteenth century are sometimes abysmal. Freedom was hardly ever freedom for all. Even the very radical republican constitution of the first year maintained the distinction between active and passive citizens, between citizens truly capable of citizen's rights and second-class citizens - which included, moreover, all female citizens without exception... It took long struggles to wrest universal suffrage, in small steps. All these freedoms, moreover, are rather formal: the political right of a worker and that of his boss who owns newspapers and is ready to spend astronomical sums of money to run a campaign have no common measure. All this and much more can be said, but if the reality is sometimes far from the fine speeches, this does not remove any value from the speeches: we believe that the movement of history is that of the widening and deepening of democracy, and first of all of political democracy, and these last decades would seem to confirm it. Contested vigorously in the thirties of the last century, democracy has hardly any opponents left. The so-called "totalitarian" dictatorships have all collapsed. The military regimes that were still important in "Atlanticist" Europe in the early 1970s (Spain, Greece, Portugal) have given way to almost irreproachable democracies. Latin America seems to be learning about democratic regimes, and left-wing governments can last more than a few months without being overthrown by bloody military coups, more or less piloted by the US secret services.

One can quibble, but the general line is clear: democracy, supported by the market economy, has triumphed. "The end of history," said Fukuyama. There are some recalcitrant, capitalist Chinese who maintain the political structures of the "totalitarian" and "communist" state, but what changes since the death of Mao! The "Muslim world" is boiling over and democracy is not a highly prized value there. But progress will come... so much for the optimistic discourse. To which the grumblers object that the Tarpeian Rock is close to the Capitol and that this apparent apogee of democracy is nothing but the sign of its decline already well underway.

The three meanings of democracy

First of all, we must know what we mean by democracy. For the Ancients, and this is still the meaning of the word in the 18th century, democracy is the power of the people and this power only exists if it is exercised directly by the people. Athenian democracy resides in the fact that the assembled *demos* directly makes decisions, appoints and dismisses its leaders. The popular power is direct and without separation between legislative and executive. The Greeks distinguish the *laos* from the *demos*. The *laos is* the population, the people as a whole of the inhabitants - this is what will be aimed at by the setting up of institutions and practices that Michel Foucault classifies under the term "biopolitics". The *demos* is the people transformed into a political body. The *laos* is formless, it is the plebs of the Romans. It must be structured, organized by a "montage" which is the work of the "clerics" (*klericos*) - hence a "liturgy", a staging intended for the *laos*. This opposition is redoubled: a Greek is either a simple private individual, *idiotes*, member of the *laos*, or a citizen, *politis*, as part of the *demos*. Democracy would be the government of the people, by the people, for the people? The people as object or recipient of the government, it is the *laos*, whereas the people as agent ("by the people"), it is the *demos*. This distinction is very far-reaching in the questions which concern us particularly here.

It remains to know who is part of the people and who is not. The Athenians had a rather restrictive definition of it: neither slaves, nor masters, nor women were part of it. However, the Athenian democracy remained a democracy and not an aristocracy or an oligarchy, because the "small people", what will be called "plebs" in the Romans, plays a decisive role there. Not everyone was a citizen, of course, but the quality of citizen was not linked to wealth, nor to a particular social status. There are "nobles" in Athens as in Rome, families who take pride in their "race", but a poor craftsman can also be a citizen, even if his chances of accessing the supreme magistracies are rather reduced - for example, in Rome, the tribunes of the plebs are not plebeians.

There is a second meaning to the word "democracy": it is no longer a question of knowing whether the people as a whole exercise power through their assemblies or their means of control, but what interests are really taken into account in the conduct of public affairs. If the *demos* is the people, the majority of the people is naturally composed of the "little people"; in Florence, we spoke of the *popolo minuto*. In the assembly, everyone is there, rich or poor, noble or artisan, but in reality, there is a division that persists, a division that, without being as old as humanity, probably goes back to prehistoric times, to the Mesolithic and the beginnings of the Neolithic, between the "great" and the people[5]. Machiavelli makes

---

5. See Brian Hayden's little book, *L'Homme et l'Inégalité - L'invention de la hiérarchie à la préhistoire* (*Man and Inequality - The invention of hierarchy in prehistory*), CNRS editions, 2008.

this the fundamental division in all political regimes and Vico explains the history of republics, the transformation of tribal governments into aristocratic republics and of aristocratic republics into popular republics by the conflict between the strong (the "giants", the "heroes", the *gentes maiores*) and the *famoli*, the plebs[6]. "History up to our days is the history of the class struggle": this central thesis of the *Communist Manifesto* of Marx and Engels is so common, taken up again so often by the greatest, that it imposes itself, in spite of the repeated attempts to stifle this unpleasant truth. From this follows the second meaning of the word "democracy": there is democracy when the interests of the largest part of the people prevail, that is, the interests of the poorest.

In a more modern sense, democracy is identified with the respect of democratic freedoms, that is to say, both individual and political freedoms - in short, the "1789 freedoms". Today, this understanding prevails and it is the concern for individual liberties that is the main concern. The classical liberal interpretation has finally imposed itself. Personal freedoms and, above all, property rights are the freedoms of first rank, which must take precedence over political freedoms in the event that they come into conflict. It will be seen that even on this point, there is much to be said and basic individual liberties, the "1789 liberties", are not doing very well.

In an ideal republic, these three meanings of the word "democracy" should not contradict each other: freedom guaranteed to all presupposes a certain equality, not only of rights, but also of fortunes, and thus it requires a policy that avoids too great inequalities and prevents the poorest from being condemned to a misery destructive of the social order... The ideal of the Keynesian state with social-democratic tendencies, which inspired Western European and (partially) American governments during the so-called "Thirty Glorious Years," implements, or at least endeavors to implement, these three dimensions of democracy:

1. It broadens access to public life for all: women are allowed to vote, the age of majority is lowered and participation in public life is

---

6. See Vico (G.), *La Science nouvelle*, Fayard, 2001, translated by Alain Pons.

encouraged, notably through mass political parties - Italy and Germany provide quite remarkable examples, even if they are very dilapidated today;

2. The interests of the poorest are taken into consideration to an extent never seen in previous historical periods, with social protection, protection against unemployment, retirement, vacation rights, massive development of secondary and higher education, etc. The main demands of the minimum program placed at the end of the *Communist Manifesto* of Marx and Engels seem to be satisfied or in the process of being satisfied!

3. Individual liberties are guaranteed. The Keynesian state defends private property. But the various forms of freedom of conscience and personal liberty take on great importance: freedom of morals, abolition of almost all forms of censorship, recognition of the right of each individual to live the life that seems right to him or her without having to bend to traditions and "good morals" dictated by religious convictions.

In the 1970s, even when left-wing politicians dressed themselves up in all sorts of "socialist", "communist" or even "revolutionary" garb[7], their only ambition was to defend and develop this model, which neither John Stuart Mill nor Lord Keynes would have disowned, and which was theorized by John Rawls. It will be objected that this ideal democracy that has become a reality is itself the result of political and social conflicts that are often very violent and that it has remained confined to the richest part of the capitalist world, which is true. The program of the National Council of the Resistance, the Italian Constitution and the work of the First Republic, the great reforms of Clement Attlee in Great Britain, to take only these salient examples, were variants, more or less radical, of this same political orientation. And even today, this orientation remains the ultimate reference for many currents of the "radical left" or "anti-liberal".

---

7. Let us remember that, until the beginning of the 1990s, the French Socialist Party defined itself as a "revolutionary party"...

In contrast to this period and this "model", the great turning point of the 1980s appears to be a regression on all fronts. Equality is called into question, both by the valorization of performance, of competition, of "winners": the rule is *vae victis*. The poor are losers (sorry, *losers*) and therefore to give them a voice would be to let society be run by those who are unable to do so because they are incapable of personal success. Social protection is considered a burden, an unproductive expense for a humanity that will soon be considered supernumerary.

This is why a democracy deserted by the popular classes becomes the only possible one: a "pacified democracy", rid of this "egalitarian passion" that liberals have always mistrusted, rid of the plebs, in short, a democracy rid of the *demos*. When a president of the Republic, somewhat imprudently, boasts that "in this country, when there is a strike, no one notices anymore", he is delivering the secret of contemporary politics: it is necessary to let the "big ones" decide among themselves and to outlaw, once and for all, the "tumultuous republic" dear to Machiavelli.

This explains the meaning of the great transformation of our time: government is replaced by governance, a matter of administration reserved for experts, which camouflages the violence inherent in the government of men under the hypocritical mask of technical management. Saint-Simon (echoed by Marx) dreamed of a society where we move from the government of men to the administration of things. In a certain way, we are there, but the dream has turned into a nightmare.

See the process dialectically

One might object to this black-and-white picture that the past is always more beautiful than the present - Machiavelli indicated the reason: the past is the time of youth, and when one grows old, when the ills of age make themselves felt, one regrets the vigor of youth. This is exactly what seems to be happening in politics today in most of the layers and groups opposed to "neoliberalism".

The idyllic vision of the glorious era of the welfare state, while not without real foundations, has the serious defect of not grasping reality dialectically.

The accountant makes two columns, the credit and the debit, and will judge the health and robustness of a social and political regime by trying to determine whether the credit column is really longer than the debit column. The dialectician, on the contrary, will try to understand the link between the "positive aspects" and the "negative aspects", to understand their dialectical unity in order to grasp the historical development in its reality.

Let's remember what is too often forgotten: the Trente Glorieuses were not so glorious and the redistribution machine of the welfare state worked as much in one direction as in the other: the habit of watering where the ground is already wet is well established. The Gaullist regime was not a paradise for the working class - even if the situation was much better for the Communist Party than it is today. Political democracy was exercised freely only to the extent that it was certain that the results of the elections would suit the "masters of the world," and if not, stabilization maneuvers and coups d'état were undertaken again. Latin America in the 1960s and 1970s was not part of the paradisiacal "world of yesterday". Nor was Greece of the colonels... nor even Italy, which was agitated by the action of the secret services, especially those of the United States, but not only. No nostalgia for a time of progress or a time of revolutionary hope. It is more relevant to try to understand how today came out of yesterday.

To understand what really happened, to reconstruct the link between events, to make a history of the half-century that followed the defeat of Nazism, is a task of which we have only very partial glimpses and which deserves to be seriously tackled - even if many elements are still missing, precisely because they are too close to us. But there is a second, properly philosophical or theoretical dimension, which consists in looking at political principles and their own dynamics. I will summarize this in three theses:

1. There is a close link between individualistic liberal demands and the destruction of collective protection systems;
2. The common feature of the past and the present is that democracy has only ever existed as a form of oligarchy;

3. Liberal individualism is its own gravedigger and leads to the strengthening of the state it claims to fight.

The liberal individual versus the republic

We are talking about "liberalism" here, but the word is so ambiguous, so polysemous, that it is better to begin by specifying its uses and by saying what we mean by "liberal individual". Classical liberalism, coined in the seventeenth and eighteenth centuries by the great philosophers of modern Europe, covers several distinct but closely related issues.

In the first place, liberalism appears with the push of the new commercial and industrial classes against the feudal system and the multiple hindrances it imposes on what Marxists would call the "development of the productive forces." It is a liberalism often reduced to simple economic liberalism (freedom of the market or "laissez-faire"), but which encompasses many other aspects.

The respect of the right to property and the freedom to get rich from one's industry are themes shared by Hobbes, Locke and their followers, but also by Montesquieu and Turgot. One has always had the right to get rich, and the Catholic condemnation of money was nothing but a tartuffery... But as soon as the Reformation legitimized the will to get rich as being in accordance with divine purposes, the taxes levied by an unproductive clergy and the insistent "protection" offered by the men-at-arms became intolerable burdens for those who perceived themselves more and more clearly as the living forces of European nations. All the philosophy of these two centuries is traversed by the question of money, the legitimacy of interest and the defense of the owner's right. Even the philosophers who are classified among the most radicals bear witness to this.

Spinoza constructs his politics by showing how ambition and the love of wealth can be brought into play in such a way as to guarantee freedom, concord and peace in the republic. Alexandre Matheron calls the Spinozist ideal state a liberal state, and this term must be understood in all its meanings. Moreover, to know what a liberal state is, Spinoza himself gives the example of the main trading power of his time:

> "Let's not look too far for examples, because we have enough in front of us. Hasn't the city of Amsterdam experienced the benefits? This does not prevent it from developing continuously, in all fields, under the admiring gaze of other peoples. In this flourishing republic and splendid city, people of all national origins and religious sects live in perfect harmony! When it comes to making an investment, the citizens are only concerned with whether the man they are dealing with is rich or poor, whether he can be trusted or whether his reputation is that of a deceiver. Once fixed on this, they do not care at all what religion or sect the other party adheres to, for, supposing one were ever to go before the judge, this consideration would serve neither to win nor to lose the case[8]."

This is what Vico reproaches Spinoza for when he says that "Benedict Spinoza speaks of the republic as if it were a society of merchants[9]".

A severe moralist - and by no means a libertine - Diderot, in many ways a Spinozist, is not only one of the most determined representatives of Enlightenment materialism and atheism, but also a defender of "good luxury"... and of free trade, as long as the exchange remains fair. The *Letter on the Book Trade* is a plea for the freedom of publishing and for the defense of copyright...

This first form of liberalism, which seeks to free civil society from the shackles of the feudal system, must be understood in its complex aspects. Marxists generally consider the development of liberal ideas as the expression of the aspiration to power of a new dominant class that gains ideological domination before directly seizing political power. Liberalism is explained by the desire of this new class to rule society according to its own will and to enrich itself without limit - enrichment becoming the reward for activity and talent. This aspect is undeniable and there is some

---

8. SPINOZA (B.), "Traité des autorités théologiques et politiques", chap. XX, in *Œuvres*, La Pléiade, Gallimard, 1954, p. 906.
9. VICO (G.), *op. cit*, § 335.

truth in the traditional interpretation of "historical materialism". But at the same time and for the same reasons, liberalism must stand up against all forms of parasitic activities, against the rents of the Church that serve to feed "lazy monks", against taxes, duties and a thousand and one ways of extorting money from those who work, trade and finally make the nation live. Not wanting to be held to ransom and only paying taxes by controlling their use is a liberal claim, but also a claim of political freedom in general. Turgot, the great French liberal, never questioned the absolute monarchy, but he united in a coherent plan the liberalization of the grain market, the abolition of guilds, an ambitious tax reform that led to the liquidation of the tax privileges of the nobility and the clergy, the royal corvée, and an action in favor of religious tolerance. The immense majority of the nation would have gained from the application of the project of this daring reformer... but the united forces of the noble reaction were able to defeat him.

In other words, the claims of economic liberalism - freedom of enterprise, freedom of trade and reduced intervention in "private" affairs by outside agencies - are not only about establishing the rule of the free fox in the henhouse. They are also a rejection of a certain type of domination. This liberal freedom is not only the anti-feudal and anti-absolutist demand of the rising bourgeoisie. It will also be that of the revolutionary or radical movements, often libertarian (and not liberal) of the end of the nineteenth century and the beginning of the twentieth against "the plutocrats", the army and the Church. It was also the demand that swept away the bureaucratic regimes in the USSR and in the countries of the East.

I have had occasion to hypothesize that the "liberal turn" of the 1980s was made possible because the layers of the dominant class that had an interest in it were able to mobilize the dominated for "freedom" by arguing that the bureaucratic constraints of the welfare state weighed as much on the wage earners as on the bosses. The Keynesian-Fordist growth of the three decades following the Second World War was essentially based on a techno-scientific management of firms and the generalization of the Fordist production chain. It is too often forgotten that the first shocks to this model came from the revolts of young workers - for example, during the strikes in Caen and Rennes in 1967[10]. Faced with this revolt against the conditions of Fordist production, the dominant classes proposed more "freedom": a change in the hierarchical model ("shortening the chain of command"), management by objectives, development of individual initiative and participation in groups to improve working conditions and productivity. The slogan "all entrepreneurs" is a scam, but it is based on real aspirations, which we will discuss later. Is it possible to untangle the skein, to separate economic liberalism as an ideology justifying the omnipotence of capital and the aspirations for individual initiative, autonomy in work, the elimination of bureaucracy and open or underhand forms of parasitism? Answering this question is decisive if we want to draw the main lines of an alternative to the omnipotence of capitalism.

Secondly, liberalism is intimately linked to a certain form of political organization and a certain conception of law to which the names of Locke, Montesquieu or Tocqueville are attached. But here again, it is the complexity of the definition that must be noted. Although it has been historically closely linked to the economic liberalism we have just been talking about, classical political liberalism has its own specificities: Turgot does not ask the properly political question, although he has the support of the "philosophers" who are most often supporters of political liberalism. To define this political liberalism, we must proceed by oppositions and differences.

First of all, political liberalism is opposed to monarchical absolutism. It is the political liberalism of the *Glorious Revolution,* so called because it was above all an unrevolutionary arrangement between the dominant classes to get rid of the unfortunate spectre of a real revolution, that of 1642, when for the first time representatives of the people condemned a king to have his head separated from the rest of his body. This liberalism expresses the will of the dominant classes not to be entirely subjected to the monarchic political power. But whether this political liberalism is equivalent to

---

10. See COLLIN (D.), *Le Cauchemar de Marx*, pp. 76-77.

political freedom is far from clear. It claims freedom from monarchical state power, but not freedom for all, not freedom in general. Starting from the conflicts between the British imperial power and the American *insurgents*, then between northerners and southerners, and drawing on a vast documentation, Domenico Losurdo shows that liberalism and slavery can coexist without major difficulties.

> "The so-called champions of liberty label as synonymous with slavery and despotism a fiscal imposition implemented without their explicit consent, but they have no qualms about exercising the most absolute and tyrannical power at the expense of their slaves[11]."

Losurdo cites John Millar, a disciple of Adam Smith and a prominent representative of the "Scottish Enlightenment":

> "It is singular that the same individuals who speak with refined style of political liberty and who consider as one of the inalienable rights of mankind the right to impose taxes, make no scruple of holding a large proportion of creatures similar to themselves in such conditions as to deprive them not only of property, but of almost all rights. Fortune has perhaps produced no situation more than this capable of ridiculing the liberal hypothesis or of showing how little the conduct of men is, at bottom, directed by philosophical principles[12]."

Without reducing liberalism to this dimension alone, Losurdo uses the category of "democracy of the race of lords", which gives a good account of this democracy reserved for a small minority combined with the oppression of a mass of slaves or plebs considered to be made up of inferior men (as the Irish were often considered by the English) or of men who were barely human, as the Amerindians were considered. Hence these apparent paradoxes: some of the *insurgents* opposed the "mother country" because it began to question the slave trade; with an unintentional sense of humor, Washington addressed his fellow citizens and called on them to fight

---

11. LOSURDO (D.), *Controstoria del liberalismo*, Editori Laterza, 2005, p. 12.
12. MILLAR (J.), *The Origin of the Distinction of Ranks* (1771), cited by LOSURDO (D.), p. 13.

against the British Empire "so as not to be miserably oppressed like our Negroes"... or those southerners, fully penetrated by the argumentation of the great liberal theorists and who defend the right of slave owners against the tyrannical law of those northerners who want to emancipate the slaves. The most famous case is that of John C. Calhoun, vice-president of the United States from 1825 to 1832, who developed a coherent political philosophy, claiming in particular John Locke, in which the southerners will find all the necessary justifications during the Civil War. Fighting both to defend the autonomy of the Southern states - against the "tyrannical" centralization wanted by the Northerners - and against the abolitionists, "blind fanatics", Calhoun is the ardent defender of the law that obliges the abolitionist states to hand over runaway slaves. Calhoun supports the paradox that freedom is never more secure than in states founded on slavery. There is no need to twist Calhoun's texts to find in them an astonishing anticipation of the famous "freedom is slavery" maxim typical of the totalitarian system of *1984* imagined by Orwell.

As early as 1790, it was the liberal Burke who launched the ideological offensive against the French Revolution - at a time when, let us remember, it had merely established a constitutional monarchy, strongly inspired by the English model! But what Burke could not support was the first article, which declared all men free and equal in rights. Burke sees there only an abstract freedom which will make the bed of despotisms, to which he opposes the freedoms of the English. It should be noted that all counter-revolutionary criticism, from Rivarol to Maurras, via Joseph de Maistre, will take up the central core of Burke's polemic, while being less verbose on the liberties of the English...

This liberalism defends a certain conception of freedom, a freedom without limit for those who by nature have the right to enjoy this freedom without limit. And this is why it is anti-monarchist since monarchy limits the freedom of the "race of lords". It is therefore an aristocratic liberalism.

But liberalism can also be defined in opposition to democracy. Democracy being the power of the people, the people tend to assert their interests and impose them by law and by the force of government. And so the people can become tyrannical, putting into question individual liberties. Benjamin Constant thematizes the opposition between the liberty of the Ancients conceived as the participation of the people in the exercise of political power and the liberty of the Moderns centered on the defense of individual liberties. It is on the basis of this opposition that he argues for the necessity of a censal suffrage: if those who have no property and no ability to acquire and keep property are in power, they will necessarily take measures to share the fortunes and to support the plebs at the expense of the "productive classes", i.e., the richest. Unlike Calhoun-style slavers, liberals like Benjamin Constant supported equality of rights in general: no one could be arbitrarily deprived of his liberty or property, all must be equal before the law, etc. But equality must stop at the end of the day. But equality must stop where the exercise of political power begins. In short, it is a question of protecting freedom from democracy. As Henry Sidgwick says in his Elements of Politics (1897): "there is no certainty that a representative legislative system, chosen by universal suffrage, would not interfere more with the free action of individuals than would an absolute monarchy."

It is quite common today to denounce insidious forms of return to censal suffrage, which is associated with the Restoration period in France. However, censal suffrage, in one form or another, was the rule in all the democratic revolutions of the eighteenth century. The French Revolution did not establish universal suffrage: in 1791, we have a complex system of censal suffrage. 1848 established a universal suffrage... male quickly limited. And above all, until the 20th century, female citizens were only passive citizens, forbidden from political rights and often even civil minors. Not to mention the age limits - until very recently, one was soon old enough to be an exploited worker or a soldier destined to end up as cannon fodder, but to be a citizen, one had to wait until 21.

In truth, the distinction elaborated by Sieyès between active and passive citizens remains the fundamental distinction around which the political life of liberal democracies is ordered, whose organization is conceived throughout to protect the dominant from popular tumults. This is why liberalism accommodates authoritarian states, provided that business can be conducted according to stable rules known to all and that property rights are respected. Nevertheless, and the experience of the last few decades seems to point in this direction, one can think that the capitalist classes, especially the one that Leslie Sklair[13] calls "TCC" (*Transnational Capitalist Class*), clearly prefer a democratic state, which is generally less costly and whose public life, also regulated by a particular form of supply and demand, is ultimately more in line with the general objectives of capitalism. And as long as the spectre of social revolution no longer haunts the big metropolises, there is no reason to resort to a fascist or dictatorial state.

Third, political liberalism could be defined in opposition to the republic. Isaiah Berlin has contrasted "negative freedom" (that of the moderns) as freedom from hindrance or freedom from interference, with positive freedom, freedom as self-realization, which is part of the ancient civic humanism of Aristotle and Cicero. The most radical and restrictive definition of negative freedom is probably found in Hobbes:

> "And according to the proper, and generally received, meaning of the word, *a* FREE MAN *is one who, for those things which he is able to do by his strength and intelligence, is not prevented from doing what he has the will to do.* But when the words *free* and *liberty* are applied to something other than *bodies*, they are used abusively. Indeed, what is not subject to movement is not subject to impediments, and therefore, when we say, for example, that the path is free, the expression does not mean the freedom of the path, but the freedom of those who walk on this path without being stopped. [...]

> "The Athenians and the Romans were free, that is to say that their republics were free; not that individuals had the freedom to resist their own representative, but that their representative had the freedom to resist other peoples, or to invade them. Nowadays, the word LIBERTAS is written in large letters on the towers of the city of Lucca, and yet no one can infer that a private individual is freer there or more exempt from serving the

---

13. See SKLAIR (L.), *The Transnational Capitalist Class*, Blackwell Publishing Ltd, 2001.

Republic than in Constantinople. Whether a Republic is monarchical or popular, freedom remains the same[14]."

Conversely, for the ancient philosophers, who are sometimes classified as "civic humanists", freedom exists only in and through participation in civic life. Cicero develops this ideal in *Des Devoirs* and in *The Republic*.

> "Nature has so imperiously imposed upon men the obligation of virtue and has inspired in them such a passion to defend the existence of the community, that this force has triumphed over all the attractions of pleasure and leisure. It is not enough to possess virtue, as one can know a technique without using it; a technique, even if one does not practice it, one keeps the theoretical knowledge of it; virtue, on the contrary, consists entirely in its application; and its highest application, it is the government of the city and the integral realization, in facts and not in words, of the principles that these people proclaim in their corners." (*Republic*, I, *II*, 1-2.)

> "Freedom cannot dwell in any state except in one where the supreme power belongs to the people. It must be recognized that there is no more pleasant state, and that if it is not equal for all, it is not freedom either. Now how can freedom be equal for all, I do not say in a kingdom, where servitude is not even concealed, and is not in doubt, but also in states where citizens are free only in word?" (*Republic*, I, *XXXI*, 47.)

> "Freedom does not consist in living under a just master, but in having none." (*Republic*, II, *XXIII*, 43.)

Man is therefore free only in a free city. This freedom finds its highest realization in the participation of citizens, as equals, in civic life. It is public life which is the highest expression of freedom. But this participation in public life is, at the same time, a moral duty (see *Duties*) : the citizens form a community bound by moral feelings. Echoes of this ancient conception

---

14. Hobbes (Th.), *Leviathan*, chap. XXI : "De la liberté des sujets", edition Sirey, 1971, trans. F. Tricaud.

can be found in the austere republicanism of Jean-Jacques Rousseau. Liberals like Berlin reproach this conception with being conducive to despotism. In the *Social Contract, there is* a famous passage:

> "So that the social pact is not a vain form, it tacitly contains this commitment, which alone can give force to the others, that whoever refuses to obey the general will will be forced to do so by the whole body: which means nothing else but that he will be forced to be free; for such is the condition which gives each citizen to the Fatherland guarantees him from all personal dependence; a condition which makes the artifice and the game of the political machine, and which alone renders legitimate the civil commitments, which without it would be absurd, tyrannical, and subject to the most enormous abuses." (Book I, chap. VII.)

This passage is often interpreted as a justification of the "despotism of liberty", to use Hegel's expression, of which the revolutionary terror of the Committee of Public Safety would have been the application. My point is not to know whether Rousseau deserves this reproach or not: by asking him questions that he himself could not ask, by asking him questions after the French Revolution, we are condemned either to try to make the dead speak, that is to say to indulge in an exercise in philosophical spiritualism, or to admit that no satisfactory answer can be given. On the other hand, it is certain, because experience has taught us so cruelly, that the opposition between the man who should be according to the order of reason and the miserable empirical being who is rarely reasonable and who constitutes the real subject, not of moral and political philosophy, but of real political life, has led inevitably to tyranny. And of this we must acknowledge the liberal critics. The man does not live only of politics. The nobility of civic commitment, the ability to put the common good before one's own selfish interests, the ability to follow right reason rather than passions, are far too rare to be the basis for a sensible politics and morality.

According to a very dialectical scheme, republicanism can be presented as the overcoming of the opposition between negative freedom (freedom of non-interference) and positive freedom. Without completely repeating here what I have developed in other works[15], we can simplify things by saying that republicanism takes up the communitarian ideal of freedom by law - which is that of civic humanism - while maintaining that individuals do not necessarily want to participate in public affairs, may legitimately want to take care of their private affairs and only expect the republic to protect them against all forms of domination.

The first formulation of modern republicanism is probably found in Machiavelli[16]. In essence, Machiavelli divides the nation into the people and the great ones and characterizes them politically as follows: the "great ones" want to govern (and want to rule everything according to their own natural way) while the people want above all not to be dominated and to remain free, which implies that freedom cannot reside in participation in government! This is why, according to Machiavelli, it is in the people that one must place the guard of freedom, precisely because they do not aspire to govern or to dominate. Clearly, for Machiavelli, a republic is not a direct democracy where the assembled people run the city's affairs on a daily basis. Machiavelli's people have no slaves to work for them, they must spin wool, forge swords, make clothes or bread, care for their families, defend their wives and children. And freedom, for Machiavelli, lies first of all in the security that allows him to carry out all these activities. But at the same time, there must be institutions that allow the people to choose the rulers, to eliminate those who are obviously incapable of defending the republic, to protect themselves against the inevitable arrogance of the great. Whereas in Hobbes, and in a certain way also in Rousseau, acceptance of the social contract entails uncon-ditional submission to sovereign power, in Machiavelli, since sovereign power always depends more or less on fortune (and not on a fictitious contract), this power has legitimacy only insofar as the people accept it,

---

15. See, in particular, COLLIN (D.), *Revive la République !*, Armand Colin, 2005.

16. As much as the author of the much misread and misunderstood *The Prince*, Machiavelli is the author of the *Discourses on the First Decade of Titus Livius*, a long meditation on republics. See COLLIN (D.), *Lire et comprendre Machiavel*, Armand Colin, 2008.

and it is subject to what Philip Pettit will call a "principle of guaranteed contestability[17]". Thus the great founding moment, for Machiavelli, is the demonstration of the Roman people withdrawing to the Aventine (494 BC) and finally obtaining the creation of the institution of the tribune. Machiavelli is not a modern democrat, that is to say that he does not tell beautiful democratic stories to embellish a somewhat less glowing reality. He says what is and sticks to the "effective reality of things". And this reality is that it is always an elite that governs - there is no counter-example in any developed society[18] - and that, consequently, the problem of freedom is that of the protection of the citizens against the tyrannical tendencies of any power, that of the submission of the rulers to the laws, and finally the guarantee of *vivere civile*, that is to say, of a free life in a free republic. Good institutions are those that keep this ever precarious balance between the defense of liberty and the necessity of government.

While liberals consider that the law is basically only a necessary restriction of freedom, republicans consider that freedom is always a freedom through law. While liberals consider that rights belong to the individual, defining them almost independently of any social life, republicans consider that it is social life that allows these rights to exist and that man is by nature a social being, and that it is only in society that he can develop and assert his uniqueness and autonomy. There are, however, commonalities between liberals and republicans: distrust of all-powerful political power, even when that power is democratic; the tyranny of the majority is a tyranny like any other - and sometimes even more terrible: tyrants who came to power through mass movements have generally been much crueler than those who had to make do with a coup d'état

---

17. PETTIT (P.), *Républicanisme, une théorie de la liberté et du gouvernement*, translated from English by J.-F. Spitz and P. Savidan, Gallimard, 2004.
18. In some minimal societies, such as the Nambikwara, of whom Lévi-Strauss speaks so movingly, it seems that the social hierarchy is almost non-existent. But these few marginal examples cannot make us forget everything we know about human history and even prehistory. Brian Hayden (*op. cit.*) traces back to hunter-gatherer societies the domination of an elite, made possible once food became relatively abundant.

Democracy, oligarchy, elites and control of the masses

or a palace revolution. The principle of separation of powers, claimed by the vast majority of liberals, is an intangible principle for republicans. But republicans take the principle of separation of powers a step further: not only must citizens be protected from arbitrary encroachments by the state, but also the public space must be protected from arbitrary encroachments by economic powers. Republicanism also presupposes the protection of individuals against other dominations than political domination, for example the domination of parents over children, of bosses over their employees, of men over women, in short all the dominations that develop almost spontaneously in situations of asymmetrical relations, all those situations in which it is freedom that oppresses and the law that liberates.

Thus liberalism is not alien to democracy - it intersects with democracy in the third of the senses we distinguished at the beginning of this chapter... but it does not require that the individual rights it claims to defend be the same for all. He is not totally alien to the republic: the concern to put limits on state power and the separation of powers are republican themes, as is the defense of individual autonomy. It is therefore not very relevant to be "anti-liberal" as many groups and currents of the left, and especially of the "left of the left" or the anti-globalist left, have proclaimed themselves since the 1980s. An anti-liberal can be accused of being hostile to individual freedoms or to the "rule of law" and, in fact, the radical left has often tolerated all sorts of blatant violations of the most elementary freedoms as long as they were carried out by governments claiming to be revolutionary, anti-imperialist, or anything of the sort. To add to the confusion, it should also be remembered that a liberal in the French (and European) sense has little to do with a liberal in the American sense: for example, John Rawls defines his own doctrine as "political liberalism", whereas it is often very close to republicanism (as Rawls himself acknowledges) and constitutes a fairly good theoretical formulation of social-democratic policies. And finally, Serge Audier and some others devote their efforts to the rebirth of a "liberal socialism" that is not the capitulation of socialism to liberalism, but a socialism that is both radical and capable of integrating the achievements of political liberalism[19].

From the multiplicity of meanings of the word "liberalism", it follows that it is not clear what a "liberal" is, and hardly any more what an "anti-liberal" is. However, it is possible, in order to clarify ideas, to define the core of philosophical or political positions which, rightly or wrongly, are called or referred to as "liberalism" and which it is appropriate here to define.

The first feature of this liberalism - and in this it is the heir of the contractualism of the classical age - is an anthropological conception of man as an isolated individual, self-sufficient, an "atom" which will be connected or not to other atoms. The man in the state of nature of Hobbes, Grotius or Rousseau is a man of this kind - even if the philosophical and political conclusions of these authors diverge greatly (at least if we take at face value Rousseau's polemics against the first two). It is in this anthropological thesis that the most extreme forms of liberalism, such as Robert Nozick's libertarianism, are rooted, as well as *homo œconomicus*[20], the "being of reason" around which the socio-economic ideology of neo-liberalism has been built from the 1980s to the present. It should be pointed out that this thesis has for Rousseau only a heuristic fictional value ("let's put aside all the facts", he says), whereas Hobbes considers that man in his state of nature, this man who loves nothing less than the company of other men, is man in his essence, which manifests itself as soon as he is no longer bound by the bonds of fear of sovereign power.

If men are by nature isolated individuals, they live in society only as a result of the accidents of history or as a result of rational calculation, not by nature. All social contract theories are based on this idea: men accept the constraints of social life - they agree to obey a common law and give up their natural freedom - because they find benefits in union. While Rousseau wondered whether the Republic outlined in the *Social Contract*

---

19. Liberal socialism found its best defenders in the Italian thinkers and politicians of actionism (the "Action Party" is one of the Italian anti-fascist parties) like Carlo Rosselli or Guido Calogero.
20. See the precise and forceful book by ANDRÉANI (Tony), *Un être de raison. Critique de l'homo œconomicus*, Syllepse, 2000.

Democracy, oligarchy, elites and control of the masses

was not a regime made for gods rather than men[21], for Kant, "the problem of the institution of the state, difficult as it may seem, is not insoluble even for a people of demons (provided they have an understanding)[22]". Men eventually reach morality only because a clear understanding of their interest has put them on the right path, even if morality, according to Kant, makes disinterestedness its cardinal virtue. Between Hobbes and Kant, the differences are wide and seem almost insurmountable. However, there seems to be a common ground concerning human nature. Kant's "unsociable sociability" is in some ways similar to the fundamental unsociability of Hobbesian natural man.

It is not without reason that the ultraliberal Robert Nozick presents himself as a "Kantian". Certainly, if one studies seriously Kant's philosophy and his attempt to understand the metaphysics of morals in all its subtleties, it soon becomes clear that Nozick's Kantianism is, to say the least, usurped. But he shares with Kant certain axioms that Kant himself has in common with many philosophers of the seventeenth and eighteenth centuries. Kant begins his universal doctrine of law with "the private right of yours and mine in general".

> "Mine in law (*meum juris*) is that to which I am bound in such a way that the use that another could make of it without my consent would harm me. The subjective condition of the possibility of use in general is possession"[23].

The Kantian definition directly links two kinds of rights: rights as immunities or exemptions (not being harmed, not being obliged to do something) and rights as powers. But this very general definition has important and problematic consequences. After arguing that "it is possible for my arbiter to take for mine any external object", otherwise freedom, as formally defined by practical reason, would be in contradic-

---

21. It is certainly to him that Kant is thinking when he speaks of those who claim that the republican constitution "should be a state of angels" (*Project of Perpetual Peace*, VIII-366 - the pagination refers to the Berlin Academy's *editions*).
22. KANT (E.), *Project of Perpetual Peace*, 105, VIII-366.
23. KANT (E.), *Metaphysics of Morals*, "Universal Doctrine of Law", § 1, in *Works III*, p. 494.

tion with itself, Kant asserts that the arbiter's external objects can be of three kinds:

> "1° a (corporeal) thing outside of me; 2° the arbiter of another in view of a determined act; 3° the state of another in relation to me, according to the categories of substance, causality and community between me and external objects according to the laws of freedom[24]."

In other words, property defines not only a relationship to the things in my possession, but also relations between individuals. The right of ownership thus encompasses the things I can use, the obligations of others towards me (in contracts, for example), and the status of certain individuals (Kant gives the example of a woman, a child or a servant). From this point of view, the theory of property is thus, more generally, a theory of social relations as a whole.

In the end, Nozick does not deviate much from Kant when he makes the right to property the essential right of man, the one that defines him as an individual separated from other individuals. In order to think about the link between individuals, it is necessary to define the conditions that are properly the object of a theory of justice. This one concerns only three subjects:

- the original acquisition of possessions: here Nozick takes up Locke's theory, modifying and completing it;
- the transfer of possessions: what are the legitimate means of acquiring a possession?
- the treatment of injustices, i.e. the principles of reparation when justice has been violated.

The first two problems define an "empowerment theory" that allows for a complete formulation of the distribution theory.

> "First, a person who acquires possession in accordance with the principle of justice regarding acquisition is entitled to that possession;

---

24. KANT (E.), *op. cit.* § 4, p. 497.

"Second, a person who acquires possession in accordance with the principle of justice governing transfers, from someone else entitled to that possession, is entitled to that possession;

"Third, no one is entitled to a possession except by (repeated) application of the first two propositions[25]."

Nozick insists that these principles do not define a *pattern of* distribution.

"Almost every suggested principle of distributive justice is organized into a pattern: to each according to his moral merit, or according to his needs or marginal production, or how hard he fights to get there, or the weighted sum of the above, etc. The principle of empowerment that we have outlined is not organized in a model[26]."

One can have models that account for this or that particular distribution (for example, in economics), but not a general model of distribution. Such a model would be contradictory to Nozick's basic principles: for example, to generalize "to each according to his merit" would be contradictory to the right I have to bequeath my possessions to my children, independently of any appreciation of their moral merit - Nozick takes up the very debatable, but always unproven, idea that the right of ownership includes the right to test. But, as Bobbio convincingly shows, no one can determine in what a natural right to test lies. It may be thought that the living person disposes of his property as he wishes, and that the will merely carries out the wishes (the last wishes) of the living person. But precisely, the execution of the will is based on a legal fiction: the expression of a will that no longer has a subject capable of willing, a detached will. One could also suppose that the properties following the "natural" lineage of human reproduction automatically go to the children or, failing that, to the closest relatives. But in this case, the right to test is limited, since the father - in this case - is not free to disinherit his children in order to bequeath his property to his mistress or to

---

25. Nozick (R.), *Anarchy, State, Utopia*, PUF, 1988, coll. "Libre échange", trans. Évelyne Dauzac de Lamartine, p. 189.
26. Nozick (R.), *op. cit.* p. 196.

a passing tramp. Finally, just as naturally, one might think that the property of the living person, resulting from his membership in society and having been guaranteed by the public authorities, returns to the community at his death to serve the public good. Nozick dismisses this discussion because it would fundamentally undermine his individualist presuppositions.

For Nozick, it is the principle of freedom that will always overturn all models of distribution. Suppose we give to everyone according to their work. No one can stop me from spending my money to support my favorite basketball team. The money of thousands of fans can then end up in the pocket of this or that star, who will then be much richer than the principle of "to each according to his work" would have allowed. The examples could be multiplied. Nozick shows that any model of distribution can only be maintained by violating the fundamental rights of the individual. Indeed, principles of justice in models always require redistribution. Yet:

> "Taxation of property from labor is on a par with forced labor. Some people find this thesis obviously true: taking the earnings from n hours of work is like taking n hours from that person; it is like forcing that person to work n hours for someone else. Others find this argument absurd. And even these, if they object to the mention of forced labor, would object to forcing unemployed hippies to work for the benefit of those in need[27]."

Nozick's positions seem so contrary to some of our ordinary moral precepts and so unrealistic that they seem to refute themselves. However, if the minimal state he defends is not really taken seriously by any political leader, his theses constitute the theoretical underpinning of neo-liberal policies directed towards a generalized privatization of the social functions of the state. These ideas have been widely disseminated in all the upper strata of modern societies. The collection "Libre échange", in which the first French translation of Nozick was published, clearly announces its color and claims to be a militant collection aiming at defending "the authentically liberal point of view in France". It is true that in France,

---

27. Nozick (R.), *op. cit.* p. 211.

Democracy, oligarchy, elites and control of the masses

liberals are more likely to claim to be followers of von Hayek than of Nozick, *catallaxia* and the holistic point of view it implies being more easily accepted in Durkheim's country. Libertarian liberals are quite rare and, despite efforts to appear very modern, they have an unfortunate tendency to fall back on the obsessions and even the style of the old French reactionary right - they are more concerned with denouncing the influence of Freemasonry, civil servants, socialists, communists, trade unionists than with supporting the liberalization of the drug trade as David Friedman does. But it is different in the United States where libertarians play a significant role and are quite distinct from the "moral majority" and more generally from the conservative right. A good example is Ron Paul, a senator from the Republican Party, who was a testimonial candidate in the 2008 US presidential election. If one is looking in Europe for something that corresponds to the ideas synthesized by Nozick, one will find it rather on the side of the "societal left" (to whom one sometimes applies the rather all-purpose term of "bobo"): for example, concerning the legalization of the use of soft drugs, this left often takes up David Friedman's arguments in their entirety.

Nozick's theses do not lack attractive aspects. Nozick denounces the "paternalistic" conceptions of political power, which, by treating individuals as children, claims to want their good, even in spite of them. His theory makes individual freedom a cardinal virtue and can therefore be presented as a theory of individual emancipation, a liberating theory. When he writes that "people tend to forget the possibilities of acting independently of the state[28]", this is not liberal-capitalist: any "old-style" Marxist or any anarchist could take this up: "Producers, let us save ourselves", says *The International.* The replacement of the emancipation of the workers, which, according to Marx, will be the work of the workers themselves, by the statization and the taking over of all social life by state or parastatal institutions, is something that would have horrified the socialists and communists of the 19th century - Guesde and Lafargue, founders of the "French Workers' Party", virulently

---

28. Nozick (R.), *op. cit.* p. 31.

denounced those of their reformist comrades who wanted to nationalize all industry and transform workers into civil servants.

A serious critique of libertarianism requires going to the heart of the matter, that is, to anthropological considerations. Nozickian anthropology is based on an archaic conception of the state of nature, straight out of the fictions of classical age "jusnaturalism". Individuals leading a separate life and legitimately appropriating the product of their labor, this is one of those "robinsonnades" that Marx mocked. Nozick claims this "robinsonnade" tradition[29]. He goes so far as to write that "each person represents a miniature society[30]". This means 1° that he exists by himself and without relation to other "miniature societies"; 2° that he has no other limit than himself. Pierre Legendre has shown that this conception of "the individual become *mini-state*" is not an alternative to totalitarianism, but only the way in which "ultra-modernity has turned the totalitarian card upside down, in the form of the irruption of the dogmatics of the subject-King[31]."

There is no need to go into further detail in the critique of Nozick's book[32]. The difficulty that libertarians have in transforming their ideas into practical political ideas is that, first, they have to support politically people with whom they disagree profoundly - for example, American libertarians are more likely to be on the Republican side (theoretically anti-interventionist in economics) than on the Democratic side (theoretically more interventionist and redistributive), and so they have to put quite a bit of water in their wine in order to find common ground with the bigots of the "moral majority. The second problem with libertarians is that they collide head-on with the most deeply held Christian moral traditions. Thus, a consistent libertarian should find nothing to object to when an individual uses drugs to the point of committing suicide, more or less slowly. Everyone is master of his own life and, libertarians add, a free market in drugs would be an advantage over the present underground market, reducing the causes

29. See NOZICK (R.), *op. cit.* at 231.
30. NOZICK (R.), *op. cit.* p. 232.
31. See LEGENDRE (Pierre), *La Question dogmatique en Occident*, Fayard, 1999, p. 67.
32. See COLLIN (D.), *Morale et justice sociale*, Seuil, 2001.

of delinquency. As far as relations between individuals are concerned, the rule is quite simple: everything that is done between consenting adults is licit. Thus, prostitution should be considered as a service that does not need to be regulated[33] and even less forbidden. The only acceptable criterion is always consent: David Gauthier wants to found a "morality by agreement" since contracts are sufficient to define norms acceptable to all. Half seriously, half provocatively, some libertarians call for a free market in adoption: if poor parents sell their children to rich people who want to adopt to satisfy their "desire for a child," there should be no regulation against it. It is a transaction between free people in which no one is harmed, neither the poor parents who receive money and are relieved of a burden they could not bear, nor the rich adopters who see their desire satisfied, nor the child who will be able to receive a better education and will have better prospects in life... Some libertarians even call themselves frankly anarchists and claim that they are the only consistent anarchists. They call for the "liquidation of the power of politicians", which is pure anarchism, as one can read on some libertarian websites.

For the most part, however, libertarians refuse to draw these extreme and yet logical consequences of their own theses. They are content to limit their claims to the economic and social sphere, denouncing collective systems of social protection, unemployment benefits, public schools, etc. If each individual is a small society on his own and if he is totally sovereign, then it is only in the economic and social sphere that he is able to make his claims. If each individual is a small society in himself and if he is totally sovereign, it is indeed an attack on his freedom to force him to subscribe to social security or to pay taxes which will be used to finance a public school which he has not chosen and which he may not need if he has no children. In all these respects, it must be recognized that the libertarian theses have been widely heard, even if not always with the radicalism and systemic

---

33. On this subject, see the debate between Ruwen Ogien and Michela Marzano. To Ogien's minimalist ethics, Michela Marzano opposes an "ethics of autonomy" which cannot be reduced to consent. For the theses of MARZANO (Michela), *Je consens donc je suis... : éthique de l'autonomie*, PUF, 2006.

spirit of this school, whose dogmatism is often quite astounding. The growing privatization of the public sector, and in particular of health and schooling, is a fairly universal trend. Even when this privatization remains limited (as in France at present[34]), the general tone of public discourse is one of "responsibility": you are responsible for your health and therefore you must pay a fixed price for each medical consultation and for each drug in order to force you to act as a responsible patient. You are also responsible for the future of the planet and you are given all kinds of advice to preserve the environment. You are responsible for your professional future and you must therefore learn to "manage" yourselves. And so on.

The interesting paradox is this: the fundamental ideas of libertarians are disseminated in the form of an omnipresent discourse of guilt, and freedom, when put through the mill of government policies, appears to the vast majority as a regime of restriction. But the most serious thing is elsewhere: liberalism pushed to the limit explodes not only the republican forms of *welfare*, but also the very idea that men make society and that they find in social existence the very possibility of happiness. Individuals leading separate lives must be indifferent to each other. They are bound by no other duty to other members of the community than to respect their property. Nozick and his followers never fail to teach the little moral lesson that is essential to their theory: envy must be banished, as the only way to prevent the libertarian society from unraveling as soon as it is constituted, into a Hobbesian world where "man is a wolf to man". But as Rousseau already pointed out, envy is inevitable as soon as men live in society and inequality reigns among them. Moreover, the economic system preferred by liberals and libertarians, capitalism, functions on the basis of envy. The development of consumption is not so much based on the satisfaction of needs as on the desire of each person to have the same thing as his neighbor.

Liberal-libertarian ideas still find expression in the refusal to pay taxes: to pay taxes is to affirm one's membership in a community for which all

---

34. Many North Americans are convinced that France is one of the most socialist countries in the world...

its members are co-responsible. The anti-tax revolt of the wealthy classes - which, for example, has brought the very modern and trendy California into the Republican camp, alongside the backward hicks and millionaire preachers of the "moral majority" - is one expression of this phenomenon so well analyzed by Christopher Lasch[35].

Not all liberals share the complete and systematic doctrine of Nozick and his epigones. But in asserting the absolute rights of the individual as owner, they are led to reject all the constraints imposed by membership in a common political community. Vico thought that in ancient societies, the "barbaric" and "heroic" societies, the *gentes maiores*, the chiefs, the strong men and more generally the noble classes held the *famoli*, the plebs, to be strangers, and with great insight the Neapolitan philosopher wondered about the Latin term *hostis*, both host and enemy: the plebs are the host of the possessing classes - and as such they have no rights - and they are their potential enemy. The development of liberalism has resurrected this figure of a foreign plebeian towards whom the ruling classes, those who possess wealth, have no duty and all rights.

Contemporary liberalism therefore has little to do with that of Montesquieu or Tocqueville. The author of *The Spirit of the Laws* can still be rightly claimed to be a descendant of republicanism, whereas contemporary liberalism is irreducibly hostile to the republican spirit, since it makes the political community at best a necessary evil, at worst a straitjacket that the possessors have the right to break, thus transforming all social life into a merciless war of the possessing classes against the *famoli*. But this unrestricted freedom that liberals claim for themselves turns against the most elementary forms of freedom, first and foremost the classical "liberal" freedoms.

Let us conclude provisionally: contemporary liberalism accomplishes what is in potential in its classical seeds. As the leading edge of a movement that aims at mastering the world, the liberal current

---

35. See LASCH (Christopher), *La Révolte des élites et la trahison de la démocratie*, preface by Jean-Claude Michéa, translation by Christian Fournier, éditions Climats, 2003.

46

has profoundly shaken the old social and ideological structures, and for a while it could appear as a liberator or as the natural ally of all emancipatory currents. But now that the capitalist mode of production dominates the whole world without serious competition, contemporary liberalism will reveal itself as the main enemy of freedom... and thus of old liberalism. In other words, the tactical complicity of republicans and liberals may well be obsolete, and republicanism will emerge as the heir to the best of the liberal tradition - the defense of rights, the control of government - against the kind of liberalism that dominates in the age of "absolute capitalism."

The really existing democracy is an oligarchy

We have just been reminded of the extent to which liberalism and democracy have not always gone hand in hand and why liberalism has often been a "democracy for the race of lords". We must now question democracy itself.

If democracy is the exercise of power by the people as a whole - government of the people, by the people, for the people, as Abraham Lincoln famously defined it - such a government exists almost nowhere. Even leaving aside the question of the definition of the people, i.e., its boundaries, the manner in which citizenship is acquired, the only truly democratic democracy is direct democracy, or at least government under the direct control of the people. Examples of such a government are quite rare: a few decades of Athenian history, the Paris Commune, the Russian soviets for a brief period, the insurrectionary government in Budapest in 1956... Why have these experiences been so few and so short-lived?

What is called democracy in modern times is a kind of government that the ancients (Aristotle, Cicero, Polybius) and less ancient ones such as Machiavelli would have called "mixed government", that is, a regime in which the popular element, the aristocratic element and the monarchical element are combined, in varying proportions. Classical republicanism generally advocates a mixed form of government. Representative democracy, even in its most parliamentary forms, is by definition a mixed system: the popular element lies in the fact that the people decide who can and cannot be part of the governing aristocracy. Instead of a hereditary aristocracy or a competitive aristocracy, we have an elective aristocracy.

Let us be a little more precise. Parliamentary democracy is never purely parliamentary - except for the never-applied Constitution of 1793 - since the government is a separate organism (by virtue of the principle of the separation of powers) and this government has over the years taken on an increasingly monarchical character, even in regimes officially classified as parliamentary: for example, in Great Britain, Germany or Italy. In other words, even in parliamentary democracy, there is a monarchical element in addition to the popular and aristocratic elements. *A fortiori*, presidential (USA, Russia) or semi-presidential (France) regimes can be assimilated to monarchies where the monarch is elected for a limited period of time and is, more or less, controlled by a parliament.

The popular element of our mixed systems is more or less important. The frequency of electoral consultations, the way in which the various fractions of the people are represented, the existence or not of parties genuinely linked to the working classes, the existence or not of referendum procedures all play a part. It should also be noted that the popular element tends to become less important almost "spontaneously", through citizens' lack of interest in politics. In large democracies, it is increasingly common for electoral consultations not to mobilize even half of the registered voters - not to mention citizens who could be voters but are not, because they do not even ask themselves whether they are registered on the electoral rolls.

We live, therefore, neither in a democracy nor in a mixed regime in the sense of the republican tradition, but in regimes that are more and more clearly oligarchic. Oligarchy is, in the typology of the Ancients, a degeneration of aristocracy. The latter is, according to the etymology, the government of the best, the government of those who, by their qualities, deserve to govern and govern for the common good, whereas oligarchy is the government of the few for the interests of the few, and the main "merit" of the governors is to be rich[36]. Georges Sorel[37], who had the experience of the parliamentary republic before his eyes, wrote:

> "Democracy rests on the existence of a solid hierarchy; the oligarchy of big arrivistes needs an ardent troop of low officers who never stop working in the interest of their chiefs and who derive little material profit from their activity; it is necessary to keep this sort of little nobility in suspense, by lavishing them with marks of sympathy, by exciting in them feelings of honor, by speaking to them an idealistic language. The greatness of the country, the domination of natural forces by science, the march of mankind towards the light, these are the nonsense that is always to be found among us, in the speeches of democratic orators[38]."

We have before us a great deal of empirical evidence of the growth of this oligarchy born in the soil of "democracy". But aristocracy itself is a very indeterminate term. Who are the best? The most deserving? But as Aristotle points out, there is a general disagreement about what merit is. Traditionally, aristocracy is presented as the government of noble families, of the most honorable "races". The merit of the aristocrat in the ancient world, as in the European monarchies, lies in birth: virtues are supposed to pass from fathers to children, perhaps through seminal liquor... To this aristocracy of blood, characteristic of unequal societies, modern republicans wanted to substitute an aristocracy of virtue and knowledge. On the one hand, the election is supposed to allow the elevation to the rank of legislators the most virtuous citizens. On the other hand, the republican meritocracy organizes the selection according to the criteria of knowledge: the entrance exam to the Grandes Ecoles, which train the "normaliens" and the "polytechniciens" in order to make the best servants of the State.

---

36. See on this subject in *The Republic*, VIII, 550d-557a the still current description of the "oligarchic man".

37. A theorist of revolutionary syndicalism and the general strike, Sorel kept away from the main stream of socialism, which he saw becoming mired in parliamentarianism. He is an author worth reading (or rereading) today.

38. SOREL (G.), *Les Illusions du progrès*, L'âge d'homme, 2007, p. 182.

This idyllic picture has only a distant relationship with reality. The masters of the Old Regime were very often able to obtain the anointment of popular suffrage - in some campaigns, the squire, "our good master," frequently made a suitable deputy to the assemblies of the republic. In the absence of noble titles and landed property, some big bosses could easily convert the general equivalent into votes and thus do what was necessary to attract the good graces of the "sovereign people". In other words, the election, under the guise of popular sovereignty, provides a new veneer for the dominators of old. The anointing of the Lord and the anointing of universal suffrage come together (*vox populi, vox Dei*).

It is true that the people, the "low people", the *popolo minuto*, were able to find authentic representatives in democratic regimes, whether or not they came from their ranks. From the radicals to the socialists, from the socialists to the communists, the Third Republic allowed the social ascension to the highest functions of the petty bourgeois, the professors, the trade-union leaders and even the workers. But it would be a mistake to confuse the social ascent of elements representing the people with the people's accession to power. In the mechanism of the renewal of the elites, universal suffrage played its full role, that of organizing and conso-lidating the social and political consensus. Frequenting the gilded salons and dinners of good society, the revolutionaries were wisely domesticated - but perhaps that was all they asked for, since they had already fought to become leaders, spokesmen, general secretaries, etc.? The extension and radicalization of democracy did not overthrow oligarchic domination, but only broadened its bases. It is not just a question of direct political personnel. Union leaders play their own game, often far more politically important than that of the "workers" parties. In return, numerous posi-tions, however modest, are available to any trade unionist who wishes to make a career - from the simple works council to the thousand and one companies dependent on social organizations, via the Economic and Social Council.

Since the 20th century, oligarchy has taken on new forms. It has become largely globalized and lives more and more independently of its former "national bases" and, on the other hand, it exerts its influence directly through the media, television or Internet, which tend, more and more, to make the candidates and to make the elections.

The formation of a transnational capitalist class is analyzed at length by Leslie Sklair in his book, *The Transnational Capitalist Class*[39]. The interest of this work is that it does not limit itself to the analysis of the structuring of capital on a global scale - a task in which a certain number of Marxists such as François Chesnais excel[40]. He tries to draw out the ideological specificities as well as the links between individuals and groups that make such a class appear, not only "in itself", but also "for itself". For Sklair, this cultural-ideological dimension is even essential and allows to understand the power and the capacities of resistance to the crises of this transnational capitalist class:

> "The first cultural-ideological task of global capitalism is to ensure that as many people as possible consume as much as possible by inculcating beliefs about the intrinsic value of consumption as a 'good thing' and key behavior of a 'good life.' Thus [...] the captains of industry have been reinforced by the captains of conscience[41]."

While traditional Marxism considers ideology as a simple "superstructure", concentrating its features on the "infrastructure", i.e. the relations of production and the relations of class, Sklair underlines the importance on the part of the dominant classes, of what one could call "ideological struggle" and whose object is nothing else than the "colonization of the consciences". There is a new phenomenon here: the national capitalist classes each governed according to their own natural way, and did so by relying on different, even frankly conflicting, ideologies. Thus the German and French ruling classes in the nineteenth and early twentieth centuries used very different ideological resources, precisely because the struggle for hegemony in Europe was at stake. These contradictions between the capita-

---

39. Sklair (L.), *op. cit.*
40. See Chesnais (F.), *La Mondialisation du capital*, Syros, 1994.
41. *Op. cit.* p. 11.

list powers for the division of the world - one of the essential characteristics of imperialism according to Lenin - take a subordinate place today:

> "for the global capitalist system, considered as a whole, these internal struggles of the ruling class are less important than what binds the members of that class together, taken as a whole, that is, their common interest in the protection of private property and the rights of private individuals to accumulate it with as little interference as possible[42]."

Just as national ruling classes are formed through an institutional network of schools, clubs and marriages (of love, of course!), so the existence of transnational firms develops this type of relationship and allows the effective formation of a transnational class conscious of its own interests. Sklair breaks down the Transnational Capitalist Class (TCC[43]) into several strata:

- executives of transnational corporations (TNCs) and their local representatives);
- bureaucrats and "globalized" politicians;
- Globalized professionals (technicians, scientists);
- merchants and the media.

The first of these groups is the dominant group, and the other three form the foundation. The CTC can also be defined politically. Its members oppose not only those who reject capitalism, but also those sections of the national ruling classes who reject globalization[44]. Apart from transnational firms, purely national firms now represent only a very narrow sector. Even firms that are state-owned or have some kind of monopoly on the national terrain are increasingly behaving like TNFs. Sklair considers the definition of multinationals in the early 1970s as domestically based firms operating abroad to be outdated. The interests of CTC members are primarily focused on the international arena, and both TNFs and the international

---

42. Sklair (L.), *op. cit.* p. 12.
43. Sklair uses the abbreviations TCC for *Transnational Capitalist Class* and TNC for *Transnational Corporations.*
44. The Anglo-Saxons use the term *"globalization"*, but the term used in France is "mondialisation".

institutions they rely on (e.g., WTO) emphasize free trade and the development of export strategies. In terms of power, Sklair notes that:

> "The concept of a transnational capitalist class implies that there is a central inner circle that makes decisions on a broad systemic scale, and that it connects through various channels with subsidiary members in communities, cities, countries and supranational regions[45]."

To explain this mechanism by which a restricted core assures its domination, Sklair appeals to the Gramscian concept of hegemony. It is a much-used concept, perhaps too much so, but Sklair is not wrong to use it since the ideologues of the parties of this new class themselves use the reference to Gramsci. What is meant by the term hegemony? In fact two things: the ideological battle and a strategy of class alliances. A dominant class cannot dominate durably by force alone. It must also benefit from the consensus of the dominated, and to do this, it must strive to make the majority share its general views, its conception of the world as much as its moral ideas and its long-term perspectives. What is elaborated in *think tanks*, clubs and more or less discreet foundations must then irrigate the whole social body, become the common language of the major media, but also of the school and of all the places where the thoughts of those who will have to implement the policy decided by the ruling classes are formed. The ruling class must then appear as the bearer of the interests of much wider layers. If the nation is no longer the cement of this class alliance, other mobilizing themes must be found. A certain cosmopolitanism serves as a common background for the ruling circles and the new intellectual classes that have developed in the last decades with the new extension of world trade and the new information and communication technologies. This cosmopolitanism is the bearer of impeccable moral ideals: it is hostile to all discrimination that could prevent an individual from realizing his or her ambitions, whether it be discrimination based on gender, skin color or sexual orientation. But this refusal of discrimination is only the obverse

---

45. SKLAIR (L.), *op. cit.* p. 21.

of a medal whose reverse side is the acceptance of inequalities. Thus, we can see political leaders condemning racism or discrimination against homosexuals and, almost in the same speech, attacking the egalitarian ideals of the French Revolution, which would have handicapped this country by undermining the culture of responsibility at its base. The link between the two sides of the discourse is clear: as soon as there is no more discrimination (as contemporary globalist cosmopolitanism demands), the poor are poor by their own fault, and, consequently, national systems of solidarity no longer have any reason to exist, all the more so as they are revealed as brakes on the development of the only stimulus to progress that is competition. If there had been only the "economic liberalism" side, the CTC would never have been able to establish its domination. Friedrich Hayek's Mont Pelerin Society, however clever its strategies for penetrating political circles, could never have won ideologically. It is the alliance with a large layer of the upper middle classes that ensures its success, those upper middle classes that want, for themselves and for their children, to consolidate the positions acquired by what they believe to be their skills.

The oligarchic drift of advanced capitalist societies, of those which, precisely, boasted and still boast of their democratic character, is therefore not only a consequence of the almost irremediable rotting of any political regime. On the contrary, it corresponds to a profound renewal of the ruling elite, a renewal of which we have not measured the full extent and which shifts the lines of political, social and cultural cleavages. To understand this, we need a theory of the formation of the ruling classes.

The new elites

It would be necessary to return to the philosophical and sociological theories that have sought to understand the formation, maintenance and eventual disappearance of elites. In Italian culture, the question of elites plays an important role, often neglected elsewhere. From Machiavelli to Gramsci, through Vilfredo Pareto, Gaetano Mosca and Roberto Michels, these authors have given often divergent, but always stimulating approaches to the formation of the ruling classes and the means they use to establish their hegemony and renew themselves. Compared to the traditional Marxist analyses which stick to class relations, reduced to the property relations of the means of production and exchange, the analyses on the formation of elites have the advantage of emphasizing the phenomena of domination which are not directly linked to the relations of production as well as the internal transformations of the ruling classes, which should interest those who want to reflect on politics in strategic terms.

In the course of the last century, two types of phenomena have developed and flourished, perhaps converging, but distinct. In the first place, the bureaucracies that emerged from the workers' and anti-capitalist movement took on an ever greater role in the management of capitalism on a global scale. From the beginning of the 20th century, Roberto Michels was able to analyze the increasingly conservative role of the apparatuses of the social-democratic parties and the trade unions. The triumph of the Bolsheviks in Russia in 1917 allowed for the development of a new "revolutionary" bureaucracy that could be said to have all the characteristics of a new ruling class. Trotsky and the orthodox Trotskyists fervently argued that the bureaucratic caste that ruled the USSR was not a new social class, but a parasitic and counterrevolutionary outgrowth on the healthy body of the Soviet "workers" state. With the establishment of political and social regimes similar to that of the USSR in Eastern Europe and later in China, North Korea and Cuba in 1959, the Trotskyist thesis, which assumed the exceptional and aberrant character of the development of the Soviet Union, could no longer be supported. The majority of Trotskyists, however, clung to it against all reason. However, the discussion about the nature of the USSR and its ruling bureaucracy, which began in the ranks of the communist (including Trotskyist) left, soon made it clear that the USSR and the so-called "socialist" countries presented new, unprecedented forms of domination. James Burnham, a brilliant Trotskyist intellectual, evolved quite rapidly after the German-Soviet pact and the invasion of Poland and Finland by the "red" army. Taking up ideas put forward by the Italian Bruno Rizzi (who was also close to Trotskyism for a while),

Democracy, oligarchy, elites and control of the masses

but without acknowledging his debt, Burnham saw the emergence of a new class, that of organizers, of which the Soviet bureaucracy was the first example. Just as Rizzi had analyzed "the bureaucratization of the world", so Burnham announces that the development of this new layer of organizers (or managers) concerns all countries in one form or another.

In another, more optimistic way, these conclusions are corroborated by economists and political scientists such as J.K. Galbraith or Maurice Duverger, who support the theory of a convergence between capitalist and socialist regimes, a convergence achieved through the democratization of socialist regimes and the state social organization of capitalist countries. These two authors, typical of the "Trente Glorieuses" ideology, insist on the development of a new ruling elite of "managers".

The fall of the Soviet Union and the "neoliberal" turn in capitalist societies have relegated Burnham and Galbraith's theories to the background. But one wonders whether a new elite has not come to power in the last thirty or forty years, a new elite that is being formed by absorbing some parts of the old ones (for example, those who occupied the field during the time of the welfare state) and by simply ousting others, those who took advantage of the high culture. Whereas the old-style technobureaucracy, that of socialism or the Stalinist system, as well as that of the authoritarian states or the welfare state, was visible and even claimed its own existence as a manifestation of historical progress, the new elite denies its own existence, conceals the ties that bind its members, the processes of selection of new members, the exorbitant legal privileges it enjoys.

There are certainly a number of partial studies of the elites of the early 21st century. We have already mentioned Leslie Sklair's work on the transnational capitalist class. Roberto Michels' investigations of workers' organizations should be revisited, focusing on the unions. Beyond the tendency towards conservatism that Michels was talking about, the trade union apparatuses are today, almost everywhere in the world, integrated into the functioning of the capitalist mode of production. They are less and less organizations whose aim is the defense of the "material and moral interests" of the workers and more and more cogs in the state apparatus, of which they co-manage decisive sectors, such as social protection in all its forms. At the same time, it is no longer necessary for unions to have members and militants. They need only be "representative", according to criteria agreed between union leaders and governments.

Here an incident is necessary: it is not a question of repeating the leftist discourse on the "betrayal" of the union "bonzes". The trade union apparatuses have evolved according to the resultant of the forces that are exerted on them. On the one hand, a working class that is progressively losing all consistency, to the point that one can say that there are still many workers, but that they no longer form a class conscious of its own objectives; on the other hand, the upheavals of the capitalist mode of production and the displacement of relations within the capitalist class: on both sides, the trade union apparatus loses its support and tries to negotiate its survival and to defend the interests of its constituents in a situation where, globally, everyone has admitted that the capitalist mode of production is without serious competitors and that the only real perspective is to negotiate within the frameworks set by global capitalism.

This is the same movement that is leading to the end of the mass parties that dominated the last century. The social democratic parties were the first such parties, no longer informal gatherings behind a few individuals, no longer simple coalitions of interests behind a powerful protector (as were the factions of the old republics), but structured organizations, with their own ideology and discipline, which contributed in their own way to the circulation of elites. The fascist parties took up this principle of the mass party, as did the communist parties: Lenin, setting out in *What to do?* the principles of what was to become Bolshevism, was inspired first of all by the German social-democratic model and the ideas of Kautsky. The major European Christian Democratic parties also sought to be mass parties on this model, notably in Germany and Italy. The case of the British *Labour Party* is somewhat different, since it is a party that was first created as the parliamentary representation of the trade unions. In any case, all these mass parties have disappeared or are in agony. The Italian case is spectacular: in a few years, the powerful PCI, which formed a real counter-society, especially in the regions it controlled, has broken up and been replaced by a simple electoral apparatus. In its place, there are electoral apparatuses, populated by professionals and elected officials, without doctrine, with committees of experts providing programmatic axes and ideological justifications. "Registered voters" are called upon to participate in the choice of the leader through "primaries", a mode imported from the United States where they have a completely different history. This new organization, which we do not hesitate to call "participatory democracy" in a very Orwellian way, consecrates the separation of the mass of citizens, who are less and less citizens in the original sense of the term, from a ruling elite that unites the economic elite, the political elite and the media elite, with individuals navigating from one of these spheres to the other according to circumstances.

It must be recognized that the ideal of a democracy in which everyone is "alternately ruler and ruled" (Aristotle) is an unattainable ideal in the complex and vast modern social formations. Democracy in its modern sense has always been representative. The general will is exercised through the will of the representatives: a primary figure of political alienation according to Rousseau, but an inescapable figure as soon as the republic is no longer "of a size limited by the extent of human faculties, that is to say, by the possibility of being well governed, and where each one is sufficient for his own job, no one would have been obliged to entrust to others the functions with which he was charged: a state where all individuals knew each other, the *obscure* maneuvers of vice nor the modesty of virtue could have escaped the public gaze and judgment, and where this sweet habit of seeing and knowing each other, made the love of the fatherland the love of the citizens rather than that of the land[46]."

But in the *Social Contract*, Rousseau makes this remark: "If there were a people of gods, they would govern themselves democratically. A government so perfect is not suitable for men." (L. III, chap. IV) The *Social Contract* is underpinned by a model of direct democracy, since the general

---

46. ROUSSEAU (J.-J.), *Discourse on the origin and foundations of inequality among men*, Dedication.

will can only result from the will of all bodies forming and the will of the citizen cannot be represented: I can always delegate to someone the accomplishment of some task, but I cannot delegate to anyone to will for me what I should will. In other words, representative democracy, in all its forms, is already a form of political alienation, that is, a loss of original freedom: "man is born free and everywhere he is in fetters." But Rousseau is aware that the pure model of the government of the sovereign people is practically impossible, or, if it exists, it is quick to be corrupted.

In fact, revolutionary democracy, the direct expression of the "little people", the one dreamed of by anarchist socialists (Proudhon's communes) or that of revolutionary Marxist councillors, has been shattered by reality. In the first moments of an insurrection, on March 18, 1871 in Paris, in Russia in 1905 and in February 1917, in Hungary in 1956, the committees, councils, soviets, organs of direct democracy give form to the popular movement, they are the mediation that allows to transform the revolt into a political movement. But, very quickly, they turn into either assemblies of impotent chatterboxes or organs of manipulation of the masses by well-organized minorities. The first reproach is addressed by Marx to the Paris Commune whose procrastination was fatal. The soviets under Bolshevik control illustrate the second reproach. Indeed, dominated classes make very bad dominating classes. The popular assemblies, whatever they are, after the excitement of the first days, become the theater where the smooth talkers, who are not often from the poorest backgrounds, confront each other. The strength of the people, which is felt in the great revolutionary moments, is reduced as soon as it is a question of stabilizing the situation, of making decisions. This is why a new elite emerges - in the most favourable situations - without which direct democracy will be diluted and liquidated. In Portugal in 1974 and in Eastern Europe in the 1980s, all combinations met. The direct-democratic organizations in Portugal never managed to emerge as an independent force and broke up. Workers' unionism in Poland fell under the control of a political faction linked to the Catholic Church. In the GDR and Czechoslovakia, the demonstrators were never able to come together as an autonomous political force, giving way to politicians from the former Stalinist apparatus. Nowhere did the dominated classes - although they were politically literate - succeed in establishing new, living democratic institutions in the long term. Once again, it is necessary to discard the reassuring explanations that each time discover particular circumstances that give reason for the failure of the popular movement. Neither the betrayal of the leaders, nor their lack of historical insight, nor this or that weakness specific to the people of a given country can explain why politics always remains the business of minorities, the majority being at most a supporting force. Man does not live by politics alone! He must most often be concerned first of all with living, with making his children live, and political passion is a passion too elaborate to touch the majority of humans, except in rare moments, and from this point of view, the most stable form of majority participation is representative democracy, as imperfect as it may be with respect to a conception of democracy made for the gods.

The question is therefore to determine how democracy can remain democratic when it is representative, i.e. when the people must entrust an elite of elected officials (but that is an elite!) with the task of carrying out the functions that democracy would like it to be entrusted with. The two minimal conditions are, first, the regular control of the elected representatives, on the basis of a broad political discussion and the holding of honest and fair elections and, second, the regular renewal of the political class, by drawing on the pool of the popular classes. These two conditions are either non-existent or drastically limited in most democratic states. Long terms of office were unknown in the old republics, which often set a maximum term of six months or one year for those who had the power to govern. Today, the shortest terms of office are in the United States and are four years. In France, they are between five and six years, leaving ample time for those in office to flout their commitments to the people. Electoral systems are designed in such a way that very large sections of the people are excluded from participating in the vote. A "majority" party can win with one-third of the votes cast, minorities are ruthlessly suppressed in the name of governmental stability, while abstention is on the rise in all democracies and the number of unregistered citizens is increasing. The so-called power of the majority is now only the power of the minority, strong enough to organize its maintenance in power by preserving the appearance of free elections - but not hesitating to resort to rigging and ballot stuffing in case of emergency, as the 2000 presidential election in Florida showed.

The essential problem, therefore, is not that of the separation between the governors and the governed. This separation is a given that cannot be eliminated. The realist theorists start from the existence of a political class, of an elite, of a vanguard party, of an active minority, let's call it as we want. The question of political freedom is precisely that of the relationship between the masses and the elites, or between the people and the great, to use Machiavellian language. There is a democratic republic when the people can freely choose their leaders, can control them - that is, when there are mechanisms to protect them against the abuse of power - and can challenge their decisions[47]. Conversely, oligarchy means the monopolization of leadership positions by a minority of the rich who are able to eliminate the influence of the people or corrupt them. The dominant trend today is this.

"Neoliberalism" and financial oligarchy

Let us beware of the generally misleading use of the term "liberalism" instead of "capitalism". There is an honorable liberalism that must be defended, and anti-liberalism serves as a banner for so many dubious enterprises! However, the term "neoliberalism" can refer to what the

---

47. The idea of a power exercised directly by the lower class - the "dictatorship of the proletariat" among Marxists - is, from this point of view, extremely paradoxical. The proletariat, by definition, is a subaltern class; the dictatorship of the proletariat would be the domination of a subaltern class, which is a logical contradiction. This class that exercises its dictatorship is no longer the proletariat, but simply a new political ruling class. To understand this, we need to read or reread George Orwell's *Animal Farm*: after the animals chase the farmers away, the pigs soon convince the other animals that specialists are needed to run the farm. And the pigs soon stop walking on all fours: "four legs are good, two legs are better"...

Democracy, oligarchy, elites and control of the masses

Italians call "liberism", that is to say an ideology whose different variants converge on two theses:

- The "free" market is the best system for allocating resources for production to achieve economic growth and common prosperity;
- The state should intervene as little as possible in all areas that could be advantageously left to free enterprise and individual responsibility - this includes most public services and social protection, which should be replaced by private insurance systems.

Reduced to its regalian functions, in other words to the protection of private property, the State should progressively replace the rule of law and sovereign power with modalities of "governance" that give pride of place to negotiation between "actors", to bargaining, in cenacles where the elites co-opt each other and escape all popular control. The European Union is a model of this "governance" without government. This "neo-liberalism" has a liberal façade, but only a façade. It is not a return to the "Manchester system" as the defenders and opponents of the policies implemented since the late 1970s have said. The reality of today's capitalism is not a mad attempt to implement a centuries-old liberal utopia.

First of all, the entanglement between the state and big business is more total than ever. If the Keynesianism of the decades following the Second World War may have appeared to be a kind of state capitalism - in the PCF, it was called CME, State Monopoly Capitalism - the turning point at the end of the 1970s modified its forms, but not its profound reality: the links of American President Obama with the great financial institutions of Wall Street, such as Goldmann Sachs, are well known, as is the dismantling of the French nationalized sector... for the benefit of senior officials linked to the business world. Whereas in the 1970s, studies abounded showing the role of the arms economy in the functioning of the capitalist mode of production, there seems to be much less interest in it, but it continues to be as essential as it was during the Cold War. The importance of "gun merchants" and military orders remains decisive. It is also often difficult to understand what is really at stake in privatization and the introduction of competition in public services. Officially, it is a question of reducing the scope of the state in favour of private initiative. The orthodox liberal doctrine would imply that the state should be confined to its "regalian functions". In practice, it is something else: former public services are entrusted to private companies (e.g., highways) or transformed into private companies (e.g., La Poste, France Télécom, EDF/GDF), but these companies, which are entrusted with public service missions, remain linked to the state by all sorts of contracts, a state that often continues to own part of the capital and directly supervises the appointment of their CEOs. The public authorities continue to provide these companies with guarantees, particularly financial guarantees. For the private capitalists who invest in these sectors, it is an investment without serious risk: the management of personnel is that of the private sector, the users are transformed into "clients", but in case of problems, it is the public that pays. Public-private partnerships" (PPPs) are expanding rapidly in all sectors. Far from being a "de-statization", the "liberalization" of the public sector is, on the contrary, a transformation of state management, which is increasingly modelled on that of a company - and, significantly, elected officials at all levels willingly compare themselves to managers. There is, more than ever, a continuum between the state and capitalist enterprises, with state coffers being able, if necessary, to make up for the cash-flow failures of private companies: the rescue of virtually bankrupt banks after the bursting of the *subprime* "bubble" gave a striking illustration of this.

Neoliberalism is not a return to entrepreneurial capitalism based on production, but the excessive development of all forms of parasitism. Financial deregulation allows all kinds of audacity in speculation. The outsourcing of management functions through auditing firms, consulting firms, coaches, etc., creates pseudo-companies that have no other purpose than to involve new layers trained in *business schools in* the sharing of surplus value, partly at the expense of employees, but also of productive capital, and to contribute to an enlargement and diversification of the elite, whose flashy success plays a prominent ideological role. This development of parasitism stems from the very functioning of the mode of production:

Marx showed that the domination of finance and its side effects, such as speculation and finally the constitution of a unified financial market on a global scale, are not mysterious processes, separated from what happens in the "engine room" of production. The development of "fictitious capital", of which government bonds were for a long time the most complete form, has found new ways with the unprecedented growth of the "derivatives" market. Financial capital can be divided into two categories that are usually confused and yet are radically different in nature:

1. Medium- and long-term loans that finance productive investments and whose interest is basically a deduction from the surplus value produced in the production process;
2. Phantom capital, represented by receivables that are exchangeable for future cash commitments, the value of which is derived entirely from the capitalization of anticipated income with no direct counterpart in earning capital.

Let us follow Marx's reasoning for a moment.

> "The form of interest-producing capital makes any definite and regular money income seem to be the interest of a capital, whether or not it comes from a capital[48]."

The "fictitious capital" is based on a retrospective intellectual operation, which supposes an inversion of means and ends, an operation proper to the process of production of ideological representations. "Monetary income is first transformed into interest, and, from there, we also find the capital that is its source." Marx is content here to describe the concrete functioning of the capitalist mode of production. Thus the sale price of a piece of real estate is calculated by considering that this property is interest-bearing capital, the latter being represented by the rent. But this process has an important consequence: "any sum of value appears as capital, as soon as it is not spent as income; it appears as a principal sum by contrast with the

---

48. Marx (K.), *Capital*, book III, chap. V, p. 1161, in *Œuvres II* [By "Œuvres" we mean the Rubel edition in the Pléiade collection].

possible or real interest that it is capable of producing." The example of government debt sheds light on the consequences of this process:

> "The government must pay its creditors a certain amount of interest each year for the capital borrowed. In this case, the creditor cannot cancel his loan, but he can sell his claim, the title that assures him of ownership. The capital itself has been consumed, spent by the state. It no longer exists. What the creditor has is (1) a title of ownership, (2) what follows from it, namely, a right to an annual levy on the proceeds of taxes, and (3) the right to sell that title. "But in all these cases, the capital that is supposed to produce an offspring (interest), the payment of the State, is an illusory, fictitious capital. This is because the sum loaned to the state not only no longer exists, but was never intended to be spent as capital."

For the creditor, lending money to the government to obtain a share of the tax proceeds, or lending money to an industrialist at an average interest rate, or buying shares to receive dividends, are equivalent transactions.

> "But the capital of the public debt is none the less purely fictitious, and the day the bonds become unsaleable, the very appearance of that capital is over."

But public debt is not the only form of fictitious capital. "Fictitious money capital" includes all varieties of interest-bearing money market securities, insofar as they circulate on the stock market, as well as shares. To this must be added the many "new financial products" which all, in one form or another, aim to "securitize" credit and to circulate debt securities as capital. In this category, we must include "high-risk products" such as *junk bonds*, which are highly leveraged because they are based on bad debts. *Subprime* mortgages, which were the factual cause of the 2007 crisis, fall into the same category: they are the "securitization" of bad debts - linked to the indebtedness of poor households for the purchase of their homes. Households unable to meet the escalating debt are forced to sell their property and it is expected that foreclosing and reselling the property will provide a good "return on investment", as the housing market is expected to rise continuously. The system worked until household debt led to massive foreclosures of unpaid homes that had to be resold in a crowded market. The bankruptcies of individuals thus led to the bankruptcies of credit institutions and the crisis spread through a financial system addicted to derivatives (in 2005, the amount of transactions on the derivatives market was nearly 30 times the amount of transactions on the "normal" financial markets). But if the machine has jammed, it is because the so-called "real economy" (as if, from a capitalist point of view, speculation on the financial markets was an unreal economy!) was showing signs of serious exhaustion. The financial economy produces nothing, it is only a means of pumping out the surplus-value produced in the productive system for the benefit of the capitalist stratum that today dominates all the others, financial capital. One can dream of a reinvigorated, "moralized" capitalism, but this is only a dream.

A third aspect is the role of the mafias and *rogue capitalism*. Honest capitalism, the virtuous Christian boss, the impeccable exploiter, has always been accompanied by an army of adventurers, shady financiers and real crooks. Balzac and Zola (cf. *L'Argent*) give numerous illustrations of this. But what in the end was only the scum of the movement, the "dregs of bourgeois society" of which Marx speaks when he tries to understand the social roots of Bonapartism, has become an essential component of the global functioning of the capitalist mode of production. The difference between honest business and shady business has become very thin: the drug economy and the sex economy are non-marginal integral parts of the global economy as a whole. *Offshore* financial centers provide the interface between the light and dark sides of the economy.

The whole is locked by devices of ideological and social control like no other social formation has known before. We return to this in the following chapters. But this control implies transformations of the legal system and an expansion of the role of the police that contradict all the most venerable liberal principles.

Thus, neoliberalism appears not as the achievement of liberalism, but as its negation - or, if you like, as a self-destructive achievement. The liberating potential of the first liberalism, that which attacks the absolutist state and promotes the civil rights of individuals, seems to be exhausted. The question we will have to ask is what social forces and political strategies can guarantee what is worth saving in the liberal heritage.

Far from the soothing discourse on the unceasing progress of democracy, or even its definitive triumph, let us note that political freedom is threatened by the ever-increasing power of oligarchies. Political freedom, in accordance with the republican ideal, is one of the disappearing political values. We take for democracy what is only a caricature of it, i.e. a mixture of demagogy and organized stultification of the masses - according to recipes that the Rome of the decadence of the Republic and the Empire had already tested. An uncompromising critique of these oligarchic "democracies" is indispensable. Chains covered with flowers.

But it is futile to dream of a people's power, a democracy of councils, a federation of communes or any other formula that can be drawn from the arsenal of revolutionary utopias. The state is necessary - at least on a conceivable human horizon - and freedom can only be defined in this relationship to the state. If politics is the business of minorities, how is it possible to combine in a way that preserves freedom this dialectic between the people and the great of which Machiavelli spoke? We will come back to this in the last part.

Chapter II
The end of negative freedom
and the surveillance society

Many liberals, such as Isaiah Berlin, believe that freedom should be limited to negative freedom, that is, the freedoms and rights to do what does not harm others. I am free, negatively, only "insofar as no one interferes with my action[49]". Conversely, they consider dangerous and potentially tyrannical the demanding conception of freedom as self-realization through political action, as it is found both in ancient republicanism (Aristotle or Cicero) and in modern theorists of radical democracy such as Rousseau[50]. Without going into detail here, one can, of course, admit that most liberal freedoms are essential ingredients of any extended conception of freedom: freedom of conscience, freedom of expression of one's opinions, freedom to come and go without being accountable to the police, freedom from spying, freedom from arbitrary imprisonment, rights of defence, right to privacy, rights of the person, to engage in whatever occupation seems good, etc. The (non-limitative) list of rights and freedoms understood under the Berlin concept of "negative freedom", all these "freedoms of the Moderns", should be fully claimed by all those who militate for a radical transformation of social relations and think it necessary to substitute the

---

49. Berlin (I.), "Two Concepts of Freedom", p. 171.
50. Berlin claims that Rousseau formulated the basic principles of communism, fascism and all totalitarian orders... Just that!

social appropriation of the means of production for capitalist property. Even the right to private property should be guaranteed in a socialist or communist society as soon as one can distinguish between private property and capitalist property. The inability of the communist movement of the 20th century and of the various revolutionary movements to understand the importance of this heritage of classical liberalism is one of the deep causes of the failure of these movements[51].

Yet it is precisely at the moment when today's liberals are trumpeting the news of their definitive ideological triumph that we are witnessing an unprecedented regression of these fundamental liberal freedoms. It is as if they were just a propaganda tool to be waved in the face of the "communist danger", but a tool that has become completely useless now that the monster has collapsed.

There are three particularly crucial aspects. The first concerns freedom of expression, and it is all the more strange that the regression of freedom in this area was largely initiated under pressure from the "societal left" movements. The second concerns the obsession with security and the generalization of surveillance, propagated by those who claim to be the most liberal and who never stop praising the risk society. The third is the indefinite extension of the law's domain, in a world where the magical belief in the powers of the law prevails over any other consideration and where everyone always finds a good reason to make yet another small law, nibbling away at freedoms.

Thought police and speech police

In the "novlanguage" of *1984*, "the expression of unorthodox thoughts was almost impossible". "A person educated only in Novlanguage would no more know that *equal* had once had the secondary meaning of *politically equal* or that *free* had once meant *politically free* than, for example, a person

---

51. On this point, we refer to the conclusions of our books, *Revive the Republic!* and *Marx's Nightmare.*

who had never heard of chess would know the special meaning attached to *queen* and *rook*[52]."

Political correctness" was first imposed from the left and from the United States. Oppressed "minorities" or victims of massive injustice demand consideration and words are seen as a way to ignore this injustice or to despise this handicap. Nothing is more understandable: social violence is also expressed in language. Being an African American is different from being a nigger, and it is surely better to be *gay* than queer. Through the battle of language, it is a question of recognition.

Recognition: this is a theme that has become central to political and social demands as well as to moral philosophy. Axel Honneth, a German philosopher who has put this concept at the center of his thinking, starts from Hegel and his "dialectic of master and slave" to make social conflict a conflict for recognition: by confronting the one who wants to dominate me, I want him to recognize my value and my dignity. For Honneth, a continuator of the Frankfurt School, recognition, however, cannot be purely verbal; it is linked to and gives justification to social radicalism. There is something profoundly right in this approach: even in the most elementary social demands, there is always something to do with recognition. When workers go on strike for wage increases, the material results of the strike rarely match the costs. From a strictly utilitarian point of view, the strike is rarely a good calculation. And even then, we are talking about a country and a time when strikes are generally peaceful and the right to strike is protected, because losing one's life for a few pennies of increase is the worst calculation. It is thus that, in the strike, there is another spring, moral, this claim of recognition: "we are men and not dogs", says an old revolutionary song.

It is therefore understandable why recognition is at the heart of the demands of those who see themselves as groups that are victims of domination and oppression. Things get worse when recognition becomes

---

52. ORWELL (G.), *1984*, translated from English by Amélie Audiberti, Gallimard, Folio, p. 435 and 436.

an abstraction, erected as an absolute independently of the social and political conditions of the moment, and tends to substitute itself for justice. No doubt it is absurd to oppose social justice and the struggle for recognition, as Nancy Fraser rightly shows[53]. The fact remains that this is in fact what is happening. On the one hand, recognition replaces social demand and, on the other hand, oppressed groups are engaged in the competition for recognition.

In social struggle, the dominant know from long experience that paying the dominated with words is the cheapest. Recognition is what is most easily given. Black Americans continue to break all the records for poverty, unemployment, lack of education, and massively populate the prisons... but they have the satisfaction of no longer being despised... in the official language at least. The workers are renamed "collaborators": it doesn't cost a cent more. Wal-Mart's "collaborators" have become emblematic of the new overexploitation of workers (some authors speak of the "Wal-martization" of companies) and should be prepared to look for work elsewhere if, by chance, they feel like collaborating with their co-workers in order to create unions...

All *political correctness* works on this model. While we pretend to recognize the value of a particular group, we practically devalue it. The policies of "positive discrimination", or *affirmative action* according to the American expression, only recognize the injustice done to a group in order to lock it in better. In France, the ZEP recognizes the difficulties of "socio-cultural" origin of children from poor neighborhoods... in order to better provide them with an education for the poor, an education that sometimes has little to do with the one from which the children of the bourgeoisie and petit-bourgeoisie of the wealthy neighborhoods can still benefit. My son, who attended one of these ZEP schools, had found the right explanation: ZEP means "Zone d'éducation péjorative". The truth comes out of the mouths of children... Thus the recognition granted by

---

53. FRASER (Nancy), *What is Social Justice? Reconnaissance et redistribution*, translated from English by Estelle Ferrarese, éditions La Découverte, 2005.

the dominant ones reveals itself as a new, more hypocritical and more repulsive form of social contempt.

But the secondary benefits that the dominant classes derive from the recognition granted do not stop there. Not only is social peace bought very cheaply, but recognition also legitimizes the cutting off of freedom of expression. Unable to obtain an end to racial discrimination in hiring - because this would mean infringing on the freedom of capitalists to hire whoever they want - the sanctimonious anti-racists focus on the speech they want to ban. Racial slurs are punishable by law. And one thing leads to another: macho language or homophobic slurs are in the crosshairs. The irascible driver who sends other motorists to Sodom and Gomorrah will no longer be fined for traffic violations, but could be sent to court for homophobic insults. But there is no reason to stop at name-calling. Even a formally very polite speech can be equated with contempt for a group. For example, a member of parliament was fined quite heavily for homophobic remarks, on the grounds that he had considered homosexuality not to be a normal moral behaviour. In the absence of social transformation, the "bourgeois" justice is summoned to condemn the words and the remarks that express non-conforming ideas.

It is not enough to police the language of ordinary life or public discussion. History must be attuned to the demands of "recognition". Certainly, the oppressed and the victims need to have their history as oppressed recognized. It is certain that, too often, the history taught officially is the history seen by the dominant. But this official history is often followed by another kind of official history, which is equally entitled to distort the facts. Only the values have been reversed. As early as 1989, the orientation law adopted on the proposal of Lionel Jospin required that the programs make a suitable place for the criticism of colonization. In 1991, the Gayssot law outlawed any challenge to the commonly accepted reality of the genocide of Jews and other human groups (Gypsies, homosexuals, etc.) in Europe. In both cases, the good intention is not in doubt. But good intentions lead to the destruction of the very freedom and democracy they claim to defend. For freedom of speech and freedom of criticism are the elementary conditions of freedom itself. If there is an official truth that is indisputable under penalty of criminal prosecution concerning the extermination of the Jews of Europe, why should there not be a historical truth in general? Many historians and defenders of human rights, anti-fascist, anti-racist, anti-colonial activists, such as Pierre Vidal-Naquet or Madeleine Rebérioux, denounced the Gayssot law from the start. For Madeleine Rebérioux :

> "The text of the Gayssot law is highly questionable for three reasons:
> - it entrusts to the law what is of the normative order and to the judge in charge of its application the responsibility of telling the truth in history, whereas the historical truth rejects any official authority. The USSR paid dearly enough for its behavior in this area for the French Republic not to follow in its footsteps;
> - it almost inevitably leads to its extension one day to other fields than the genocide of the Jews: other genocides and other attacks on what will be called "historical truth";
> - it allows the negationists to present themselves as martyrs, or at least as persecuted. Already, Garaudy is publishing a new edition of his book in "samizdat"[54]!"

Pierre Vidal-Naquet stated:

> "I have always been absolutely against this law, along with the great majority of historians. It risks bringing us back to state truths and turning intellectual zeros into martyrs. The Soviet experience has shown where state truths lead. The 1972 law against racism is more than enough[55]."

One cannot suspect Pierre Vidal-Naquet of being too indulgent towards revisionists and negationists. His position is one of simple common sense. As soon as the truth needs the powers of the police and the judiciary to make itself heard, it is no longer a question of truth, but of something that is the antithesis of it, the "truths of the state," as Vidal-Naquet puts it. Let us clarify this further to avoid any confusion. Revisionism and

---

54. *Le Monde*, May 21, 1996.
55. *Le Monde*, May 4, 1996.

negationism are, at best, the products of deranged brains. But as such, they are not incitements to racial hatred. There is a major difference between saying (I) "All Jews must be killed" or "Jews are inferior beings" and (II) "Extermination camps never existed." The statement (I) is a direct call to action, while (II) is just the statement of a fool or a bastard. There is often a connection between (I) and (II) statements. Those who say (II) out loud are actually thinking (I). But until the Gayssot law, a clear distinction was made between the former and the latter, and only the former were punishable by law (as was the call to murder).

This elementary common sense of historians was unfortunately not heard by the left as a whole, which pretended to show its intransigent "anti-fascism", an "anti-fascism" all the more noisy because there was no serious fascist threat, except in the minds of those for whom this shoddy anti-fascism takes the place of politics.

Once the mechanism has been set in motion, it is only natural that hatred of thought and hatred of freedom will be allowed to run free. The memory of slavery becomes a political issue: rightly, Blacks can show that their ancestors were the victims of a cruel colonialism, denying their human dignity by transforming them into beasts of burden. History will have to be rewritten. Western societies, even under a liberal guise, have always been busy perpetrating the genocide of colonized peoples and there is no serious difference between Nazism and slavery. A law, the Taubira law, passed in 2001, will begin to lay the legal groundwork for an official history of slavery. In his book *Les Traites négrières - Essai d'histoire globale*, the historian Olivier Pétré-Grenouilleau argues that the slave trade was never a genocide, because there was never any desire other than mercantile on the part of the slave traders, and certainly not that of exterminating their "merchandise. His book, published in 2005, was the subject of much controversy and was even prosecuted for revisionism and denial of a "crime against humanity". The fact that the affair ended in a tailspin does not change its profound significance. Where a debate among historians could have been opened, the intervention of the courts is required to nail the impertinent. In this case, it is all the more interesting that Pétré-

Grenouilleau raised a well-known historical problem: the slave trade was not invented by Westerners. It was the Arabs who set it up long before the West had the idea of using African slaves to work in their American colonies. And when the West took over from the Arabs, they could only do so with the active complicity of a number of African kingdoms...

When, in 2005, the right-wing majority had a law passed on the sly requiring that the teaching of history expose the positive role of colonization, the left took six months to notice the problem, but ended up protesting against this attack on the rights of historical truth. But it was in no position to lecture, since the laws of 1989, 1991 and 2001 had already seriously undermined the principle of freedom of research in history.

Although it is not yet the subject of an article of law, there is one area where today the criminalization of non-conforming thought is in the process of being criminalized: it is the analysis of Israeli politics. Twenty years ago, there was a clear distinction between anti-Zionism and anti-Semitism. Important groups, often composed of activists of Jewish origin (from the *Bund*, for example), were anti-Zionist and not at all anti-Semitic. There was even an anti-Zionist party in Israel, the *Matzpen*, which survives today in certain radical currents opposed to the policies of the ruling parties in that country. To be anti-Zionist is simply to consider that the creation of the State of Israel was a diversionary operation aimed at dividing the working class of European countries (this was the position of the *Bund*). Anti-Zionists still consider it a colonial fact based on a terrible lie: the land of Palestine would have been "a land without a people for a people without a land". Anti-Zionism is thus similar to all the radical revolutionary currents that hold nationalism to be a trap, intended to divert the working masses from the class struggle. Rosa Luxemburg, for example, opposed the socialist leaders who made Polish independence from Russia the central point of their program. It should therefore be possible to pass severe judgment on the Zionist movement without being anti-Semitic. This question is no more taboo than the French colonial policy in Algeria, for example: very few people label criticism of French policy in Algeria until the early 1960s as "anti-French racism". But for Israel, the same method does not apply. What Israeli historians today can afford to do, to destroy the legends of Israel's birth and to confront their country with its own colonialist past, has become almost impossible in Europe or the United States. Even mild criticism of the policies of any government in Tel Aviv is equated with anti-Semitism.

That anti-Semitism takes the mask of anti-Zionism is obvious. No one will deny that a devious anti-Semitism remains alive and well, and that it is only exposed through coded language. Nor can we forget that there is an old anti-Semitic tradition on the left that can be traced back to Alphonse Toussenel, but from which Proudhon, the founding father of anarchism, is far from being exempt. The "socialism of fools" (in the words of August Bebel, one of the founders of German Social Democracy) that is anti-Semitism can still be successful in Europe. But it is also clear that Israel's policies feed anti-Semitism. The campaigns on the theme of "criticism of the Israeli government = anti-Semitism" correspond to specific strategic objectives and are part of the weapons of ideological warfare. A war in which the fate of the peoples of the Middle East (including the Israelis) counts for little in comparison with the interests of imperialist domination, in all its forms. An indirect proof of this can be given: by a curious phenomenon of contagion, what is true for Israel is now more and more often true for the United States. The denunciation of "anti-Americanism" has become a literary genre. Only those who speak badly will recall Mr. Bush's grandfather's unwavering support for fascism in general and for Hitler's regime in particular. Only the bad tongues will recall that even under the bombs, the German army never ran out of oil. Amazing, isn't it? Only the bad tongues will recall that the hysterical anti-Semites of yesterday have often become the most unconditional supporters of Israel. Only the bad tongues will point out that the "friends of Israel", especially those who sit in Washington, are also friends of the oil monarchies and of the main organizers and financiers of anti-Semitic propaganda in the Muslim world - Saudi Arabia plays a very important role here as a hotbed of anti-Semitic propaganda, but we must also mention the Al Azhar mosque in Cairo.

Backlash or logical complement: the same methods are now applied by the fundamentalist Islamist movements: any criticism of Islam as a religion is considered as "Islamophobia", and thus indirectly as a kind of racism, symmetrical to anti-Semitism. And as a consequence, criticism of Islamism is equated with criticism of Islam and Islamophobia. A certain number of Christian hierarchs have understood this and are trying to silence any manifestation of anti-Christianity under similar pretexts. A united front of priests, rabbis and imams. One is surprised that Nietzsche is still on sale!

Let's summarize: criticism is forbidden, of slavery, of anti-slavery, of colonialism and anti-colonialism, of Judaism, of Islam, of Christianity, of Israel, of the United States and of the Arab states... Silence in the ranks. However, you have the right to say all the bad things you want about Cuba, Iran, North Korea, and by an old reflex, you can even attack Russia! No doubt these latter countries deserve to be severely judged, but let it not be known that human rights are more badly treated in Cuba than in Saudi Arabia, that women's rights are better respected in the Arab Emirates than in Iran, or that North Korea is really more dangerous to peace than Pakistan.

One could multiply the examples, keeping to France: one does not need to go to the United States to see how the single thought, mass conformism, the most ridiculous and fussy puritanism exert their ravages in a democracy transformed into a plaything of pressure groups and oligarchies of all kinds. From the French right, this hostility to freedom of expression is not really surprising. Only young people can be unaware of the heavy conformism that reigned under Gaullism, at a time when Jacques Rivette's adaptation of Diderot's *La Religieuse* was being censored, at a time when François Maspero - for the political works he published - and Jean-Jacques Pauvert - for his erotic works - were being sued. The "party of order" is in its role.

More worrying and surprising seems to be the rallying of a part of the left to the all-out repression. But when you look at it closely, it is not so surprising. If the right defends property much more than freedom, the left has been more often than not elitist and authoritarian. There are hardly any organizations as undemocratic as the unions and parties of the left, except for the parties of the right! "Democratic centralism", this Russian export, seemed to be incompatible with the temperament of the French, which is often said to be rebellious and a bit anarchistic. However, for several decades, the Communist Party succeeded in imposing a formidable discipline of conscience on hundreds of thousands of citizens, adults, independent, who tried voluntary servitude. It is not much better with the socialist party - in its various forms - which, without the strength and efficiency of the PCF, has a solid tradition of bureaucratic party with semi-feudal mores.

Basically, this French left, which has long since given up on shaking off the yoke of capital and the state and has nothing to propose but to put flowers on the chains of oppression and domination, is fundamentally inclined to despise freedom. As long as the right and the left were in frontal opposition (according to the logic of the Cold War), there was still a space for freedom in this very conflict. But with the end of the hopes, illusions or mystifications of "French socialism", an end that can be traced back to the autumn of 1981, not to say to May 21 of the same year, the day President Mitterrand took office, the exhaustion of the right-left conflict gradually led public life to conformism, to the complete triumph of the language of wood. Thus, it became impossible to distinguish by style and vocabulary the texts of the congresses of the right-wing parties from those of the left-wing parties.

This undivided domination of a thought common to all the ruling classes, of the right and of the "left", is not specifically French. It is true that, in some respects, the phenomenon is aggravated by the institutions of the Fifth Republic, this elective monarchy that personalizes power to the maximum and depoliticizes public life. But the same normalization of thought is taking place almost everywhere. Unlike the totalitarian enter-prises of the 20th century, we are not dealing with an intolerant ideology advocating the exclusion and elimination of deviants. The Stalinists or the Nazis have enemies and know that one can hold tongues, but not the thoughts of individuals. This is why they proceed to purges and mass exterminations: a tribute from vice to virtue, classical totalitarianism does not really believe in the possibility of shaping minds once and for all. The contemporary single-mindedness, on the contrary, takes seriously the totalitarian speeches and wants to realize them: it believes that it is really possible to shape the minds, to form them according to the needs of the dominant political, social and economic system, and that it is possible to reach this goal in consensus, without the need to use torture, executions and the omnipotence of the political police.

Thus, it seems, one should no more discuss the principles of the "market economy" (a kind euphemism for "capitalism") than those of democracy. If you discuss the former, you are in fact a hidden enemy of the latter and therefore an unknowing Stalinist or Nazi: on this theme a literature is produced that is as insipid as it is repetitive, but which benefits from wide publicity in media that are increasingly directly controlled by the masters of this famous "market economy". The MEDEF is leading an obstinate offensive against what still resists the single thought in the French educational system. The market economy is no more debatable than democracy, according to an official of the employers' organization who called for Marx to be removed from the economic and social science curriculum in high schools. In July 2006, Mrs. Parisot, the new president of the organization, heir to the "Comité des forges", of sinister memory, did not hesitate to mobilize Sartre and the *Reflections on the Jewish Question* to condemn any attack against the bosses which would be akin to a kind of racism, because it would designate a group for public vindication...

Let us specify: there are classic and well-known cases of repentant "leftists" who have become men who are as fanatical on the right as they had been fanatical on the extreme left. Others have followed another slope that has led them from social revolution to "societal leftism", naturally compatible with all forms of liberalism. The former are classic examples of the all-too-predictable transformation of the young revolutionary petit-bourgeois into the old reactionary petit-bourgeois. Listening to them, one begins to sing the old Jacques Brel song: "the bourgeois are like pigs...".

The second type is much more interesting because it is very clearly in touch with the reality of domination today: oppression must be dressed up in the garb of revolt. The American or French "neocons" remain extremists, partisans of violent revolution - even if now it is the US army that carries this "revolutionary violence". The societal leftists converted to neo-liberalism, on the contrary, express the normal regime of the system of domination today. They are positioned in its center of gravity. "Living dangerously": a romantic ideal for an adventurous youth, a Nietzschean ideal, is perfectly appropriate at a time when precariousness at work is becoming the rule - life itself is precarious, says the inimitable Mrs Parisot, who defends the development of the "separability" of workers... a typical expression of the novlanguage to designate the right to lay off without constraint. The old capitalists were willingly a little, a lot and sometimes passionately racist. The new ones are in favor of "miscegenation", which gives an elegant justification to globalization and the destruction of social achievements. We know how advertising exploits this *new age* ideology in the service of *business as usual.*

Let's take the area of morals. "In the old days, workers often lived "à la colle" and children were born out of wedlock more often than not. Marriage was a matter for the bourgeoisie, who wanted to unite assets and much more rarely hearts. Chagrined moralists often complained about the bad morals of the poor. Between working-class women and girls of ill repute, the amalgam was made without much precaution. In truth, workers and bourgeois did not belong to the same world, did not live according to the same values nor the same rules, and in the working class remained vivid the memory of the independence of yesteryear, the independence of the free worker, the independence also of the "cheminot" - the one who goes out on the roads and works wherever the opportunity arises - the independence of the one who is not tied down anywhere. Anarchism in France, the *wobblies* in the United States, testified to this state of mind. And morals were one expression of this opposition between two incompatible worlds. It is thus that the opposition or the working-class exteriority could join the artistic or bohemian criticism of the bourgeois way of life.

To be against the bourgeoisie was also to be against bourgeois marriage, against hypocritical conventions, for freedom also in the field of sexuality.

As soon as the workers, however, had to come to terms with the idea that capitalist exploitation was not just a bad moment to pass, as soon as they were strong enough to impose an improvement in working conditions, without being strong enough to overthrow the system, as soon as they could therefore have the hope of integrating into the overall functioning of capitalist exploitation under less bad conditions, we witnessed a "normalization" of working-class mores. The rise of trade unionism after the First World War led to a clear improvement in the condition of the workers, which at first translated into a rapid decline in women's work: the housewife became the ideal of the successful worker. The "bad manners" became the prerogative of the petty bourgeois and the communist party became the guardian of the workers' morality, under the watchful eye of Jeannette Thorez-Vermeersch.

Today's good morals almost magically resolve all contradictions: against the old moral order, it goes without saying that sexuality is plural. One can be stupidly hetero, but it is rather trendy to be *gay*: one takes again the American word according to the same processes of euphemization which make that one does not speak any more about the Blacks, but only about the Blacks. But it is also interesting to be lesbian, "bi" (implied bisexual) or "trans". There is even an association of *gays*, lesbians, bi and trans, which should be called GLBT (which does not mean "Bolshevik Leninist Workers Group".

Sexuality is plural: let's not exaggerate! Because it is not sure that it is still sexuality. One also takes again the American fashion of the *gender studies* and it is the notion of kind (grammatical or metaphysical category) which replaces the good old sex whose fault is to evoke almost naturally parts of the body, penises in erection, clitoris, breasts, vaginas and all the excretions which generally accompany their meeting. The new "gender" plurality is hygienic!

But above all, the new sexuality must be normalized. In the past, people fought for the right to make love without going before the mayor and the priest. "J'ai l'honneur de ne pas te demander ta main", sang Brassens. Today, the crucial demand, the one that is unanimously (or almost unanimously) supported by liberals and social democrats all over the world, is the demand for homosexual marriage! "Let's engrave our names on a parchment" chant the guardians of the new moral order. Let's leave aside the complex questions that this demand raises about the meaning of legal norms and the techniques of reproduction of life. Let us remember the most important thing: there is no longer any question of having on one side the legal, juridical, moral order or whatever one wants and on the other side disorder, contestation, revolt. Revolt and contestation must also be integrated into the order, become one of the legally determined modalities of the application of the order itself. Homosexual marriage is the demand that no human activity should be outlawed, that the smallest mark of non-conformity should disappear and that all extravagances of the body should receive the state's blessing. Homosexual marriage, a new and astonishing extension of the "biopower" that Foucault, one of the first, had theorized.

This unique thought is an astonishing magma! The mayor of Paris, an avowed homosexual, has had a major Parisian landmark renamed after... Pope John Paul II. The conflict is outlawed. With the single thought, secularism must be "open" to become compatible with clericalism, freedom must pass under the forks of the multiplication of regulations in any subject and out of subject, the opposites must merge in a great general embrace. Even if it means that the truth and the reminder of reality are purely and simply censored. The great offensive against psychoanalysis, an offensive of which Deleuze and Foucault were undoubtedly the initiators, is now inscribed in the contemporary configuration of societal leftism retransformed into dominant thought. Freud must be a swindler, because psychoanalysis reminds us that it takes a man and a woman to make children and that the assembling of kinship is always done under the control of this real constraint: unbearable denial of the "right" of homosexuals to have children! Freud must be denigrated and pilloried, as was done for Marx, because Freud analyzes the "malaise in civilization" and allows us to dismantle the lies of the obligatory happiness of the market society. We need a so-called "black book of psychoanalysis" because we need to finish with the ruthless critics of contemporary society, the "Freudo-Marxists" of the Frankfurt School, Adorno and Horkheimer or Marcuse, whose *One-Dimensional Man* is more than ever current.

While the "masters of suspicion" are sent back to hell, the good old spiritualist philosophy that dominated the French university for so long is back in the limelight. The "analytical" mandarins who want to "professionalize" philosophy, to make it a technical discipline, an appendix to the hard sciences or to psychology, are also working to defuse all the potential for contestation of this very old intellectual exercise. Critical psychology and psychoanalysis have been reduced to the bare minimum, leaving room on the shelves of bookstores for personal development manuals, alongside treatises on how to raise your dog and your children or how to be comfortable in your sneakers. Let's not talk about the "economic sciences" section, which is confusingly uniform in terms of doctrine, apart from a few superficial variations.

The standardization of thought is, of course, a recurring trend. No era has really escaped it. Perhaps even our rationalist belief that truth is derived from the exercise of reason pushes it. But in our time, and perhaps for the first time, the standardization of thought takes place without any reference to truth. Bellarmine must have been right against Galileo, because the Church held the truth. And it was in the name of the truth constructed by reason that the fight against the Church was waged. Stalin was right, because scientific socialism was supposed to tell the truth. Even in Orwell's *1984*, when the party wants Smith to admit that 2 and 2 make 5, if the party believes that this is the truth, we are still in a relationship, albeit a perverse one, with the truth. The single thought, "Nietzschean" to the devil in that, is indifferent to the truth. This is its strength. Efficiency, usefulness, frivolity, prosperity, pleasure, personal fulfillment, happiness and longevity, all this is invoked by this dominant ideology, but the truth almost never. But freedom begins when we know that 2 and 2 make 4 and we can say it: Orwell's lesson must not be forgotten.

However, one should not confuse this liberticidal conformism with a return to the Victorian order and to the compact rituals of 19th century bourgeois sociability. The conformism having to adorn itself with the ornaments of the revolt, from now on everybody is on first-name terms, the president of the Republic can speak a French of the level of a school playground, the marks of the most ordinary civility can be erased. In the age of transparency, restraint has become hypocrisy, and frankness is demanded. That is to say, a brutality of social life that conforms to the spirit of war of each against each of capitalism.

The security obsession

One of the essential themes of science fiction is that of the society of generalized surveillance. *Big Brother is watching you: the* omnipresence of the figure of totalitarian power. Yet, paradoxically in appearance, this generalized surveillance is at the heart of the development of our "liberal" societies, at the heart of societies where the denunciation of totalitarianism is a universal credo - there should even be a daily "quarter-hour of hate" against totalitarianism. The imperative of security is gradually, insidiously, enclosing the whole of society in a steel cage and gradually destroying what is the basis of modern individuality, the separation between private and public life.

All this is becoming well known. The enumeration of the methods of surveillance and of the legislative arsenal has been done elsewhere often enough that it is not necessary to return to it. What deserves explanation are the arguments by which the constant reinforcement of the apparatus of surveillance and control of individuals is legitimized. The totalitarianism of the 20th century was justified by an affirmation of the absolute legitimacy of state power: the state is the absolutely sovereign reality outside of which there is nothing that deserves to exist. Mussolini, Hitler and Stalin, each in his own way, repeated this. The totalitarianism of the 21st century, the one that is quietly being put in place, with our assent, hypnotized as we are by the virtual reality that the media offers us, is a "liberal" totalitarianism, an officially anti-state totalitarianism, a totalitarianism that we must accept in defense of freedom.

There are two systems of justification that differ in their degree of sophistication, but which are both based on the same liberticidal ideology. First degree, the "café du commerce" type: "I don't care if they search my car because I have nothing to blame myself for". An argument of an insignificant stupidity, but which it is nevertheless increasingly difficult to fight. "I don't care if they apply the death penalty, because I'm not guilty!" Or: "We can use torture on criminals, since I am not a criminal." Or, "We can look at who I vote for, since I am always on the side of power!" This argument (if it can be called that) asserts that all individuals are guilty without knowing it - as the police chief tells the commissioner played by Bourvil in Jean-Pierre Melville's *The Red Circle*. The intelligent politician does not speak in this way: he knows that this language tramples on any idea of the law. Indeed, the Declaration of the Rights of Man of 1789, to name but one, is without the slightest ambiguity. Here are some articles whose spirit is clearly opposed to the security ideology:

> **Article IV** - Liberty consists in doing whatever is not harmful to others: thus, the exercise of the natural rights of each man has no limits except those which assure the other members of society the enjoyment of these same rights. These limits can only be determined by law.
>
> **Article V** - The law has the right to defend only those actions that are harmful to society. Everything that is not forbidden by the law cannot be prevented, and no one can be forced to do what it does not order.
>
> **Article VII** - No one may be accused, arrested or detained except in the cases determined by the law, and according to the forms it has prescribed. Those who solicit, dispatch, execute or cause to be executed arbitrary orders, must be punished; but any citizen called or seized by virtue of the law must obey immediately; he makes himself guilty by resistance.
>
> **Article IX** - All men being presumed innocent until proven guilty, if it is deemed necessary to arrest them, any rigor that is not necessary to secure their person must be severely repressed by law.

All those, parliamentarians as well as ministers, who for decades now have not only authorized, but also incited the police to solicit, dispatch or execute arbitrary orders, should have been punished for violation of the fundamental principles without which the State "has no constitution" (cf. Article XVII).

But the security demagogue is educated. It is therefore in the name of human rights that he proposes to tear human rights apart.

> **Article II** - The purpose of every political association is the preservation of the natural and imprescriptible rights of man. These rights are freedom, property, security, and resistance to oppression.

Safety is one of the fundamental rights, and from there on, a remarkable ideological travesty will be carried out.

First oversight: safety is replaced by security. But these two terms have different meanings and connotations. Individual security - for this is what the Bill of Rights clearly refers to - is a legal term that designates an "element of individual liberty consisting in the guarantee against arbitrary arrest, detention and punishment[56]. Security is therefore first and foremost the protection of the individual against the arbitrariness of political power! And this "right" is then used to legitimize the arbitrary power of the State in order to ensure the "security" of citizens. But security is something quite different from the immunity from arbitrariness that security designates. Security is the absence of danger or the prevention of danger. Sometimes one term is used instead of the other, but they can be radically antinomic: in a country where rights are violated, I am safe to stay at home without making politics, precisely because I do not have security from the police!

This evasion is coupled with a far from innocent change in the order of rights. On the right and on the left, it has become fashionable to assert that security is the first right, which commands all the others. In the spirit of the Declaration of Rights of 1789, it is quite the opposite. Freedom is the

---

56. CAPITANT (Henri), *Vocabulaire juridique* (included in the *Trésor de la langue française*: http://atilf.atilf.fr).

first of the rights, and it is for this reason that the list of rights begins with freedom and ends with resistance to oppression: when freedom and all its conditions (property, security) have been limited or suppressed, one must then recover one's rights by all possible means! The Constitution of 1793 went even further: it was not content to make resistance to oppression a right, it made insurrection against tyranny "the most sacred of duties"! In any case, the texts of 1789 and 1793 are authentically republican texts in the sense that the primary function of the State is to guarantee freedom against domination.

Security is at the forefront of political principles not in the republican tradition, but in the thought of Hobbes, an uncompromising supporter of the omnipotence of sovereign power. For the author of *Leviathan,* the mission of sovereign power is to ward off the violence of a "state of nature" characterized by the "war of each against each". Without the security guaranteed by this absolute power, life would remain miserable, disgusting and short. But, unlike the modern ideologists of the security state, Hobbes speaks the truth: if the primary function of the state is security, then it is impossible to speak of freedom. If citizens retain the power to challenge the sovereign from behind, quarrels will resume at the first opportunity and we will immediately fall back into the state of war from which we had wanted to emerge. This is why there is no serious difference between an absolute monarchical power and a republic. According to Hobbes:

> "Although the name of liberty is engraved on the towers and gates of cities in large letters, yet it does not concern individuals, but the body of the city; nor does it belong to a republican city any more than it does to such and such a city which is in the heart of the kingdom[57]."

Moreover, Hobbes attacks the idea of political freedom at its root:

> "If one wishes to be free while everyone else is enslaved, what else is there to claim dominance?"

---

57. HOBBES (Th.), *The Citizen*, GF-Flammarion, 1982, trans. Samuel Sorbière, p. 202.

The claim to freedom would thus be just another way of claiming domination. The strength of Hobbesian thought lies not in its normative value, but in its ability to describe the dynamics of the modern state, in a society that is, ultimately, our own. The natural reality of man is war, whose civilized form - if one may say so - is economic war, a true war of each against each. But the possessing classes seek security in order to guarantee their property and to enjoy the wealth they accumulate while keeping for themselves the freedom to act as they please. It is therefore a question of the will to dominate and nothing else.

Once the ideological trappings are gone, what is left of this endless debate on security that would require the trimming of all fundamental freedoms one by one? First, we need to establish the facts and then discuss the policies to be implemented. As far as the facts are concerned, we are in a state of confusion. We talk about the rise of insecurity on the basis of statistics which we do not know exactly what they measure and which are susceptible to all sorts of manipulations depending on the displays chosen by the ministers. No one can say whether there is really more or less insecurity than there was thirty years ago, since we do not know how to quantify this insecurity. At the beginning of the seventies, the road killed 18,000 people per year. Today, the figure is slightly above 5,000. The progress in safety is therefore considerable. In comparison, the figure for blood crimes, about 2,000 attempted homicides per year, is very stable, and homicides related to robberies or attempted robberies remain very low, with a downward trend for several years; the rate of homicides and attempted homicides even fell at the turn of the millennium: it was 3.6 incidents per 100,000 inhabitants in 2000, compared with 4.5 in 1990. The main factor of insecurity is parents for their children, husbands for their wives, lovers for their mistresses and all the combinations that follow[58], to which we add madness, drink and other drugs. But nothing to do with the savage hordes that would attack our lives to take our property! At least in our country.

---

58. We almost added "and vice versa", but this is not correct: 85 to 90% of homicides are perpetrated by men. Female poisoners and stabbers are still rare! But in this field also the equality between men and women progresses...

Second aspect: what is violence? Battles between young people have always existed, and if some of them are now widely publicized (for example, rivalries between gangs of neighbouring housing estates in a particular Parisian suburb), we forget that they were much more general a century or two ago. From one village to another, confrontations could be systematic between teenage gangs. But it happened in the countryside, out of sight, and especially out of sight of adults, and no newspaper talked about it, and the blows and wounds were treated as best they could, but without calling the ambulance. In high schools, violence between students has certainly decreased considerably since the fifties and sixties, if only because of the reduction of boarding schools. Anyone who has undergone the rites of hazing knows what it was like; it still exists in a few chic prep schools, some military schools and some grandes écoles without shocking our anti-insecurity critics: sadism, cruelty, humiliation, sexual violence, that was and still is hazing. Today, a couple of slaps or a racist insult are classified as violent incidents and increase the statistics for the greatest happiness of the patent exploiters of the world's misery. Perhaps it should only be noted that school violence today is more often violence against teachers and against the representatives of institutions in general. This would be a new phenomenon to analyze in detail. But here again, we must beware of perspective effects. When Brassens sings: "Or, sous tous les cieux, sans vergogne / C'est un usage bien établi / Dès qu'il s'agit d'rosser les cognes / Tout le monde se réconcilie", he is relying on an old popular background of hatred against the powers that be, the police and the judges[59].

We could talk about sexual violence. Here again, the criminalization of certain behaviors considered unimportant in the past is evident. Michel Foucault gives many examples of this process. Here is a significant one:

> "One day in 1867, a farm worker from the village of Lapcourt, a little simple-minded, employed according to the seasons at one place or another, fed here and there by a little charity and for the worst work, lodged in the

---

59. If a rap group sings the same thing replacing "cognes" by "keufs", what will we hear against this intolerable rise of violence of young people against the police...

barns or stables, was denounced at the edge of a field, he had, from a little girl, obtained a few caresses, as he had already done, as he had seen her do, as the kids of the village did around him; it is that at the edge of the wood, or in the ditch of the road which leads to Saint-Nicolas, one played familiarly the game which one called "of curdled milk". The parents reported him to the mayor of the village, the mayor reported him to the police, the police took him to the judge, he was charged by the judge and submitted to a first doctor, then to two other experts who, after writing their report, published it. What is important about this story? It is its miniscule character; it is that this daily life of village sexuality, these minute buccaneering pleasures could have become, from a certain moment, the object not only of a collective intolerance, but of a judicial action, a medical intervention, an attentive clinical examination, and of a whole theoretical elaboration. The important thing is that this character, until then an integral part of peasant life, was measured, the cranium was studied, the facial bones were examined, the anatomy was inspected for possible signs of degeneration, he was made to speak, he was questioned about his thoughts, inclinations, habits, sensations and judgments[60]."

It has recently been discovered how common "pedophilia" may have been in institutions that cared for children and adolescents, especially religious institutions. What is now considered a crime was known for a long time, but deliberately ignored, because it was part of the more or less inevitable natural phenomena. For a part, one can therefore think that the figures measuring insecurity are on the rise simply because our societies are more and more policed, that is to say, at the same time more penetrated by the rules of respect for others, more intolerant of abnormal behavior and more and more subject to the power of the police, to the systematic control of all acts of "deviance". Is it necessary to totally deny this insecurity which occupies so much the media, especially in the periods of election campaign? Probably not. Laurent Mucchielli points out:

---

60. Foucault (Michel), *La Volonté de savoir (Histoire de la sexualité, I)*, Gallimard, 1976, p. 43-44.

"In reality, what is increasing in French society are intermediate assaults (beatings that are rarely very serious, however, since they only lead to time off work or hospitalization in one case out of twenty), which are concentrated in and around the poor neighborhoods of large cities, with the perpetrators as well as the victims most often being young men who fight among themselves. Finally, it should be remembered that the crimes that most often plague the daily lives of the French are not interpersonal violence, but theft and burglary. These attacks on property represent two-thirds of all crimes recorded by the police each year, and we know how much the increase in social inequalities serves as a crucible for them."

A diagnosis that deserves to be qualified, but which can serve as a basis for discussion. There are, in fact, sectors of our societies in which the conditions of ordinary life have seriously deteriorated, both in absolute terms and in relation to the boisterous ease and security enjoyed by the privileged classes. Thus, aggregate statistics may mask considerable disparities between the affluent classes, who generally live more securely than they did a few decades ago, and the poor, who experience a considerable deterioration in their living conditions, not only materially but also socially.

Mass unemployment and rampant poverty in the former working class neighborhoods of the big cities have created a breeding ground for the wandering of a whole segment of youth, left to fend for themselves, and for the development of delinquent or frankly criminal activities. In addition to poverty, there is social contempt and racism, both in its direct forms (insults, police checks on faces) and in all kinds of discrimination, in hiring, in housing, etc. What is surprising is not the phenomenon itself, but the fact that, all in all, it remains so little developed. At least in the countries of "old Europe". We know that this is not the case in the United States, Russia, South Africa or Brazil, to mention only the best known of these countries, where the war of each against the other remains the rule.

After the right, specialist in the tchatcha of insecurity, a whole part of the left has blown the same trumpets. The "angelism" of a left that saw prevention and education as the remedy should be ended. The American myth of "zero tolerance" strikes everywhere. The result is well known: repressive measures have become considerably heavier, prisons are over-crowded, especially for petty criminals who should not be allowed to mix with serious criminals. The Declaration of Rights of 1789 stated:

> **Article VIII** - The law shall establish only strictly and obviously necessary penalties, and no one shall be punished except by virtue of a law established and promulgated prior to the offense and legally enforced.

The inflation of laws is accompanied by the inflation of penalties - even if they are sometimes unenforceable - and leads to the inflation of police action (especially when, as in the Soviet five-year plan, the police operate on "numbers"). We learn in the press that a pre-adolescent caught stealing a chocolate bar in a supermarket can be taken into custody and his family's parental authority can be entrusted to a judicial agent, called a "referent". We are not yet back to the galleys for stealing a loaf of bread, but we are getting closer and closer to it every day. And we don't have a Victor Hugo to talk about our miserable people.

The revolutionaries of the past considered that thievery was only one of the consequences of social organization based on private property. Obviously, if private property is abolished, thieves will disappear immediately, since theft can only be defined in relation to property. But this rather simplistic Proudhonism is not very satisfactory. As it has become more and more difficult to steal cars, specialists in the resale of luxury vehicles now have to assault the driver to steal his keys and escape, having first put him in no condition to call the police, because the time is long gone when one could start a car with two crocodile clips! Hence the recent statistics that show a worrying rise in violence against people. Violence against people should therefore be considered not as distinct from property crime, but as a consequence of it.

In any case, even in a society without capitalist ownership of the means of production, private property should be ensured and it should be protected just as people should be protected in their physical integrity since individual private property is closely linked to self-ownership. So, even if the question of insecurity is ideologically agitated, manipulated to better manipulate, it remains and above all will remain, even with a society much better organized than ours, a serious question. It is only necessary to ask it correctly. When it is said that security is the first freedom, it is at best a verbal pirouette: security is an imperative which, whether we like it or not, limits freedom insofar as it entrusts a special body with the protection of citizens. This special body must have the means to enforce order - it has the "monopoly of legitimate violence" as Weber would say - and therefore it is already potentially in a position to abuse these special rights against citizens, honest and dishonest alike. To be sure, the policeman who arrests the thug who was assaulting an old lady is protecting the old lady's liberty, and his interference with the thug's freedom of maneuver cannot reasonably be understood as an infringement of liberty - here the republicanist argument for a protective state is fully legitimate. But this will not prevent the question of protecting citizens from police abuses - abuses that may even be committed "in the right cause". In a television police series, *Boulevard du Palais*[61], the sympathetic Inspector Rovère, a tormented alcoholic and defender of widows, orphans and prostitutes abused by their pimps, does not hesitate to take many liberties with the Code of Criminal Procedure in order to lock up the guilty and clear the innocent who have been unjustly accused. Although the adventures of Inspector Harry Callahan that made Clint Eastwood's acting fame have often been seen - from the left - as a fascist apology for police violence and self-defense, it may well be that Harry Callahan and Rovère are closer to each other than one might think. They both embody that very dangerous temptation of all police: to defend the law and justice by violating the law and the fundamental rights of citizens. And I have taken here examples of fiction, of police officers animated by feelings of justice, incorruptible and insensitive to the charms of careerism! That is to say, I have pointed out the questions that arise even under the most favorable conditions. One can understand what happens in real conditions, which are generally less favorable.

---

61. The characters of this series were created by the late Thierry Jonquet.

There is an insurmountable conflict between freedom and security: guards are needed to protect the freedom of the good people, but who will guard the guards? Let us ask the question in this way and stop telling tales to little children; only then can we arbitrate in full knowledge of the facts between equally legitimate but conflicting demands. However, the logic of current public security policies is not to pose the problem in these terms, it is to swallow up all freedoms in this one and only pseudo-freedom that is security.

Body control: biometrics

So many pages have been written about subjugation, the control of bodies and biopower, so many scholarly essays, that I hesitate to add a few paragraphs on this subject. But it is necessary. Michel Foucault, independently of the conclusions that he draws from it and that one can discuss, had the merit of bringing to light the fundamental modification that takes place in the modern era when one passes from classical politics, which is satisfied with the threat of death to obtain obedience, to biopolitics, which manages the production and the reproduction of life. From population statistics (in Buffon's *Natural History*, for example) to public hygiene, through treatises on the education of young people - including the ravings of Tissot - a whole new regime of population control is put in place. In terms of repressive control, the great turning point was the introduction of fingerprints. The technique of identifying individuals by fingerprinting was invented by a British colonial administrator in India and later perfected by Francis Galton, Darwin's cousin and promoter of eugenics. It is completely in line with the development of these techniques of control of the bodies which develop with the modern times and the rise of the capitalist mode of production.

Before the invention of biometric methods, the identity of an individual - that is, his or her identity with respect to the political order - depended solely on custom (everyone knows him or her in the village, for example) or on written attestations: I have an official paper, duly signed, which attests

The end of negative freedom and the surveillance society

that I am indeed who I claim to be. That the register in which births, marriages and deaths are registered is called "civil status" is an accurate name, for a "civil status" in the sense of Hobbes' or Rousseau's theories of the social contract is a text in which the names of human beings participating in the "body politic" are inscribed, and this inscription makes them persons, that is, subjects of the civil order, who would otherwise be nothing but indistinct individuals in the natural order. Men are not a herd under the leadership of a shepherd. Men are talking animals, and the law only says so. In any case, this is how, from Aristotle to modern political theorists, the political condition of man was seen. With the invention of fingerprints, it is no longer writings that make a man, but something that marks him in his flesh. In ancient times, convicts were branded with a red iron; the Nazis generalized the process by tattooing a number on the deportees, most of whom were destined for extermination. But contemporary society does not even need these barbaric procedures, devoid of the slightest technical sophistication. It looks for natural traits in each individual that become, through the intermediary of biometric means, so many painless marks: a much more efficient management of the herd.

Fingerprints were only the first step in a process that has developed with computers and image recognition. As long as fingerprints are taken by a registrar issuing a passport or by a police officer during an arrest, we are still in the realm of craftsmanship, especially since comparing a suspect's fingerprints with those we have somewhere in a file remains a complicated affair, and we can only implement all the complex workings of the police machine in the context of a criminal investigation. But with computer technology, combining databases, image digitization, image recognition and network communications, we have not only a quantitative change, but a qualitative change, which is well expressed by the DNA fingerprint. We will come back later on to the meaning of this obsession with DNA or the "genetic code", revealing the "butcher conception of humanity" (always the herd). For the time being, the police, under any pretext, are building up files of potential suspects. Indeed, as in *The Red Circle*, "all men are guilty".

Because biometrics is becoming more widespread. A much simpler method than fingerprints or DNA prints is iris recognition. It can even be implemented without the knowledge of the persons concerned. It appeared in science-fiction movies and is becoming more and more widespread, especially for authorizations to move around in premises under surveillance or in computer security: no more need for a password that can be forgotten or that can be hacked: the user looks straight at his computer!

In the novel *Unbearable Happiness*, Ira Levin[62] imagines a happy society, free of misery, conflicts, and all forms of violence, including those born of the sexual impulse, now placed under state control. The individuals who violate the law are no longer considered as criminals to be punished, but as sick brothers or sisters who must be looked after. To avoid any disorder that would jeopardize this harmonious society, individuals are equipped from birth with electronic bracelets that must regularly pass through readers that identify the position of the bracelet wearer. Today's reality is based on yesterday's science fiction.

There are many excellent reasons for developing these biometric technologies: no one can want criminals to go unpunished or the innocent to be mistaken for the guilty; the security of industrial, transportation, or telecommunications facilities is clearly a much more rigorous imperative than it was a century or two ago. The integration of all technical systems on a global scale leads to constraints for which technical solutions are found that, in turn, reinforce this integration. The nuclear industry and telecommunications provide good examples of these processes. In this self-reinforcing mechanism, freedom, in its most immediate sense, is inevitably crushed. Technical advantages are paid for at a high price. This is yet another point on which Rousseau clearly perceived the enslaving rather than liberating potential of "the progress of science and art".

---

62. Levin (Ira), *Unbearable Happiness*, J'ai Lu, 2003.

Indefinite extension of the law's domain and regression of civility

In truth, the question of security is not a false question, a propagandistic diversionary maneuver orchestrated by the right, as many on the left believe, but a fundamentally ill-posed question, posed in a perverted manner by both sides.

The rise of insecurity and the rise of the feeling of insecurity (two expressions that are undoubtedly true and correlated) stem from a fundamental social cause that we must try to understand: the almost total triumph of capitalism. In the society of the 19th century, the whole of the social formation is dominated by the capitalist mode of production, which is still far from having penetrated the whole society. The family - and in particular the bourgeois family - functions according to rules that are not those of the capitalist mode of production, that is, the conversion of all wealth and all social value into a general equivalent, in other words, into a value that has a market value. The great transformation, accomplished in the course of the 20th century, subjects almost all spheres of social life to the domination of the logic of capital.

Let us explain: all known class societies are based on the extortion of the social surplus by one or more dominant classes; they are therefore exploitative societies. This is not what specifically characterizes the capitalist mode of production - ancient societies also extorted the social surplus from their slaves, their serfs or even their burghers, who were condemned to pay tithes and other taxes from which the ruling classes were exempt. Historically, capitalism is not the most repressive social organization either. On the contrary, it has often made freedom the banner of its intensive and extensive extension. It certainly uses repression, even the most cruel, when it deems it necessary. It can temporarily hand over the reins to hordes of killers (the death squads) or rely on a "supreme savior" no matter what the cost. But for capitalism, the normal regime, the least costly, in any case, is democracy. The capitalist mode of production is characterized by the transformation of all social relations into relations between things measured by their (market) value. Where social relations were regulated by tradition, by magical beliefs, by conventions, by power relations, by blood ties or those of passion, the capitalist mode of production has substituted a single law: the law of value. The wealth of our societies is presented as an immense accumulation of commodities, says Marx from the first lines of *Capital.* The law of value is expressed by the omnipotence conferred on the general equivalent, that is, money.

Georg Simmel[63] has shown the liberating dynamics of monetary exchange. The owner of wheat can only exchange his wheat for a suit of clothes if he finds a suit producer who loves wheat! The owner of money can buy what he wants and from whom he wants. When the serf begins to pay his chores and tributes in money, he begins to free himself from serfdom. Money undoes all traditional relations of subordination. This paradox is very well exposed by Simmel: the circulation of money develops the intricacies between the activities of all individuals, but, at the same time, it makes each one less dependent on the other individuals. Dependent on all, one ends up being dependent on no one. The neutral medium of money neutralizes all personal relationships. Simmel sees the negative effects that this development of monetary relations can have, but, as an heir of the Enlightenment, he sees in it above all the progress of freedom, in all the meanings that one can give to this term. That relations between men become relations between things, they gain in objectivity, according to Simmel.

Certainly, things do not themselves mutually determine their value. We are here, as Marx analyzes in a famous chapter of the first section of *Capital,* in the midst of commodity fetishism: relations between men take the fantastic form of relations between things. This phantasmagoria cannot, however, be dispelled by showing the real, as one dispels the magician's illusions by showing his "tricks". The exchange of things for their value, this very ancient exchange which only takes on its full reality with the full development of the capitalist mode of production, is a process of

---

63. See SIMMEL (G.), *Philosophie de l'argent*, PUF, 1987, coll. "Quadrige", 1999, translated from the German by S. Cornille and P. Ivernel.

The end of negative freedom and the surveillance society

abstraction. The thing-commodity is reduced to its value, apart from its physical qualities and its use: if a bottle of cognac is exchanged for a bible, it does not matter whether one satisfies spiritual needs and the other needs spirits, only the operation that makes it possible to write "x commodity A = y commodity B = z ounces of gold" counts. The qualities are reduced to pure quantity. But by the same token, it does not matter whether the goods were made here or there, whether they required this or that concrete, particular work, this or that amount of sweat and skill. Commodities are commodities only insofar as they crystallize not human labor, but abstract labor, labor without quality. This process radically transforms all social relations, which are thus marked by this abstraction. No Westerner of normal morals would have teenagers work at home ten hours a day and six days a week for a miserable wage. But the same Westerner, even with all the precepts of Kant's morality, will buy the latest trendy electronic gadget that an American manufacturer has made in China without any remorse of conscience. Why is this possible? Simply because the social relationship has disappeared: we buy value for value commodities that crystallize abstract labor, not human, concrete labor, not sweat and suffering.

Market exchange, as a process of abstraction, makes the most fundamental social relations, those through which the conditions of human life are produced and reproduced, lose all concrete character. From then on, moral norms themselves appear quite abstract. They are no longer the necessary conditions for the life of the community, but external rules that we sometimes try to impose as best we can. If *business ethics are* only worthy of a big laugh, it is because everyone knows that ethics has nothing to do with business - except when ethics becomes a selling point for "ethical companies" (yet another popular oxymoron) and "fair trade" - so it would have been hidden from us that trade could be unfair...

In a world where "everything can be bought and sold" (let us excuse this commonplace), where job seekers are taught the tricks to "know how to sell oneself", there is no longer any place for what these classical authors called *civic friendship*, because friendship and business never mix! Our society is certainly no more violent than traditional societies, but what has radically collapsed is civility, that is to say, the set of rituals and prohibitions by which individuals recognized each other as humans with a common world. The thing is all the more astonishing and leaves us all the more bewildered since we thought that democracy and the progress of the equality of right and of the equality of conditions were on the contrary to generalize this civility which was really imposed only between equals or in the relations of the inferiors towards the superior classes.

As soon as social wealth is reduced to an immense accumulation of merchandise, the very existence of a common world disappears - this is one of the most striking effects of the so-called "globalization". We could accumulate the symptoms here.

- It is first of all the trivialization of coarseness in expression, even in public. The evolution of political life is, in this respect, very revealing. Gender equality has also made "progress" in this area: girls now swear like cartwheels, regularly referring to male attributes that Mother Nature has not provided them with;
- It is then the loss of ordinary civility such as gallantry or respect for elders (all promoted to the rank of "old fart"); and more generally the destruction of this relationship to authority that Hannah Arendt analyzed with such finesse[64];
- But it is also the growing solitude of individuals, especially in large cities, a solitude that is all the more paradoxical because the means of communication are multiplying. While monastic life is completely devalued, while cohabitation between men and women (or between people of the same sex) has become extremely easy, there have never been so many individuals living alone. The possibility that is offered to each one to choose his leisure activities dispenses with the need to participate in collective events. The multiplication of television channels and VOD programs allow each person to make his own movie without sharing his emotions with others.

---

64. See "What is Authority?" in *The Crisis of Culture*. "Authority no longer exists," says Hannah Arendt.

Individuals, according to the operating principles of the capitalist mode of production, are in competition. And not only as bosses competing for markets. As wage earners, they compete with each other to sell their labor power. As competitors, they become rivals, and rivalry, as Hobbes says, leads to a state of war. It is enough to observe, as is classic, the behaviour at the cinema cash desk or at the baker's: people queue up and the free-rider is harshly rebuked. The drivers, who do not risk the common disapproval, zigzag to be first at the toll booth or to gain three places in a traffic jam. Law-abiding in pedestrian life, possibly pestering the delinquents, the one behind the wheel becomes a thug who multiplies the calls of headlights and scorns the safety distances, because it is necessary to make room for him so that his powerful machine exhibits the power of the lord (and the lord) of the road.

The destruction of the common world thus leads to the collapse of common morality, that spontaneous morality which is distinct both from law and from pure subjective morality in the Kantian manner. Hegel makes this ordinary morality, the "good morals", according to some translators of Hegel, the most relevant indicator of the level of development of civilization. If we apply the Hegelian criterion, it is clear that we are witnessing a regression of civilization today.

We must not look elsewhere for the causes of this extraordinary proliferation of law and dispute. What could be settled by following common sense and the common *ethos* can only be settled by the intervention of law and the administration of justice. Vico makes the pertinent observation that the Romans of the Empire multiplied laws, whereas the Republic had only a very small body of legislation. The reason for this is that individuals, having lost the sense of the common good, had become more and more selfish, and more and more quarrelsome, and, according to the Neapolitan philosopher, such a state of mind directly prefigured the decadence and fall of the Romans' civilization. The parallel with our time cannot fail to be made. For Vico, this evolution and this perversion of the "right of the men" prefigured a new historical cycle where, by virtue of the law of the *ricorso*, must return the age of the barbarians.

There is a paradox to underline. Throughout history and up to the present day, cities and civility have gone hand in hand. To be "urban" is to live in the city, but it is also to know good manners, unlike the boor, who is rude and *unpolished* (i.e. not polite enough to live in a *polis*). The modern city is reversing this ancient law. The modern city is no longer the place where one is with others, where one makes society, it is the place where the individual is irremediably alone. To give an idea of what the "state of nature" is, that is to say the state of war of each against each, Hobbes evokes "the savages of the Americas". Today's modern city would give a much more accurate picture. The savage by its etymology (*silva*) designates the man who lives in the forests. It is for this reason that the American writer Upton Sinclair stigmatized capitalism by titling his most famous novel *The Jungle*. This inversion of values, this transformation of the city from a place of civility and safety to a place of savagery, is not a recent phenomenon. The city has always had its shallows and its cut-throats that formed the necessary negative of the order imposed everywhere else. The "banlieues" were the place of the banished and the "fortifs" of Paris were the land of the "Apaches". But all this mythology, from François Villon to Becker's *Casque d'or*, no longer has any connection with the modern city. Delinquency is no longer the negative of urban values, it is the caricature of the principles on which society as a whole functions. If the activity with the highest value is that of making money, how can we be surprised that those who do not have the means to legally enrich themselves through the thousand and one tricks of financial speculation do so by other means? If owning a big German sedan is the symbol of a successful life, what does it matter how you get there? Shall we lecture them? But what right do we have? Try to lecture a financier, try to shame him by pointing out that he is juggling with billions of dollars and that we cannot find a few hundred million dollars to prevent the children of Mali, Niger or Chad from dying of hunger! The financier will laugh in your face by pointing out that the moral order and the capitalist order have nothing to do with each other and that the efficiency of capitalism only requires that we follow the rules of capitalism. What does it matter if children starve! *Mezza voce*, our dollar man will whisper that these people "should have done what we did". The law of the jungle, the "selection of the fittest" according to the criteria of social Darwinism, in a world governed not by moral principles, but by Dawkins' "selfish genes": these are the ultimate principles that legitimize the *perinde ac cadaver* submission to the law of value. But these principles apply, without change, to the mafia order and to banditry in all its forms. "The workers are jerks," says Sonny, the local mob boss in Robert de Niro's film *A Tale from the Bronx*. They are "jerks" because they are content to work hard and respect the values of honesty, loyalty and a sense of work well done. The dollar man, like the Sonny in the film, is much "smarter" and therefore deserves, according to the criteria of merit accepted in capitalist society, to make a lot of money and have power.

The proximity between the dominant classes and the bandits is undoubtedly not specific to capitalism. It had already been noted in feudalism: the knight and the bandit of honor are not very far apart: Robin Hood even tells of the inversion of values since the true man of honor is the outlaw, while the king's men are repulsive bandits. The samurai were also mercenaries ready to support any cause, and the code of honor is very ambiguous. But this was a somewhat natural proximity, since these feudal ruling classes did not owe their dominance to their leadership role in production, but only to their feats of arms and their ability to impose their own dominance by force on generally unarmed populations. Their extraction of the social surplus was done directly in a form similar to plunder. In its origins, the Sicilian mafia was simply a form of feudal system - see Luigi Natoli's famous novel, *Death in Messina - History of the Beati Paoli*. Capitalism, on the contrary, was presented in its beginnings as a mode of social organization in which only work and the sacrifice of earthly pleasures are rewarded[65]. Marx and Braudel teach us, of course, that the foundations of capitalist development are not the work and sacrifices of the petty bourgeois, but distant trade based on the royal monopoly and the plundering of colonized

---

65. Cf. Weber (Max), *L'Éthique protestante et l'esprit du capitalisme*, Gallimard, 2003, coll. "Tel", trans. Jean-Pierre Grossein.

peoples: capitalism came into the world sweating mud and blood from all its pores, said Marx. However, the capitalist mode of production, when it begins to find its own basis, does not function on direct plunder, but on the mechanisms of value production. It needs the moral preconditions analyzed by Weber. But we have reached the point where the values that make the capitalist mode of production possible are in contradiction with the capitalist mode of production itself. The moral ideals proposed by the system - for example in advertising or youth entertainment - are in stark opposition to the "Protestant ethic" of work and sacrifice that lies at the heart of the process of capital valorization.

This contradiction develops in yet another form. Capitalism presupposes that private property is sacred and, at the same time, it can only function on the accelerated expropriation of capitalist private property. Some great family fortunes have survived (in France, we think of the Peugeot family, Michelin, and, for the most recent ones, Bolloré, Lagardère, Pinault, etc.), but at the same time countless capitalist patrimonies have sunk. Of the bosses of the northern spinning mills, only the Mulliez family survives, which was able to take the turn in time by moving from production to marketing. The "expropriation of the expropriators" is therefore not a Marxist utopia, but a process that is repeated before our eyes every day. The condition for the survival of capitalism is even this process of expropriation of a part of the capitalists because they can no longer organize the valorization of capital with a sufficient rate of profit. The sanctity of private property is therefore contradictory in the extreme. On the one hand, under the domination of capital, the only human right that is really taken seriously is the right to property, but on the other hand, no society has ever paid so little attention to property as capitalist society. The patrimony made of things that remind us of the existence of the lineage, of the way each generation has inscribed its mark on the world, has practically no importance anymore: what matters is capital, and it must circulate, metamorphose constantly in order to continue to grow or else it will perish.

These contradictions, which affect the very foundations of society, the social relations of production, explain the impossibility of a substantial common ethic that could spontaneously guarantee the maintenance of basic social relations. For lack of being able to found the *ethos* proper to contemporary societies, liberal philosophers put their trust in procedural theories of morality (Rawls is the most interesting example) which could serve as a basis for procedural theories of law, of a law definitively rid of any reference to the good and to ethical values. If Rawls keeps the hope that the acceptance of the basic principles of the theory of justice could form, with the help of habit, the basis of a liberal *ethos*, this concern disappears among the proponents of minimal morality or of morality by approval.

While certain moral constraints seem to be much stronger than they were in the past - the handicapped are no longer mocked - one is often led to diagnose a real collapse of the superego. The traditional psycho-social barriers that inhibit the act or at least produce remorse seem to no longer exist and it is not only hardened criminals, but also very young people who are involved. The press and the authorities then readily speak of "barbarians" or "scum" (terms that the individuals thus designated often take up). But the barbarians of antiquity were foreigners (those who spoke neither the language of the Greeks nor that of the Romans) whose civilization was profoundly different from that of the Greco-Roman world. Today's "barbarians" are not foreigners at all. They speak exactly the language that the political leaders and the media speak (recently). Their "values" are the values of the society in which we live. Their way of life is not external to the capitalist mode of production, it is an integral part of it - between the small *dealer*, the cocaine-drunk *trader* and the big bank, a significant part of whose business comes from recycling drug money, there is an essential solidarity. Gang rape by young people who are still almost children is not an extraordinary phenomenon either: the images of sexuality conveyed by pornography freely distributed on the Internet affect very deeply the formation of objectal sexuality in adolescents who are precisely and very naturally worked by "that". In the same way, we begin to measure the profoundly deleterious influence of ultra-violent video games on the capacity of discernment of young minds which remain, in a very abnormal way, in the feeling of infantile omnipotence that no law comes to limit.

However, if only for the sake of business, the ruling classes cannot resign themselves to the delinquency they provoke. They must therefore repress and multiply the laws that ensure a more or less complete control over society. And the more capitalism develops in the global arena, the more it emancipates itself from nation-states, the more individuals are "liberated" from the old communal fetters, the more they are basically individuals without belonging, the more the processes of "de-civilization", to use Alain Finkielkraut's expression, and police surveillance with all its repressive arsenal will develop concomitantly. As is often the case, commentators see only one side of the process. On the left, they attack the police state without understanding that this police state is only the necessary counterpart of the "de-institutionalization" called for and approved by the "societal left." On the other hand, the "realists", having returned from their past "angelism", starting from the observation of "de-civilization", end up approving generalized surveillance and the multiplication of laws controlling all individual activities without being able to understand that the cause of "de-civilization" resides first and foremost in the politics and the economic system which are asked to restore the conditions of an acceptable civil life.

Crisis and collapse of contemporary liberal thought

Contemporary liberal thought rests on presuppositions that ensure its coherence: the only freedom worthy of the name is the freedom not to be prevented from acting, or the freedom of non-interference; the State must intervene only when such intervention is strictly necessary (this is the "night watchman State") and leave it to contracts between private persons to arrange the order of civil society. The freedom of the market, the freedom of enterprise and the possibility for each person, according to his activity and his assets, to legally find the means to satisfy his egoistic desires should allow a peaceful civil life, advantageous for all.

But this utopia imagined in the seventeenth century has never worked and will never work. Selfish people must be non-envious, that is, they must form their own desires, but not envy others - this is one of the conditions found in all liberal theories of justice. Now, as Rousseau had already noticed, envy is a fundamental social feeling. As soon as men began to assemble in an area larger than the family,

> "Everyone began to look at others and to want to be looked at himself, and public esteem had a price. He who sang or danced the best; he who was the most beautiful, the strongest, the most skilful or the most eloquent became the most esteemed, and this was the first step towards inequality, and towards vice at the same time: from these first preferences were born on the one hand vanity and contempt, on the other shame and envy; and the fermentation caused by these new leavenings finally produced compounds that were fatal to happiness and innocence[66]."

Rousseau draws the necessary conclusions: if this first social state can only produce "compounds harmful to happiness and innocence," then it is necessary to re-found the social state by determining the conditions that can legitimize a sovereign political power. In a society of free competition, individuals spend their time comparing and envying each other. This is even the magic spring touted by liberal economists. I have to be envious of what the other person has, even if I never felt the need for it, so that the desire to "earn more" (possibly by working more...) imposes its law. The complement of the envy is here the shame: the shame, for example, of the schoolboy not having the same "branded" shoes as his little classmate. And the one who would not have felt this shame yet will feel it well in front of the flood of social contempt which awaits him. If not all individuals are ready to seize the property of others without further ado, it's because in truth, more often than not, they obey one of those morals that capital mercilessly destroys. This is why, the more capitalism becomes pure capitalism, rid of the vestiges of the societies of the past within which it first had to assert itself, and the more the latent violence of competition tends to become open warfare, the more the state must intervene, and not only as a "night watchman."

-----

66. See *Discourse on the Origin and Foundations of Inequality among Men*.

This is why today's liberals are very embarrassed: they feel that the evolution of capitalism is turning its back on their ideals, but they must nevertheless come to the rescue of the instigators of the police state and the monopolization of power in the hands of political enterprises specialized in the occupation of power (such as the "Berlusconi party" in Italy), because they are the ones who defend the free movement of capital. So liberals are forced to approve the tapping of all citizens' phones, the opening of (electronic) mail, the grossest intrusions into private life and the guardianship - "for their own good", of course - of citizens treated like children. Liberalism has historically played a positive role in promoting the rights of the individual against the state and in raising the question of the control of the sovereign power of politics, and it has done so by emphasizing the necessities of the development of capital as a factor of not only economic, but also social and moral progress. But that era is over. The needs of capital demand that the "negative" liberties, the "bourgeois" liberties, of which the liberals were so proud, be torn to pieces.

To conclude, it is necessary to answer an objection: philosophers like to play the Cassandra and announce the worst: the golden age belongs to the past. One can always object that we do not avoid this mistake and that, in fact, freedoms are more ample today than they ever were in the past. It is true that we have lost our political passions (or illusions) but, in terms of morals and daily life, individuals have never been as free as they are today, that is to say, the weight of society, tradition and the State has never been so weak. Imagine the *gay pride* under Louis XIV or even certain television programs of the time of General de Gaulle! These arguments are not without weight... but historical comparisons are always very debatable. Proponents of negative liberty should judge the extent of liberties by the possibility that the citizen has to escape the law. From this point of view, the situation in our time is particularly catastrophic. Basically, the citizen is only free as long as the possibility of making false documents to escape the police is still open to him. This possibility is now practically non-existent. Potentially, the present state is the most tyrannical state that human history has ever known. If this potentiality is not yet reality, it is perhaps only because there is no serious force challenging the existing order. Let us imagine for a minute Hitler with all the means of the modern police force: all resistance would be annihilated in advance. We should reassure ourselves by saying that democratic governments will not abuse the possibilities given to them by the gigantic means of control that are available to them today: at least, this is how all the rulers express themselves at the moment of adopting such and such a new restriction of liberties, such and such a new computer file. In short: sleep in peace, we, the good shepherds, are watching over you! No conscious citizen should accept to trust the rulers not to abuse their power. Every true liberal, a reader of Montesquieu, knows that power carries with it the abuse of power and, in political philosophy, one must always begin by reasoning about limit situations. Machiavelli, the true founder of modern political thought, asserts that whoever wants to establish a political constitution must assume "in advance that all men are wicked and that they are ready to put their wickedness into action whenever they have the opportunity to do so[67]" or that they are "ungrateful, changeable, simulators and dissimulators, cowards in the face of danger, greedy for profit[68]". Even if optimists may think that Machiavelli's assertions are not true for all men, it is almost certain - and this is not to betray the spirit of the penetrating Florentine - that they are absolutely true for rulers, for those whom Machiavelli calls "the great ones", whom he defines very simply as those who govern or who want to govern and whose fundamental impulse is to want to tyrannize the people. More than ever, we must take on board the lessons of Machiavelli, complementing them with the lessons of the history of the last century: fundamentally, our ruling elites aspire to something that the "greats" whom Machiavelli knew could not even dream of: total domination.

The rule of law was first invented as a way to limit absolutism and to allow the new ruling classes to ensure that tax money was used wisely, that is, for the benefit of these same ruling classes. This demand happened to

---

67. MACHIAVELLI (N.), *Discourse on the First Decade of Titus Livius*, I, 3, in *Œuvres*, translation by Christian Bec, Robert Laffont, "Bouquins", p. 195.
68. MACHIAVELLI (N.), *The Prince*, chap. XVII, *op. cit.* p. 152.

resonate with the anti-feudal and anti-absolutist demands of the popular classes, peasants, artisans, intellectual petty-bourgeois, etc., and we had the great revolutionary movements of the 18th and 19th centuries. But this resonance, and even this union, were fundamentally equivocal and the alliance of all classes under the leadership of the great bourgeois (the Mirabeau and La Fayette during the French Revolution) could not last. The whole political history of the last two centuries can be read as the history of the confrontations between the various political blocs that were united in the struggle against absolutism. Marx provides penetrating analyses of these conflicts[69]. Today we are in a situation in which the circles that claim to represent liberalism, that is to say, essentially the representatives of financial capital and their political clerks, have deliberately renounced everything that classical liberalism had to offer in terms of the defense of individual liberties and the control of political power, an operation carried out in the name of the "rule of law. In the previous period, repression against revolutionary or merely seriously reformist social movements was carried out in the name of "national security", a notion that legitimized military coups, the omnipotence of the political police and the institutional torture of opponents, as was the case in the Latin American dictatorships or in the Greece of the colonels, regimes that were all supported financially, militarily and logistically by the United States, those champions of the "rule of law". But at the same time, in the richest countries, social democracy or labourism was invoked, labels that even the right sometimes claimed: thus Georges Pompidou denounced communism in the name of Swedish-style social democracy and Jacques Chirac, when he was Giscard's Prime Minister, claimed his "labourism", which was not so much of a misnomer, compared to the policy that Tony Blair or Gordon Brown would practice...

This dichotomy between military dictatorship for the underdeveloped and "social democracy" for the rich corresponded to a time of serious social confrontation when the dominant class feared (probably wrongly!) for its own domination. This is no longer the case since the collapse of the Soviet

---

69. See mainly *Les Luttes de classes en France - 1848-1851* and *Le 18 Brumaire de Louis Bonaparte*.

Union and the countries of the East, interpreted (also wrongly) as a definitive victory over "communism". The ruling class thinks it can organize a total domination, ideological, legal, social and economic, sparing itself the false costs of a Keynesianism that has become far too costly and the use of methods that are too violent and that can always provoke reactions of indignation and sometimes even revolutions - which is never good for business. The new cocktail of "societal liberalism + generalized control" works rather well for the moment. It ensures that the system has the support of the upper middle class, which wants to enjoy the benefits of its position without having to endure the old shackles on morality. It accelerates the transition to a society of individuals who are independent of each other, the old solidarities of class or profession being undone. But liberalism in the classical sense of the term has almost nothing left.

Chapter III
Dialectic of alienated work

Freedom is not only threatened by political evolutions which see the democratic project reduced to a pious wish, or even to an ideology allowing to better disguise the oligarchic domination of which we have shown some features in the previous chapter. What is played out in the "political superstructure" depends to a large extent on what happens in the "engine room", that is, where the material conditions of human existence are produced, in other words, in the labor process. Two decades ago, the end of work was announced, and our misfortunes came only because we did not understand its inevitable disappearance[70]. Work was said to be "a disappearing value"[71]. The imperious development of industry and services in the emerging countries has shown that the plectrums do not play themselves (as in the Aristotelian dream) and that capital is still as hungry for labor to exploit. The French presidential campaign of 2007 was largely conducted under the sign of "labor value": the "disappearing value" was making a sudden return to the public scene.

This back and forth of the "labor value" has had the effect of eclipsing the critique of labor as alienated labor, which was one of the strong themes of the 1960s. If work is disappearing, it is useless to criticize it, it should only

---

70. FORRESTER (V.), *L'Horreur économique*, reprinted by LGF, Le Livre de Poche, 1999.
71. MÉDA (D.), *Le Travail, une valeur en voie de disparition* (*Work, a disappearing value*), Flammarion, reprinted in the "Champs" series, 1998.

be buried with great pomp, and if it becomes the supreme value again, any criticism is unwelcome. The critique of work remains, in the form of the analysis of the pathologies of work. But it is only a question of improving working conditions, of convincing the bosses that stress at work is, all things considered, not very profitable and that happiness at work is favourable to productivity! Radical criticism of work is rare. Only a few small groups, isolated from the mass of workers, seem to be the bearers of it (for example, the *Krisis* group or the *Wertkritik* current).

Certainly, in today's society, the "right to work" can be claimed as one of the only serious rights, since it is identified with the right not to die of hunger and the right to benefit from a social existence. But it is precisely the present society that is at stake, that is to say a society whose obvious crisis cannot be averted by the remedies of recovery or neo-Keynesianism, because it is a crisis that pushes to its acme the contradiction between the "generic being" of man and the situation that is made for him in the capitalist society, or the unbearable contradiction between producer and worker. There is no freedom possible as long as the largest part of the time (and by far!) of the immense majority of humans is submitted to the tyranny of work.

Work and production

Let us begin by differentiating what needs to be differentiated, in other words, by getting out of the confusion that makes us mistake slavery for freedom. In Genesis, we learn that work is the punishment inflicted on man as a result of the (original) fault of Adam and Eve. To work is to earn a living by the sweat of one's brow, painfully:

> "Then he said to the man, "Because you listened to the voice of your wife and ate of the fruit of the tree which I forbade you to taste, curse the ground for your sake. You will eat from it with hard work all the days of your life. It will produce thorns and thistles for you and you will eat grass from the field. By the sweat of your face you shall eat bread, until you

return to the ground from which you were taken: for you are dust and to dust you shall return"[72].

It is a necessary suffering and, therefore, we should accept this fate and even, if possible, find good sides to it. If men had remained in the Garden of Eden, they would have been bored, argues Kant, who sees in the fall not so much the evil as the trick of providence to force man to deploy all the resources that are within him. Marx "tells a very different story". For him, man is a producer. Marx does not say worker, but producer[73] and it is by this that men distinguish themselves from animals, it is by this that they manifest their life. The distinction is not secondary. From a certain point of view, animals also work: they spend energy to obtain the means of their physical existence: they build nests, dig burrows, hunt, harvest, etc. But this activity never goes beyond the strict framework of instinctive needs and they can only reproduce their own life. Men produce "indirectly their material life" and, in doing so, they transform themselves and the natural given into the product of human activity.

Let us assume that production is the kind of activity by which men manifest their reality, and let us now designate by "work" that which is imposed on man, without him being able to do anything other than comply with it. Production is characteristic of all known human societies. The hunter-gatherers produce the weapons that enable them to hunt, jewelry, works of art - painted caves for example, statuettes representing mainly women, musical instruments that testify to the existence of a musical art, and thus of songs and dances - and they also produce everything that allows them to embellish their own bodies: paintings on the face, scarifications, tattoos: by all these means the men seek to abolish the radically foreign character of the external nature and to recognize themselves, to make

---

72. *Genesis*, III, 17-19.

73. When he envisages the social organization that will have to succeed the capitalist mode of production, he uses the formula of the "association of producers" or of the "associated producers" and never the terminology that one will find later in the various varieties of Marxism that speak of workers' power, of workers' power or of workers' control, all formulas that one would look in vain for in Marx. It is not by chance!

visible, audible, sensitive, the interiority, that is to say the self-affectation of the spirit. In all these productive activities - and here we voluntarily mix the activities directed towards the satisfaction of the material needs and the activities directed towards the satisfaction of the spiritual needs - the man recognizes himself as a free being, a being whose nature is not to be attached to an immutable natural order.

Unlike production, which manifests the human essence, work - and here we must take Genesis literally - is a condemnation. Work does violence to the individual, instead of elevating him, it lowers him, and this is why work will soon be the destiny of the slave, while the noble man, the truly human man, will be exempt from the obligation to work and will be able to devote his life to activities that are in themselves their own end. We find in Simone Weil a radical condemnation of work, based on her experience in the factory.

> "Physical work is a daily death.
>
> "To work is to put one's own being, soul and flesh, into the circuit of inert matter, to make it an intermediary between one state and another state of a fragment of matter, to make it an instrument. The worker makes of his body and his soul an appendage of the tool he handles. The movements of the body and the attention of the mind are a function of the requirements of the tool, which itself is adapted to the material of the work.
>
> "Death and work are things of necessity and not of choice. The universe gives itself to man in food and warmth only if man gives himself to the universe in work. But death and work can be endured with revolt or consent. They can be endured in their naked truth or wrapped in a lie.
>
> "Work does violence to human nature[74]."

It is not a question of taking up Hannah Arendt's opposition between work and work. Indeed, as a collective organization of production, as a collective intellectual, modern industry is just as capable of producing

---

74. WEIL (S.), *L'Enracinement*, Gallimard, 1949, electronic edition "Les classiques des sciences sociales", p. 197.

works and a human world as the ancient craft industry. It has even done so in a spectacular way during the great era of industrial revolutions. It has erected utilitarian buildings that we now look upon as cathedrals of the industrial age. The network of railroads, railway stations, highways and airports, largely structures the urban as well as the rural landscape. The ports with their enormous transhipment equipment, the iron and steel factories or the refineries illuminated day and night by an activity that can never stop, express the Promethean effort - perhaps crazy - of men to pose as "masters and possessors of nature". But what must be underlined is the unbearable contradiction between this apology of production and human capacities expressed by modern industry, and the lowering of the worker, this dispossession of oneself, which was the price to pay for capitalist prosperity.

Work and production form a contradiction, in which there is however a unity. There is no production without, in one way or another, man submitting himself to the necessities of work, that is to say, to pain, to wear and tear on the body, to the occupation and tension of all the faculties, and this is true of artistic creation as much as of the production of consumer goods and objects of use. What gives labor in modern society its special character is the fact that it is not labor in general, taken as an anhistorical category, but labor in the capitalist mode of production. If we follow Marx, we can understand exactly what is at stake: the capitalist mode of production is based on the transformation of living labor, the expression of the worker's personal power, into abstract labor, labor reduced to a pure quantity that coagulates into the commodity. This transformation is again the transformation of a personal, subjective or material power (Marx uses these terms almost interchangeably[75]) into the objective power of capital. This is the key moment. It is not a question of knowing whether the ancient slave or the serf under the feudal system lived better or worse than the modern worker. It is a question of understanding what we call

---

75. We refer here to our books *The Theory of Knowledge in Marx* and *Understanding Marx* which develop this question.

work today in the capitalist mode of production. Marx, who is not a "historicist", does not think of labor in the capitalist mode of production as the continuation of ancient or feudal serfdom, but as the destruction of the independent producer.

This process of submission of the producer to capital is expressed in three closely related forms:

- Exploitation: what underlies the mechanism of reproduction of capital A-M-A' is the extortion of free labor: the capitalist buys labor-power at its value - that is, at the sum of the values of the commodities socially embodied in an average labor-power at a given time and in a given society. But the use of this labor power produces not only a value equivalent to that of the labor power, but also and above all an additional value - *Mehrwert* - or surplus-value that is captured by capital. It is this dimension that has interested traditional Marxism most;

- Alienation: in the capitalist labor process, the worker is not only dispossessed of the means of labor - the capitalist mode of production is based on the expropriation of the independent producer who owns his means of labor - of the product of his labor (which belongs to the capitalist), but he is also dispossessed of himself. As Marx puts it, in the "labor market," the worker sells the only thing that belongs to him, his skin, and he must expect to be tanned;

- Reification: the living work, the vital activity, of the producer is transformed into an abstraction, the value, indifferent to life. What is life is transformed into a lifeless thing (money). But at the same time, that which has no life seems to take on life as it monopolizes living labor. Marx compares capital to the vampire, which gives itself the appearance of life by sucking the blood of the living.

There have been many rather sterile polemics among Marxists about whether the category of alienation is still relevant in the scientific analysis of *Capital,* whether it is better to stick to the theory of exploitation, or whether or not to accept the category of reification - which was especially popularized by unorthodox Marxists like Lukacs in the 1920s. It seems pointless to us to try to decide. The three categories have the advantage of describing the same process under three different "attributes", of giving three formulations which are mutually illuminating and can be drawn from different parts of Marx's work.

The most important thing is that the capitalist mode of production, however one analyzes it, presents itself as a system of total submission of producers to the demands of capital. We cannot insist enough on this point: submission can be formal when the worker, deprived of the possession of his tools, comes to work as a wage earner in the factory. But when the factory - which is still only a side-by-side reunion of the old trades - gives way to the modern capitalist factory, based on the division and parcelling out of labor and the implementation of a *process* unit (for example with the introduction of machine tools whose energy is supplied by a steam engine), then submission becomes a "real submission."

In recent years, we have begun to question suffering at work and stress, leading to new forms of pathologies[76]. A series of suicides in large companies such as Renault and France Télécom have brutally demonstrated the reality of work, not in "emerging" countries with low wages and hellish working hours, but in ultramodern companies (at Renault, the suicides took place in the research center), where employees benefit from salaries that are clearly above average and from a solid social protection system. The introduction of a "management" system nicknamed "management by terror"[77] is undoubtedly linked to a managerial fashion that originated in the United States and of which the Wal-Mart chain is a good illustration. Its application at France Telecom by senior civil servants of the major government bodies can certainly be explained by the ardent desire of these hyper-protected bureaucrats to show the shareholders that they

---

76. See DEJOUR (C.), *Souffrance en France*, Seuil, 1998 and, with BÈGUE (Florence), *Suicide et travail: que faire?*

77. A management specialist, Sylvain Cascarino, summarized the principles in a short, particularly scathing text published in 2002, *Le Management par la terreur en 10 leçons* (Management by terror in 10 lessons), which can be found without difficulty on the Internet.

could become capitalists as cruel as the others and that they would not be intimidated by the old trade union and political traditions of the company sold at auction by a left-wing government with communist ministers... But whatever the explanations put forward, they all boil down to one : management by terror is the very essence of the capitalist system, which has no other function than the extortion of surplus value by any means possible. When we open *Capital,* we learn how the *sweating system*[78] worked, a system of piecework wages that pushes employees to exploit themselves and their comrades. The France Télécom system with the "PVV" (Part variable du vendeur) and many other bonuses or sanctions is nothing other than the good old *sweating system*, which proves that high technology is perfectly compatible with the methods of capitalism of two centuries ago. The methods of Taylorism have also been described in detail. To all those nostalgic for the "Glorious Thirty" and the "Fordist-Keynesian regulation" of capitalism, we should recall their cost in terms of the degradation of working conditions: the great workers' strike of May-June 1968 was not only about wages, but also and often much more about the pace and conditions of work.

Only those who see the system from the right side, that is, from the side of those who profit from it, can consider that capitalism and freedom go together. For the vast majority of workers, the loss of the condition of self-employment was perceived as a regression to the condition of slavery. It took a long domestication of the working class, but also the establishment of minimal protections against the tyranny of capital, for wage labor to become an acceptable condition, and even, at times, a condition that was attempted to be made enviable. The workers became accustomed to the idea that they would never again find their lost freedom - the Marxist prophets played their part in this by denouncing the "reactionary petty-bourgeois illusions" of those who dreamed of regaining the situation of the small independent producer. Wage-labor was presented as the necessary passage for the laws of history to be fulfilled, and thus the proletarians

---

78. See Marx (K.), *Capital,* book I, chap. XXI.

exploited by the capitalists were transformed into soldiers in the army of historical progress. The most important of these were the limitation of the working day, the prohibition of child labor, and the establishment of the first mutual aid funds. This movement will have several effects:

- forced to face the limitation of the working day, the capitalist mode of production will organize itself around the hunt for relative surplus value, that is to say intensification of work, increase in productivity, development of the division of labor and rise of the "scientific organization of work". The workers' struggles acted as a spur to accelerate technical progress;
- the workers will try to stabilize their situation within the capitalist mode of production and to make wage-earning a condition linked to rights allowing to compensate (even very partially) the dissymmetry proper to the contract of employment, contract of submission of the employee to his employer;
- the workers' organizations will develop and, becoming regular interlocutors of the employers and the ruling class, they take an increasingly conservative orientation.

Even if, officially, the idea of the emancipation of the workers by the abolition of the wage-earner and the bosses remains for a long time inscribed in the statutes of the French syndicalism, heir of the revolutionary and anarcho-syndicalist syndicalism, in practice it is no longer about that at all, it is no longer about breaking the chains of capitalism, but only about negotiating the length of the chain. Let's admit that this enterprise of domesticating the revolutionary potential of the working class has worked rather well. From the beginning of the 20th century, the great socialist or social democratic utopias[79] envisaged the bright future as a society of generalized wage-labor - instead of the abolition of wage-labor, the whole population was transformed into state-dependent wage-laborers. The catastrophe of "20th century communism" (the Stalinist system) made

---

79. See ANGENOT (Marc), *L'Utopie collectiviste. Le grand récit socialiste sous la deuxième internationale*, PUF, 1993.

this perspective unattractive, and it seems that the vast majority of workers and the organizations that claim to be part of it have come to believe that capitalism is the unsurpassable historical horizon.

The producers today are no longer the workers, but the bosses and the "new producers of value", that is, the specialists in financial speculation. This transformation of representations and language is an indicator of the historical defeat of the workers' movement and with it, a certain idea of freedom. Indeed, what is called today "free world" are societies in which, in their immense majority, individuals are placed in a situation of dependence towards a minority that holds the means of production and is therefore, in fact, not free. From this point of view, freedom in the capitalist mode of production is largely illusory.

The steel cage

Max Weber, in *The Protestant Ethic and the Spirit of Capitalism*, spoke of the "steel cage" (or "steel cockpit," depending on the translation) of modern society. Showing how "one of the constitutive elements of the spirit of [modern] capitalism, and not only the latter, but of modern culture itself, namely the conduct of rational life on the basis of the idea of *the profession-vocation (Beruf)*, was born out of the spirit of *Christian asceticism*," Weber goes on to point out that Christian asceticism was transformed into the "puritanical asceticism of the profession-vocation" that gives rise to the modern idea of professional work.

> "That the limitation to a specialized work, with the renunciation that it implies to the universality of the Faustian type of man, is in the contemporary world the absolute condition of an action having a value, that therefore, today, "action" and "renunciation" inevitably condition each other. [...] The Puritan *wanted to* be a man of the profession-vocation; we are *forced* to be so. Indeed, by passing from monastic cells into professional life and by beginning to dominate intramundane morality, asceticism has contributed [, for its part,] to the construction of the powerful cosmos of

the modern economic order which, linked to the technical and economic conditions of mechanical and machinist production, today determines, with an irresistible constraining force, the lifestyle of all the individuals who are born within this machinery - and *not only* of those who earn their living by directly exercising an economic activity. Perhaps it will determine it, until the last quintal of fossil fuel is consumed. In Baxter's eyes, concern for external goods should weigh on the shoulders of his saints only as "a light cloak that could be thrown off at any moment." But fate made this cloak a steel-hard dwelling (*stahlhartes Gehäuse*). While asceticism undertook to transform the world and to be active in it, the external goods of this world acquired a growing and finally inexorable power over men, as never before in history. Today, the spirit of this asceticism has escaped from this shell - permanently? Do we know? In any case, since it rests on a mechanical basis, winning capitalism no longer needs this prop[80]."

A remarkable text that exposes how the very development of capitalism is a dialectical development, transforming action on the world to shape it into a real prison: the unity of action and renunciation that forms the ascetic principle of nascent capitalism gives way to a mechanical development that no one really controls anymore. Weber was not the first to show the link between Protestantism and capitalism. Marx had pointed this out several times[81], for whom "Protestantism is an essentially bourgeois religion[82]". But Marx's remarks are insufficient to understand what was ideologically at work. In contrast to traditional, ancient and medieval societies, Protestantism presents itself primarily as a rehabilitation of work. Far from being the mark of an ignoble condition, it is now perceived as the vocation of man. But this revaluation of the worker, far from being the starting point of his emancipation, forges on the contrary new chains and one of Weber's interests is to help us to grasp this reversal and the contradictory figures it could take.

---

80. WEBER (M.), *The Protestant Ethic and the Spirit of Capitalism*, pp. 250-251.
81. Weber often draws his analyses from the same sources as Marx, Petty, Benjamin Franklin, etc.
82. MARX (K.), *The Capital*, book I, chap. XXVII, in *Works I*, p. 1177.

Protestantism is often associated with the intellectual progress that led to the Enlightenment and the value it placed on freedom in all its forms. This is, however, not entirely accurate. The founders of Protestantism (Luther, Calvin, etc.) had little to do with the idea of progress and were at war with many aspects of modern society. Weber notes:

> "It is necessary to take into account the fact, often forgotten today, that the Reformation did not so much mean *the elimination of* the domination of ecclesial life over life in general, as above all the replacement of the form of domination that had existed until then by another[83]."

Hence the intriguing question: How is it that the bourgeoisie in economically developed regions so often supported the Reformation?

> "In fact, it was not an excess, but an insufficiency of the ecclesio-religious domination of life that the reformers who arose in the most economically developed countries reproved. Now, how is it that it was precisely these countries that were then economically the most developed and that, within these countries [...] it was precisely the "bourgeois" middle classes that were then economically ascendant that, not content to suffer this puritanical tyranny [still unknown to them], on the contrary defended it with a heroism that precisely the *bourgeois* classes *as such* had rarely developed before and never developed after [...][84]?"

Analyzing some of Benjamin Franklin's famous texts (*"time is money"*), he emphasizes that the "spirit of capitalism" is neither eudemonistic nor hedonistic, neither in search of happiness nor in enjoyment. The virtues advocated by Franklin always seem to be oriented towards utility (one must be honest because it is better in business), but this is only an appearance. Franklin's ethics (Weber puts quotation marks on "ethics" because the term seems to him to be inappropriate) defines the "sovereign good" as the fact of "acquiring money and more money while avoiding in the strictest manner all ingenuous enjoyment" and in this conception :

83. WEBER (M.), *op. cit.* p. 7.
84. WEBER (M.), *op. cit.* p. 8.

"It is man who is related to gain as the purpose of his life and no longer gain in man as a means of satisfying his vital material needs[85]."

The "spirit of capitalism" is fundamentally this inversion of ends and means that Marx exposes when he studies the transformation of money into capital. In the elementary exchange economy, the fundamental cycle is M-A-M: commodity-money-commodity. The producer of a commodity sells it to obtain money to buy the goods he needs, and in this cycle money is only an intermediary. The capitalist cycle, on the other hand, is written A-M-A', with A' = A + dA, money-commodity-money, and here money (or, more precisely, the accumulation of money) is the finality. This inversion of the "vital teleology[86]" is what characterizes the capitalist mode of production and allows us to distinguish the obsession with capital accumulation from all the forms of greed and avarice that did not spare previous societies.

Protestantism, according to Weber, was the religion that made possible the development of this "spirit of capitalism" because, especially in its Puritan or Pietist versions, it presupposes a mental concentration and a sense of being bound to work by duty that are fully part of the attitudes required by the capitalist mode of production, both on the part of capitalists and workers. Weber underlines how this passage from the Christian *ethos*, which values disinterestedness and condemns money ("the devil's dung"), to modern utilitarianism may seem staggering. But this is precisely what makes it so interesting theoretically. It is true that capitalism has subsequently emancipated itself from this "ethic" of its beginnings, but it remains linked to a certain conception of the meaning of what one should occupy one's life with. Let us learn a lesson from what Weber explains: the transformation of liberal capitalism (which at one time seemed effectively liberating) into a machine of oppression is by no means contingent, but occurs on the contrary through a kind of "fatality" whose hard core is the asceticism of work.

---

85. WEBER (M.), *op. cit.* p. 27.
86. To take here an expression of Michel HENRY in his *Karl Marx*.

Beyond the polemics on the validity of Weber's analyses, his work on *The Protestant Ethic* allows us to make the link between Christianity and modern capitalist utilitarianism and to understand how the idea that life must be transformed into work was imposed... Marx then explains how work in its concrete diversity can be reduced to abstract work and to the general equivalent[87].

Weber helps to understand one of the most interesting and strange specificities of capitalist society as a class society. Previous class societies - slave or feudal - were societies in which the mark of the ruling class was idleness. To be exempt from the obligation to work was the supreme distinction. Work was reserved for individuals of inferior status: it was by nature servile. When they were not busy with war, the old ruling classes indulged in all sorts of games, receptions, banquets, balls and other social rites by which the unity of the ruling class was maintained. In addition to the clergy, non-members of the ruling class were also invited, admitted to join them because they too were engaged in "liberal" activities, activities without mercenary ends: these are the people we will end up calling "intellectuals", artists of all kinds, philosophers, historians, public entertainers... Nothing like that anymore in capitalist society: the ruling classes, too, are obliged to work. They are subject to the business press, to decisions to be made, to operations to be set up, to negotiations to be conducted. The trader is the one who does not have *otium*, leisure, the one who is subjected to the urgency of the business to be done, which concentrates the attention and thus forbids the mind to wander freely. With capitalism, the one who has *otium* will become a despicable being, a social parasite - monks and secular clergy, useless intermediaries between men and God, fall into this category in the eyes of the reformed. In the ancient world, beggars were unfortunate people on whom charity could be exercised, thus enabling the Christian

---

87. There is in Weber a polemic against Marxism, i.e. against the "historical materialism", ideology of the German social democracy. Moreover, Weber was rather a conservative in politics. But there is no theoretical incompatibility between Marx and Weber: the best of those who put themselves in the school of Marx during the last century were often continuators of Weber. This is the case, notably, of the "Frankfurt School".

to perform acts that pleased God and would earn him paradise; with the advent of capitalism, they became reprobates who had to be pursued and locked up like criminals and forced to work - *workhouses were* even created for this purpose[88].

What is true for the working classes and for the disinherited is also true, *mutatis mutandis*, for the ruling classes. The capitalist considers the landowner who lives off his rents as a parasite and his power as a brake on the development of industry. Under the Restoration, the industrial bourgeoisie was readily republican, hostile to a regressive social order that privileged inherited titles and the prebends of power over productive activity. A champion of the union of the working classes and industrialists, Saint-Simon even defended an alliance of producers - the disciples of Saint-Simon were to play a leading role in the industrialization of France, the development of transport and the banking networks essential to modern capitalism.

Capital, says Marx, is not a thing, but a social relation; it is this relation that distributes social functions to both poles. It is an antagonistic relation - a relation of domination and exploitation - that opposes worker and capitalist. But the capitalist is also dependent on this relation and, in some respects, is even enslaved to it. When Marx says that the capitalist is the servant of capital, he is indicating this relation of servitude. Of course, the servitude of the capitalist and that of the proletarian are not symmetrical. The functionary of capital is a well-paid slave who can enjoy the particular power that his social position gives him. But luxurious servitude remains servitude: the chief of the eunuchs in the service of an oriental despot also enjoyed privileges that were out of all proportion to the situation of the little people. He could decide the fate of a large number of servants or

---

88. See Marx, *Capital*, Book I, chapters XXVII and XXVIII, on the expropriation of free peasants and the beggar's laws. Let us note that the modern labor camp is only the extension of the barbaric methods by which capitalism has ensured its domination. Their massive use in the USSR and China, better than any subtle theoretical analysis, is a sign of the class nature of these regimes, despite the apologetic speeches of Marxists. Let us also remember that the so-called "communism" in the USSR was built from the beginning by forced labor - of which "communist Saturdays" were the most benign form.

solicitors; he had a power depending on the mood of the master, certainly, but also on his own skill in the complex games of the court. And yet, he remained a slave whose position depended on the success of his intrigues. *Mutatis mutandis*, the capitalist is not unrelated to this chief eunuch. A reversal of fortune can be fatal to him. A ruined nobleman remained a nobleman; a ruined capitalist is no longer a capitalist, but a candidate for a position as a homeless person or a person on welfare. Of course, it is rare that a well-installed capitalist becomes homeless. But it is already less rare for him to do a little tour behind the bars of a prison (VIP section)... The nineties gave some examples.

The capitalist is a dominant one, dominated also by the conditions of his domination. When he exploits "his" workers, he does not do so out of sadistic pleasure, nor only out of greed: competition from other capitals forces him to produce at least at the average conditions of profitability of capital, on pain of disappearing sooner or later. Slave owners or lords could be good or bad, gentle or cruel, and there is a whole literature on this subject. The capitalist, to some extent, has no such choice. The denunciation of the capitalist as a greedy and somewhat repulsive human type, a great classic of a certain literature and of a certain type of militancy, is, for those who place themselves in the school of Marx, a real stupidity. By guaranteeing the profitability of capital, by pursuing the objectives of accumulation, he is doing his job as a capitalist (he is fulfilling his profession-vocation) and nothing else. Certainly, around these functional imperatives there is a certain amount of leeway - a style of leadership, if you like, which changes the moral judgment or the feelings one may have towards this or that representative of the capitalist class. But these fluctuations always take place around a pivot determined by the general conditions of the reproduction of capital in a given country and at a given time.

The reproduction of capital is like an automatic mechanism that uses individuals as resources and throws them away when they can no longer satisfy the demands of the rate of profit. The evolution of capitalism since the 19th century has shown how relevant Marx's intuitions were. The firm, owned by a capitalist or a family of capitalists (patrimonial capitalism),

128

has given way to joint stock companies. The latter found a certain stability in the decades immediately after the Second World War. The firm is embodied by a technobureaucracy and teams of engineers concerned above all with the long-term development of the enterprise or firm. In this type of organization, the separation between capital, on the one hand, and the functions of organization and management of the production process, on the other, is already clearly established, but the links remain with a reference shareholder who continues to intervene in the management of the firm - this is still the case in large firms such as Michelin or PSA, where the Michelin and Peugeot families continue to play their role. In the next phase, the one we are currently in, the firm, as a unit of production and reproduction of capital, tends to be nothing more than a commodity that is bought and sold on a highly speculative market. The real owners, those who commit their capital, are most often unaware of where their money has gone: investment funds, pension funds, FCP, etc., these are the institutions that take the place of capitalists, but they do not own the capital; they can only live and prosper by skilfully making the capital entrusted to them bear fruit. The figure of the capitalist (paunchy, top hat, cigar, as in the caricatures of *L'Assiette au beurre*) is a survival. There is still a bourgeois class, but it should not be confused with the capitalist class. The largest fortunes in France do not represent much compared to the mainly American pension funds, which are in reality the property of the employees who contribute to them. For the main French companies listed on the stock exchange - the famous CAC 40 - it is estimated that 5% of the capitalization belongs to the big bourgeois families. Nearly half goes to investment funds, a small quarter to institutional investors, a quarter to strategic shareholders (mostly other firms) and a handful of shares distributed among the public of "small holders". The first fortune of France seems monstrous for those who are pulling the devil by the tail, but it is almost marginal compared to the mass of invested capital.

Liberal thinkers saw and still see capitalism as an economic and social system that gives people the freedom to choose and asks them to take responsibility for their choices. But the truth is that freedom is reduced to a mere accessory. The systemic logic of capital imposes itself on economic "actors" and leaves little room for free will and much for predestination! The extension of bureaucracy and constraints on individuals follows from this very logic of the economy. One can repeat like a mantra that "capitalism is freedom", it is as convincing as when the dumbed-down crowds of *1984* chant "freedom is slavery".

Salaried employees

Let's take the problem another way. The fundamental relationship in today's society is wage labor. It was not born with the capitalist mode of production: it is almost as old as the market economy. If the wage earner differs from the slave in that he is free to put himself at the service of one boss or another, and also free to leave him (or to be left!), his situation has always been considered as a situation of dependence, a mark of social inferiority. Roman soldiers were wage earners: it is generally the army that was the first developed form of wage employment. Rowers were also salaried during the early Middle Ages. The wage earner is a kind of mercenary, one who is employed as a mere means, indifferent to the ends and thus in a position of absolute submission.

There is, however, a great difference in content between the centurion of the Roman legions and the modern proletarian. The latter is theoretically thought of as a producer - a centurion was not a producer -, but a producer separated from his means of production. The modern proletariat was formed as a result of very violent social upheavals that brutally uprooted millions of peasants or artisans to submit them to the yoke of capital. The modern worker is an expropriated producer, and this in several senses.

First of all, he is a producer without means of production: the peasants driven off their lands, the ruined artisans and all their children will provide the labor force for the primitive accumulation of capital. Deprived of the means of production, the producer is no more than a proletarian in the Roman sense: his only wealth is his progeny, whom he quickly brings into the furnace of capitalist production. Deprived of the means of production, he is deprived at the same time of the means to provide for the needs of life by himself and he loses his freedom. The first republican constitutions did not defend universal suffrage, and republican thinkers all made, more or less clearly, the difference between the active and the passive citizen. The liberals saw this as a necessity, arising from the protection of property rights as a fundamental right. Their argument - which is found in Benjamin Constant - is the following: individuals without property make up the majority of the nation's body. If they are given the right to vote, they will be tempted to use their political power to demand reforms redistributing wealth (as the Roman plebs demanded agrarian reforms) and thus the government will be led to violate the right of property, the first condition of the "freedom of the moderns. Marxism does not say anything else, but this time with a negative value judgment: the distinction between active and passive citizens unambiguously expresses the "bourgeois" character of the 18th-century revolutions. The Bolsheviks drew the consequence of this by imposing an inverted censal suffrage: in Lenin's Russia, one worker's vote counted for ten peasant's votes and the deposed bourgeois were deprived of the right to vote. But beyond these two symmetrical arguments, there are also reasonable reasons - even if today we rightly reject them - to distinguish between the two categories of citizens. In *Oceana*, James Harrington, a "neo-Roman" and Machiavellian republican and theorist of the English revolution of 1641-1649, describes the free citizen as one who owns his land, his plow and his gun. Oceana's institution is clear:

> "The first order divides the people into free men or citizens and servants or those deemed to be servants; if the latter attain freedom, that is, subsist by themselves, they are free or citizens[89]."

To be free is to be able to subsist on one's own, that is, without being in the dependence of another - and Harrington is content with a single argument, obvious to him: "servitude is by its nature incompatible with liberty

---

89. HARRINGTON (J.), *Oceana*, Belin, 1995, p. 298.

or participation in the government of a republic. It is for this reason that he defends agrarian laws that avoid the concentration of property and allow a maximum number of individuals to enjoy the rights of citizenship by not being forced into the service of another. It can be seen that republicanist argumentation has nothing to do with liberal argumentation, although in practice they can to some extent lead to a common position, as was the case during the French Revolution. The republicans make property the means of political freedom, while the liberals make it the freedom itself. The former therefore advocate the maximum dispersion of property so that the number of free citizens increases, whereas the liberals unreservedly admit that a large number of citizens are deprived of the effectiveness of their political rights.

The relevance of the republicanist argument is largely confirmed by the entire history of the labor movement. The workers were first a plebeian race reduced to the most miserable condition and deprived of all freedom. It is only when, in collective action, the workers were able to build institutions of their own, to become, as it were, the co-owners of their mutual societies, of their unions and soon of their parties, that they succeeded in imposing universal suffrage and in making themselves heard, and even in participating in the government of the republic. But if he is a member of a mutual society, a union, a cooperative, the worker is not a wage earner, he is a citizen and a producer who seeks to regain in another form the lost freedom of the independent producer. When Marxists see in the salarization of the majority of the population a progress that leads to socialism, they commit a terrible confusion: what leads to social and historical progress - if we want to keep this very problematic lexicon - is not salariat, but the actions that individuals undertake to protect themselves from its most harmful consequences. And when Marx says that communism is the real movement (and not a plan of social engineers), this is still what he has in mind: the movement by which expropriated producers seek to combat their situation as wage earners. If therefore, as for republicanists, freedom is defined mainly through the opposition *liber/servus*, freedom/servitude, the wage condition is a negation of freedom, it is the condition of the servant. And it is still commonly recalled today: the employee is at the service of the company.

But to be a salaried employee is still to lose one's freedom in a second sense. On the surface, the wage relationship is a normal contract. I give 1 euro to the baker, the baker gives me bread that I can eat as I please or give to the ducks on my Sunday walk. The worker goes to the (labor) market to sell the only thing he has: his labor power. When he sells it, he pockets the value of this labor power, i.e. his wage, in good money. The capitalist who has acquired a commodity labor power, at its value, without swindling, enjoys it as he pleases, i.e. makes it work. Nothing could be more normal: the contract is a contract between two free persons and there is nothing more to say about it. But the labor market is not the simple exchange of commodities. Marx gives a more precise description:

"The moment we leave this sphere of simple circulation, which provides the vulgar free trader with his notions, his ideas, his way of seeing and the criterion of his judgment on capital and wage-earning, we see, as it seems, a certain transformation in the physiognomy of the characters of our drama. Our old man with the money takes the lead and, as a capitalist, walks first; the owner of the labor force follows him from behind as his own worker; this one with a sarcastic look, the important and busy air; this one timid, hesitant, restive, like someone who has worn his own skin to the market, and can only expect one thing: to be tanned[90]."

The salaried worker, unlike the independent producer, does not sell the product of his work, he sells his skin! He becomes, as the colourful and somewhat obscene vocabulary of modern management puts it, a "human resource", a thing at the disposal of capitalist production, in the same way as the machines and raw materials that he has also paid for at their value and which he uses as he sees fit. During the time for which the labor contract is negotiated, it seems that the worker proceeds to this insane operation of selling himself.

---

90. Marx (K.), *Capital*, book I, II, *Works I*, p. 726.

It is not just a question of obedience. The journeyman was under the orders of his master. It is above all a question of the loss of what makes the worker a producer. His own personal power is taken over by the capitalist production process. Engels describes the work of the workers thus:

> "Watching the machines, reattaching broken wires, these are not activities that require the worker to make an effort of thought, but on the other hand, they prevent him from occupying his mind with other thoughts. We have also seen that this work does not give any place to physical activity, to the play of the muscles. Thus it is not a question of work, but of absolute boredom, the most paralyzing, the most depressing boredom there is - the factory worker is condemned to let all his physical and moral strength wither away in this boredom, his job consists of being bored all day long since the age of 8. And with that, he cannot leave for a single moment - the steam engine is running all day long, the gears, belts and spindles are constantly buzzing and clicking in his ears, and if he wants to rest even for a moment, the foreman is immediately on his back with the fine register in his hand. This condemnation to be buried alive in the factory, to constantly watch the tireless machine, the worker feels that it is the most painful torture there is. It has an extremely stultifying effect on both the body and the mental faculties of the worker. One cannot imagine a better method of stupefaction than factory work, and if, in spite of everything, the workers have not only saved their intelligence, but have also developed it and sharpened it more than others, it has only been possible through the revolt against their lot and against the bourgeoisie: this revolt being the only thought and feeling that their work allows them. And if this indignation against the bourgeoisie does not become the predominant feeling among them, they necessarily fall prey to alcoholism and to all that is usually called immorality[91]."

---

91. ENGELS (F.), *The Situation of the Working Class in England*, translation by Gilbert Badia, Éditions sociales, 1961 - Source: MIA (www.marxists.org).

Engels does not blame only physical fatigue or the intensity of work, but the transformation of production into an activity that occupies the body without exercising it, that occupies the mind by forbidding it to think. The worker has a power of his own, a power that only asks to be actualized from his subjective determinations. But in the capitalist mode of production, this personal power is snatched away from him and converted into an objective power of capital that stands up to the worker as his implacable enemy. In the labor process, the worker is not himself, his life has become a foreign process, but a process to which he is riveted. It is this process that is called "alienation" in French, but which corresponds to two different terms in the Hegelian German that Marx speaks: *Entäußerung* and *Entfremdung*. *Entäußerung* can be literally translated as "exteriorization", putting out, and this is indeed what the producer, the craftsman as well as the artist does: he exteriorizes his own subjective power by giving it, in the form of the product of his activity, an objective existence. *Entfremdung is* the fact of becoming foreign - Lefebvre, a subtle Germanist, does not hesitate to translate this term in Hegel as "strangely", used as a noun, a term also used by psychoanalysts. Labor in the capitalist mode of production is thus both externalization and "strangeness": this is the term Marx uses in his first systematic critique of labor in the capitalist mode of production: *die entfremdete Arbeit*, which the French translators render as "le travail aliéné". In the *Manuscripts of 1844*, one can read this text which, on the descriptive level, will never be denied in Marx's later theoretical elaborations:

> "What does alienation from work consist of?
>
> "First, in the fact that work is external to the worker, that is, it does not belong to his essence, that therefore, in his work, he does not affirm himself but denies himself, does not feel at ease but unhappy; he does not deploy a free physical and intellectual activity, but mortifies his body and ruins his mind. Consequently, the worker feels himself only outside of work and, in work, he feels outside of himself. He is at ease when he is not working, and when he is working he does not feel at ease. His work is therefore not voluntary, but forced, it is forced work. It is therefore not the satisfaction

of a need, but only a means to satisfy needs outside of work. The character of work appears clearly in the fact that, as soon as there is no physical or other constraint, work is shunned like the plague. The external work, in which he strips himself, is a work of self-sacrifice, of mortification. Finally, the external character of the worker's work appears clearly in the fact that it is not his own property, but that of another, that it does not belong to him, that in work the worker does not belong to himself, but to another. Just as in religion the activity of the human imagination, of the human brain and heart, acts on the individual independently of him, that is, as a divine or diabolical foreign activity, so the activity of the worker is not his own activity. It belongs to another, it is the loss of oneself.

"So we come to the result that man (the worker) only feels himself acting freely in his animal functions, eating, drinking and procreating, or at most in the choice of his house, his clothing, etc.; on the other hand, he feels himself an animal in his properly human functions. What is animal becomes human and what is properly human becomes animal[92]."

"What does the alienation of labor consist of?" could be translated here as "What does the becoming-external of labor consist of" (*Entäußerung*). In any case, it is indeed a process: the German word as well as the French word indicate unambiguously that one passes from one state to another through an alienation or an *Entaüßerung*. What is alienated? The text is clear: it is labor. Marx does not say: "labor in general is alienating". Labor is not alienating, but there is an alienation of labor. This means that labor was not alienated and becomes alienated. If it was not alienated, it is because it was the property of someone (the worker, the man who produces his conditions of existence) and it becomes something foreign to this person, something external. This is the consequence of a social-historical transformation, not the very essence of work.

---

92. Marx (K.), *Manuscripts of 1844*, translation by J.-P. Gougeon, GF-Flammarion, 1996, p. 112. We have preferred this translation to that of Malaquais for Volume II of the *Works* in the Pléiade edition.

It is thus a question of the alienation of labor under modern conditions of production, and not of the alienation of labor in general. And this time, the French translation makes it clear what kind of alienation it is: labor becomes external to the worker. If it is external to the worker, work does not belong to his essence. Curious paradox: work is not the essence of the worker! Once again, we must be precise: Marx does not say that work in general does not belong to the essence of man. On the contrary, he affirms that work as the production by man of the conditions of human life does belong to his essence. A little further on in the same text, we read that "by the practical production of an objective world, the elaboration of non-organic nature, man proves himself as a conscious generic being, that is, as a being who behaves towards the genus as towards his own essence, or towards himself, as a generic being", and that it is by this that man is fundamentally distinguished from the animal. So if the work of the worker does not belong to the essence of the worker, it is because the life of the worker at work is not a truly human life! And it is precisely what develops all the continuation of the text.

Thus the worker does not affirm himself in work, but denies himself in it; he does not find his well-being in it, but his misfortune, etc. To assert oneself, to seek one's well-being, to develop a free physical and intellectual activity, this is what constitutes the human essence. But the worker is deprived of this because work is mortification of the body and ruin of the spirit. Therefore, the work of the laborer does violence to man's nature.

Consequence: he is at home when he is not working and he is not at home when he is working: this could seem trivial, the man at work is not at home and vice versa. In reality, two ideas are implied:

- the craftsman was at home when he worked. The transformation of the craftsman into a worker is the separation of man from his work. This is the specific alienation introduced by the capitalist mode of production;
- Man should be at home when he produces, but the worker is not at home when he works. The opposition at home/at work reformulates the theme of the externalization of work. But this suggests that

this separation is not natural, does not correspond to the essence of man, and that, consequently, we must ask ourselves whether it is not possible to reconcile man with his work.

If labor is external to the worker, then labor is not voluntary, but forced. For Marx, wage labor is a form of servitude. Marx's work abounds in comparisons between wage labor and slavery. But the slavery of the modern wage laborer manifests itself in a particular way. The ancient slave did not work to satisfy his needs; he worked simply because he was a slave, and the master fed him as he fed his horses and oxen. If the slave starved, the master lost part of his capital! The "free" worker works because he has no choice if he does not want to starve. But strictly speaking, he is no more free. Work "is therefore not the satisfaction of a need, but only a means of satisfying needs outside work." In other words, if labor were not alienated, it would be, not the means of satisfying a need, but the primary need of man. Thirty years later, Marx returned to this idea:

> "In a higher phase of communist society, when the enslaving subordination of individuals to the division of labor, and with it the opposition between intellectual and manual labor, will have disappeared; when labor will not only be a means of living, but will itself become the first vital need; when, with the multiple development of individuals, the productive forces will have increased too, and all the sources of collective wealth will spring up with abundance, only then the limited horizon of bourgeois law will be definitively overcome and society will be able to write on its flags "From each according to his abilities, to each according to his needs"[93]!"

The work of the laborer is not free because it is subordinated to an external end. And this is why, apart from this constraint, no one would seek this kind of work: work is "shunned like the plague". This is a common sense observation, as long as we specify that we are talking about salaried work, forced work. The same worker, happy to be on vacation, can take

---

93. Marx (K.), "Gloses marginales au programme du parti ouvrier allemand", *Œuvres*, tome I, Pléiade edition, 1875, p. 1420.

advantage of it... to work, that is to say, to freely spend the energy of his body and the power of his mind by tinkering, cultivating his garden, etc.!

The exteriority of labor for the worker "appears in the fact that it is not his own property, but that of another, that it does not belong to him." Indeed, the worker can only work on the condition that he does so under the orders of a capitalist who will appropriate the fruit of his labor. This argument, which comes "at last", is in reality the explanation of what precedes. If the worker is outside his work, if he is not at home when he works, it is simply because the means of labor belong to the capitalist, that labor is separated from the means of labor. Marx will later show that there is nothing eternal about this situation. This social relation has the consequence that "in labor the worker does not belong to himself, but belongs to another." Indeed, the worker does not sell the product of his work like the craftsman. From a certain point of view and for a more or less limited time, he sells himself. Selling himself, he no longer belongs to himself. He is therefore alienated! We have started from the alienation of labor and we arrive at the alienation of the worker himself. An analogy follows: "Just as, in religion, the proper activity of the human imagination, of the human brain and the human heart, acts on the individual independently of him, that is to say, as a divine or diabolical foreign activity, so the activity of the worker is not his own activity. It belongs to another, it is the loss of oneself."

The conclusion of this first definition of alienation concentrates everything that has just been exposed. Alienation, the loss of oneself, reaches its peak here! If man feels free only in his "animal functions", he has really lost himself. Man produces his own life and this is the starting point, what separates him from the animals. But if this activity becomes foreign to him, it is because he loses the sense of what it really is to be a man. And the reversal is total when man comes to take animality for his own essence. And it is not a question here of the degree of arduousness of the work or of the degree of comfort and consumption. The man who works under a constraint in order to consume is alienated during his working time, but he is just as alienated and perhaps even more so during his non-working time devoted to "leisure" (cf. *below*). Just think of those crowds who, after a week's work, wander through the supermarkets... Thus in the capitalist mode of production, non-labor time is not a real leisure, but a simple moment of recuperation, destined to the reconstitution of labor power and thus entirely subject to the alienating determinations of the capitalist mode of production. In other words, the only freedom that wage labor allows, the freedom in the name of which one sacrifices the essential part of one's time, turns out to be most often perfectly artificial.

Understanding that wage labor is not only exploitation, but above all domination and alienation is essential. Exploitation is defined by Marx as the time of free labor that the capitalist appropriates in the form of surplus value. The rate of exploitation measures the ratio between paid work and free work. If the worker produces the equivalent of his wage (v) in four hours, the next four hours (pl) are labor that the capitalist enjoys for free, even though he is not stealing from the worker whose labor power he has bought. The ratio pl/v measures the rate of exploitation. Now let's imagine that the boss has been fired and that the enterprise is a workers' cooperative. It is supposed to stop exploiting the workers - and to avoid the bias introduced by the market, let us imagine that the whole company is a kind of workers' super-cooperative: will the workers work only four hours a day? or will they double their income? - whatever form it takes? Marx answers categorically no. The complete appropriation of the product of labor by the workers (a demand which appeared in the program of the Unification Congress of German Socialists in Gotha in 1875) is a meaningless demand. Before any individual distribution of production, one must deduct :

> *"Firstly, the administrative overheads which are independent of production.*
> "Compared to what happens in the present society, this fraction is reduced to a maximum from the outset and decreases as the new society develops.
> *"Secondly: what is intended to meet the needs of the community: schools, sanitary facilities, etc.*
> "This fraction gains in importance from the outset, compared to what is happening in the present society, and this importance increases as the new society develops.

"*Thirdly*: the fund necessary for the maintenance of those who are unable to work, etc., in short, what comes under what is now called official public assistance[94]."

First of all, it is not because a part of the products of his work does not accrue to him that the worker is exploited, and, consequently, exploitation cannot be defined by the simplistic formulas that we have used as a first approximation. Or else one would be obliged to consider that pensioners exploit the working, that the unemployed exploit those who work, etc., and that all redistribution mechanisms are only mechanisms of exploitation in disguise - this is the position supported by Robert Nozick, who assimilates to forced labor and to a form of servitude any form of levy operated by the State to the detriment of those who have legitimately acquired their goods and to the benefit of those who do not work or are unable to earn a living. What defines exploitation as such is therefore not simply gratis labor, but gratis labor extorted through mechanisms of domination and processes of alienation that are all the more violent because they are masked, since all of this takes the form of monetary relations, of relations between things, as indicated by expressions such as the circulation of goods or the circulation of capital.

Here we find the third aspect that characterizes the relations of labor in capitalist society, namely "reification", that is, a process that takes on a double aspect: producers compare their individual works in purely quantitative relations, abstracting from their concrete characters, which are the relations between the values of the commodities. When two producers exchange their productions according to the proportion "x commodity A = y commodity B", the living works that are coagulated in these commodities disappear to give way to a measure that seems to characterize the commodity itself. And it is also this form that makes it possible to conceal the true nature of the wage-labor contract under the respectable appearance of an agreement between free and equal indivi-

---

94. Marx (K.), "Gloses marginales", in *Critique du programme du parti ouvrier allemand* ("Critique of the Gotha program), *Œuvres*, tome I, Pléiade edition, Gallimard, 1963, p. 1418.

duals, both driven by the concern for their own interests in respect of the law. Thus, in capitalist production, relations between men (the social character of production) appear only in the form of relations between things, and conversely, things now seem to be endowed with properties that were thought to be reserved for humans. Capital is not a thing, but a social relation; but this social relation appears as a thing and, what is more, as the most general and abstract thing, money endowed with marvelous properties, such as that of growing and multiplying of its own accord once it has entered the enchanted realm of the circulation of capital. As long as the capitalist is an entrepreneur who immediately and directly converts his money into machines, raw materials and wages to be paid to workers, there is a certain relationship with reality. Industrialists compare their efficiency by counting in labor time: they know that a car, a computer or a shirt can be reduced to labor and that producer A will be more productive than B if he produces his shirt in less time than B and that profit comes only from there: from the sweat of workers. But in the financial sphere, things are different. The investor who puts his money in an investment fund thinks that he will "make his money work". But money does not work! The interest or dividend will only fall into the investor's pocket if, at some point, the circulation stops and the capital is engulfed in the furnace of production and emerges regenerated and grown, as if by a miracle. The investment specialist believes that he has produced value, but he has not produced anything at all, he has acted as a go-between to direct capital to the right flesh merchant. Marx compares him to Shylock, the character in Shakespeare's play, *The Merchant of Venice*. In any case, he and his sponsors can only live by taking their share of the activity of those who put their shirt on.

Whereas the domination of the old exploiting classes was open, unvarnished, and based on the fear and superstitious beliefs of traditional societies, the capitalist domination that expresses itself in the wage relation (for it is the essence of this relation that Marx writes A-M-A') maintains itself only by disguising itself; it needs only a minimum of open physical force and speaks not the language of popular superstition, but that of "economic science", in order to impose it on the vulgar. Domination has taken on the appearance of freedom. And the dominant itself, for reasons we have explained above, becomes more and more impersonal.

Since the essential act is that of selling labor power, wage labor is the system in which the sellers of labor power compete with the capitalist. In a very interesting documentary broadcast by France 3[95], we can see the recruitment procedures of "collaborators" for the company Carglass (a chain of windshield replacement workshops). The candidates have to defend a (fictitious) project and then the recruiters invite them to evaluate each other. Only one of them dares to criticize another candidate... and he is hired, not because of his intrinsic qualities, but because he has shown himself to be a "killer" without remorse - we know that a little later, it will be his turn to be eliminated. The wage-earner is summed up in this scene, which is shocking for those who have some illusions or who pretend to believe that capitalism is still compatible with the fundamental values of civility. We cannot really condemn our "killer": as long as the goal is to take the job, as long as there is only one position and many candidates, all means are good to survive... And, in fact, it is not a question of moralizing. The salary system is entirely based on this competition. The competition that young people have with older workers: at the beginning of their careers, they generally have lower wages and are more dynamic; the competition that workers from low-wage countries have with those from richer countries; the competition from immigrant workers who are less demanding in terms of working conditions. Unions are calling - no doubt rightly - for "equal pay for equal work". But the work of the untrained laborer is not equal to the work of the engineer, and therefore wage inequalities are justified by the egalitarian principle of trade unionism itself. The aptitudes of each individual are, for the most part, the product of natural determinisms - the strongest man can become a stakhanovist while the weakest man will be condemned to do less work in his day - and social or cultural determinisms. Moreover, not everyone can do the most rewarding

____

95. "The killing of work," October 26, 2009.

and best qualified jobs. And, consequently, the division of labor leads to the distribution of individuals in differentiated places according to the various socially necessary jobs at a given moment. New causes of rivalries, jealousies, envy, which aggravate the competition between employees and make them even more dependent.

An incidental remark, but not irrelevant to our overall point. Marx, throughout his life, mocked "egalitarian" claims. Thus:

> "Equal pay itself, as claimed by Proudhon, merely transforms the relation of the actual worker to his work into the relation of all men to work. Society is then conceived as an abstract capitalist[96]."

He also attacks the "crude communism" of those who only envy those who have a better purse. And in the *Critique of the Gotha Program*, he argues that equality of the kind "for equal work and equal pay" remains an equality situated entirely on the terrain of bourgeois law, which is equal right.

Marx believed that, from the conditions of wage labor, a struggle was spontaneously born that began to practically abolish wage labor. By uniting in unions in order to abolish the competition between them to make a general competition to the capital[97], it would be a practical step, a real movement abolishing the existing order, that is to say, the salaried condition. Without doubt, this is a necessary first step to consider the possibility of an alternative to the capitalist mode of production, but in itself this first step remains entirely within the straitjacket imposed by capital. Solidarity within an enterprise in the face of the management representing capital is relatively easy to obtain: the bonds of common work facilitate the properly political bond that is the union organization. But to envisage a community of destiny uniting the workers of a firm with those of another firm is already much more difficult. After all, if the competing company has difficulties, the employees of the healthy

---

96. Marx (K.), *Manuscripts of 1844, op. cit.* p. 121.
97. See Marx (K.), *Misery of Philosophy*, II, § 5: Strikes and Workers' Coalitions, in *Works I*, p. 134.

company will see their position strengthened in the negotiations with their own boss... To consider that on the scale of a nation, there exists a community of interest of the employees, is already to take a considerable political step, which is not done spontaneously if one remains on the ground of the wage relationship, but requires that the interest of the whole nation be considered. *Even more* difficult to grasp is the fact that it is necessary to go beyond the competition between nations. There is undoubtedly, and this is one of the results of several centuries of capitalist globalization, a confused internationalist sentiment that is widely shared. It is combined with a background of Christian universalism (all men are brothers); but this sentimental internationalism clashes with the reality of the global division of labor. Through relocations and imports of low-cost products, workers in poor countries compete directly with the richer ones and gradually break down all the barriers that workers' struggles had managed to put up against the overexploitation of labor. And if, quite naturally, the threatened workers demand a halt to relocations or protectionist measures against the import of goods manufactured under conditions contrary to ILO regulations, to take only the examples of recent social demands, we forget that these relocated industries and *low-cost* production are the main means of survival for tens of millions of workers in the "emerging" countries, who, in essence, are simply following the path that England, France and Germany had followed before them.

Whatever way one poses the problem, within the framework of wage relations, there is no lasting solution. Paradoxically, workers' struggles have contributed to the integration of the working class into the capitalist system and to the idea that there is no alternative to wage labor and that, consequently, the only possible action is to improve the position of wage earners within the capitalist mode of production. Undoubtedly, the cage is a bit bigger, a bit better heated, the food is better than in the 19th century, but it is still a cage and its bars seem stronger than they ever were.

The critique of work

The disappearance of the currents claiming the abolition of wage labor is obvious. Socialists and communists (what is left of them) have long been defenders of wage-labour. They present themselves as the spokespersons of wage earners and propose, at best, only improvements in the wage condition and not its abolition. Even the latest addition to the French left, the "Left Party", only claims an improvement of the "balance of power in favor of the wage-earner" or to give "priority to the poorest", but there is nothing that, in any way, could make one think that this party would have any desire to get out of capitalism (even if it sometimes says that it wants to "go beyond" it). It is exactly the same for its German counterpart, *Die Linke*. The groups that call themselves "revolutionary" don't go any further - they simply overplay their hand in terms of methods of action and refuse any governmental agreement with the "reformists," while they differ little from them in terms of actual programmatic content.

Various currents call themselves "alternative" or "alterglobalists". But in general terms, they are content to colour the good old left-wing Keynesianism in green or to "secede"[98] by taking refuge in the ecological niches that the capitalist mode of production can reserve. The proponents of the dual society, already a few decades ago, had sketched out a few avenues: the increase in labor productivity should be used not to produce even more, but to allow those who have neither the taste nor the skills for work not to work. By ensuring that everyone receives a subsistence income from productivity gains, we would allow them to lead a decent, albeit necessarily frugal, life, while those who are workaholics, or those who cannot be satisfied with a frugal life and want to earn more, could continue to work as they do today.

Indeed, if one can live without working in today's society, it is only by using the very possibilities that the system offers. There is a minority of unemployed professionals who know how to use all the tricks in the book

---

98. This is the position defended by Antonio Negri and Michael Hardt in their bestselling book, *Empire*.

to benefit from unemployment benefits for as long as possible... But this assumes that unemployment insurance still exists and that the vast majority of people are in paid employment and contribute to UNEDIC! The "work refractors" secretly pray that others will not imitate them. They pretend not to see that capitalism is a system, i.e. that all the parts fit together and that those who are not directly involved in capitalist production have their situation only because of the very existence of this mode of production. The "refractory" who films other "refractory" forgets that his camera is the product of a complex production process and that he was only able to obtain it because these expensive machines were mass-produced in factories where productivity is not at all a joke. One has every right to try to break away from society, to find a corner of the countryside and live there directly from one's work, eating the vegetables from one's garden or the eggs from one's chickens. But one does not have the right to claim that this is an emancipatory proposal, and one cannot want to enjoy the advantages of this society that one claims to refuse, unless one sets up cynicism as a rule of life.

The only true critique of work presupposes the ability to break, at least intellectually to begin with, with the prejudice that radically distinguishes work from free activity conceived as leisure. The real difficulty is to know how to avoid falling into utopia. In a note from 1844, Marx gives a very good example of this utopia:

> "Let us suppose that we produce as human beings: each of us would affirm himself doubly in his production, himself and the other. 1° In my production, I would realize my individuality, my particularity; I would experience, while working, the enjoyment of an individual manifestation of my life, and in the contemplation of the object, I would have the individual joy of recognizing my personality as a real power, concretely graspable and escaping all doubt. 2° In your enjoyment or use of my product, I would have the immediate spiritual joy of satisfying by my work a human need, of realizing human nature, and of supplying the need of another with the object of his necessity. 3° I would have the consciousness of mediating

between you and the human race, of being recognized and felt by you as a complement to your own being and as a necessary part of yourself, of being accepted in your spirit as well as in your love. 4° I would have in my individual manifestations the joy of creating the manifestation of your life, i.e., of realizing and affirming in my individual activity my true nature, my human sociability [*Gemeinwesen*].

"Our productions would be as many mirrors where our beings would radiate one towards the other[99]."

Commenting on this text, Maximilien Rubel writes that it is "one of the most beautiful pages of Marxian utopia inherent in *Capital*[100]." It is indeed a very beautiful text, which would appear to the positivists and utilitarians of today as the manifestation of a disheveled idealism. By giving "the vision of a world where man, freed from private property, works according to his vocation[101]", Marx shows what a truly radical critique of work in the capitalist mode of production is. "Let us suppose...": yes, that we produce like men, in a truly human way; this is for the moment only a supposition, because we continue, with all our science and technique, to work like animals.

However Rubel is undoubtedly right to classify Marx's vision among the utopias. The individualism immediately united to the social existence, the affirmation of the I in the recognition of the you, there is there a vision of the communism deeply impregnated with Christianity. Marx never completely discarded this vision. We find it again more than thirty years later in the *Critique of the Gotha Program*:

"In a higher phase of communist society, when the enslaving subordina-tion of individuals to the division of labor, and with it the opposition between intellectual and manual labor, will have disappeared; when labor will not only be a means of living, but will itself become the first vital need; when, with the multiple development of individuals, the

99. MARX (K.), *Parisian Manuscripts*, note 22, in *Works II*, p. 33.
100. M. Rubel, notes to the Pléiade edition, *Œuvres II*, p. 1604.
101. M. Rubel, *ibid*.

productive forces will have increased too, and all the sources of collective wealth will spring up with abundance, only then the limited horizon of bourgeois law will be definitively overcome and society will be able to write on its flags "From each according to his abilities, to each according to his needs"[102]!"

But it is not clear how to completely rid individuals of their subordination to the division of labor. Since Marx considers that the greatest productive force is cooperation, which presupposes the division of labor, it would have to be admitted that it is not a question of doing away with the division of labor, but of giving individuals an education that is sufficiently versatile to enable them to exercise different professions, to engage in a variety of work, and no longer to be stultified by repetitive tasks. Two objections, however, threaten to ruin this fine ideal:

- a certain number of necessary jobs may well never be chosen by our free producers, because they are unrewarding, too tiring, etc. ;
- the complexity of work in contemporary society makes versatility rather illusory. Many jobs can only be done properly if they are done frequently and if the habit is not lost. A surgeon can undoubtedly make an excellent Sunday gardener, but a professional gardener will have difficulty being a Sunday surgeon...

In the Marxian utopia of work, as in the political utopia of the abolition of the state, there enters an unrealistic view of human nature and its inherent limitations. However, the utopia should perhaps not be completely abandoned, since it can set a kind of ideal from which instruction as well as moral education could be conceived. Nevertheless, Marx himself is more cautious in the manuscripts of *Capital*. Instead of the grandiose perspectives of the machine utopia, he substitutes the idea of our irremediable separation between the reign of necessity and that of freedom. In the text that Engels placed at the conclusion of Book III of *Capital*, he writes:

---

102. Marx (K.), "Marginal comments on the program of the German workers' party", *op. cit.*

"In truth, the reign of freedom begins only from the moment when work dictated by necessity and external ends ceases; it is therefore, by its very nature, beyond the sphere of material production proper[103]."

Man can therefore neither liberate himself through work, in general, nor free himself from work, in what it has of necessary and thus of necessarily constraining by certain sides. For work appears as an eternal necessity and constraint.

"Like primitive man, civilized man is forced to compete with nature to satisfy his needs and to preserve and reproduce his life; this constraint exists for man in all forms of society and under all types of production. With his development this empire of the natural necessity widens because the needs multiply; but at the same time the productive process to satisfy them develops[104]."

It is even a constraint that, from a certain angle, can only be expanded. Marx, here, does not seem to be promoting work (work would become a game!) since work remains in the realm of necessity - that is, the opposite of play. On the contrary, he seeks to establish a new scale of values. However, one should not consider work as a curse - it is not a question of returning to the ancient contempt of work just good for slaves. A certain form of freedom can exist within the framework of work itself.

"In this field, freedom can only consist in this: the associated producers - socialized man - rationally regulate their organic exchanges with nature and submit them to their common control instead of being dominated by the blind power of these exchanges; and they accomplish them with the least possible expenditure of energy, under the most dignified conditions, the most in conformity with their human nature. But the empire of necessity remains nonetheless[105]."

---

103. MARX (K.), *Capital*, Book III, Conclusion, *Works II*, pp. 1487-1488.
104. *Ibid.*
105. *Ibid.*

Insofar as work remains necessary, it is a question of thinking freedom on the terrain of necessity. The freedom in question is a limited freedom, it is not the free development of the potentialities that are in man, which can only be accomplished beyond the sphere of material production. It is a freedom that has two aspects:

- an understanding of the necessity to avoid waste, to rationalize the relationship between man and nature, to preserve the two sources of social wealth, which are work and land. Therefore, when traditional Marxism sees communism as the liberation of the productive forces hindered by capitalist property relations, interpreting this as the unrestrained development of production and technology, it is mistaken - once again, one might add. For Marx, capitalism, as a system of production for production (necessary for the continuation of accumulation), is an irrational system and the goal of humanity is not to produce more and more, but, on the contrary, to be thrifty;
- if the necessity of work must be eternally imposed, because man remains a natural being, it remains that man can hope to abolish the domination that his own exchanges exert on him, and thus act as a socialized man. It is therefore not only a question of transforming property relations, but of transforming the relations that individuals have with their own objectified social labor.

It is thus on the side of communication, that is to say of direct relations between men, and not on the side of work, that is to say of the relations of men to things, that human freedom can be inscribed at the very heart of necessity. Man cannot get rid of necessity, he can only organize its forms differently, in conditions conforming to his nature.

> "It is beyond this that the blossoming of human power begins, which is its own end, the true reign of freedom, which however can only flourish on the basis of this reign of necessity. The reduction of the working day is the fundamental condition of this liberation[106]."

---

106. *Ibid.*

A prosaic conclusion that has the merit of taking into account the contradictory reality of work: there is no emancipation without work, that is, without production - since work is both the natural necessity and what forces man to awaken the faculties that lie dormant in him[107] - and at the same time, there is no true emancipation except outside the necessary work time. Hence the importance of the reduction of the working day, a question that is also central to Book I of *Capital*. While this question was at the forefront of social demands in the seventies and eighties, it has now almost completely disappeared. The socialists, who instituted the 35-hour work week, under very questionable conditions, almost regret it and are ready to extend working hours by increasing the length of contributions in order to qualify for retirement. As for the other parties (in France and elsewhere), they make the increase in working hours their hobbyhorse. "Work more" is the watchword. A slogan that seems completely absurd: why should we work more when technical progress, especially automation, but also the development of cooperation through a global division of labor, considerably increases labor productivity? Why do we have to work more, even though we are asked to become thrifty to "save the planet"? Why work more, when unemployment, whether open or hidden, concerns between a quarter and a third of the potential active population, especially in Europe[108]? This manifest absurdity stems from the contradictory logic of the development of the capitalist mode of production.

Thus, discussions about work in general should not make us forget the reality of wage labor in our society, a reality that is certainly multifaceted, but, for the vast majority of workers in the countries where production

---

107. See Marx (K.), *Capital*, book I, section III, chap. VII, *Œuvres I*, Pléiade edition, p. 728.
108. The official statistics in this area are even more "phony" than those of the former Soviet Union. The 10 percent announced in France (but nearly 25 percent in Spain) at the time of writing is the result of tricks that make it possible to take out of the unemployed someone who has worked one day in the last month. We could add the number of women who would like to work or work full time and who give up, the young people who study more or less artificially, the training courses that do not train them, the seniors who are exempt from employment and we would see that we are very far from the official data.

is now concentrated, marked by conditions that are still those described by Marx in *Capital*, and, for workers in the richest countries, subject to stress, to the intensification of production, to the control of minds by the methods of modern management, and to the anxiety of losing one's job. Under these conditions, the tartuffery about "work value" is quite repugnant.

Chapter IV
Alienation and consumer society

According to the thurifers of modernity, the immense accumulation of goods by which wealth is announced in our societies would in itself be the expression of a prodigious progress of freedom. The defenders of globalization have not even hesitated to argue that the possibility of choosing between a dozen brands of cereal for breakfast was in itself an adequate expression of the progress of freedom and democracy[109]. If freedom lies in choice, then hypermarkets are indeed places of freedom as free will. In front of the immense washing powder department, Buridan's donkey would remain silent until the store closes, whereas modern man, a sovereign subject, can freely decide between all these washing powder that wash whiter than white... The multiplication of technical objects offered to our desires is also the promise of an ever greater power of action: telecommunications and modern means of transport free us from our condition of men rooted in the here and now. Metaphor of the omnipotence promised to the technological man: the remote control which opens the doors or zaps the real represented on small screens less and less small. A whole philosophical tradition made of the search for the possession of material goods a tyranny which subjected the individual; the modern consumer

---

109. We owe this essential contribution to the philosophy of freedom to Peter Martin, who was editor of the international edition of the *Financial Times in the* late 1990s. On this point, see our book, *The End of Work and Globalization.*

society answers practically by exhibiting every day the immense freedom which these goods available in profusion get - one remembers the slogan: "Moulinex liberates the woman".

The man rich in needs is the civilized man

Let's start at the beginning: the criticism of the consumer society has bad press. It is said to have been the work of spoiled petty-bourgeois students and not of workers who aspired to enjoy the benefits of consumption. Even today, under the name of "degrowth", do we not find an ideology carried by a middle class satisfied with its lot and which proposes to deliver moral lessons to the whole world? The contempt for the "sordid materialism of the masses" was for a long time the distinctive mark of the most reactionary aristocracy: are we not in danger of seeing a certain radical far-left critic join the discourse of the followers of Charles Maurras? In fact, there is no shortage of reasons to be wary of the contemptuous of consumer society. If we do not want to add a discourse of deploring times and morals to an already long litany, we must try to understand what the thought of modern times has brought as a thought of economic development and of industrial and commercial civilization, and why it has won over minds and hearts.

Modernity, since the Reformation and the 17th century, has brought about a complete reversal of moral values. Poverty is no longer virtuous and wealth is no longer shameful. For Protestantism, the accumulation of material wealth is not to be sought for enjoyment, but bears witness to justly rewarded work. The men of the Enlightenment glorify "good luxury" whose pacifying and civilizing virtues seem obvious. It is undoubtedly Hegel who makes the most subtle theory of this modern world that the "things" (Georges Perec) will invade. In the passage of the *Lineaments of the Philosophy of Right*, Hegel masterfully exposes the dialectic of needs and its civilizing virtues. We will allow ourselves to give a detailed commentary on this text as it captures the very essence of bourgeois society. Far from being the mark of enslavement to material needs, the pursuit of comfort, the birth of a "man rich in needs" (as Marx would say) is the objective expression of a true progress of freedom.

The decisive moment is the analysis of the "system of needs". Because he is talking about modern society, Hegel begins with individuals.

> " § 189. In the first instance, particularity as what is determined in the face of the universality of the will in general is *subjective need*, which achieves its objectivity, i.e. its satisfaction, by means of α) external things that are equally the *property* and product of other needs and wills, and β) through activity and work, as what mediates between the two sides."

Hegel's vocabulary, a little abrupt, allows to understand with precision the most concrete realities. The individual - the particularity - is determined "in front of the universality", that is to say in front of the society which imposes its requirements. The individual is not included in universality, he is not simply a part of a whole, he exists "determined in front of" the society. And how does the individual exist in the face of universality? By manifesting a "subjective need". That the individual thinks he needs something or feels the need for something - for a piece of bread, for a luxurious food, for a computer gadget... - this is the starting point of the system of needs that contains the seeds of the whole "bourgeois civil society".

Let us continue. The subjective need reaches its objective, "that is, its satisfaction". It is clear: objectivity = satisfaction. The ancients distinguished between true and false needs - or rather, to speak like Epicurus, between natural and necessary needs and vain desires - which is what we find in all the contemporary criticisms of consumption or among the advocates of "voluntary frugality". But nothing of the sort in Hegel. The need - any need - begins by being subjective and finds its objectivity in its satisfaction. But the passage from the subjective to the objective does not happen by miracle. It needs a mediation or rather a double mediation. Satisfaction requires external things that may or may not belong to the subject and that are (or may not be) things necessary for the satisfaction of another, and what makes it possible to obtain these external things, what mediates between the two sides, is quite simply work: work that allows the subject to produce what he needs or that will make it possible to obtain from another (through exchange) these "external things" when they are the property of another.

From this, Hegel shows that subjective need is the starting point of the sphere of exchange, "the sphere of finitude", whose rationality is "understanding": it is indeed the capacity that individuals have to calculate where their interest lies, taking into account their subjective needs, and this capacity allows for "reconciliation" within this sphere itself: each one understands that he or she needs the others and each one is thus led to respect the common rules. Even if it is a minimal rational society, we see that need already has civilizing effects.

In an addendum to § 189, Hegel notes the following:

> "There are certain universal needs, such as eating, drinking, clothing, etc., and the way they are satisfied depends entirely on contingent circumstances. The soil is, here or there, more or less fertile, the harvest years follow one another and are not alike. One man is brave, another lazy; but this swarming of arbitrariness generates from itself universal determinations, and this apparent dispersion and absence of a guiding idea is held together by a necessity which intervenes spontaneously. To discover here this necessity is the object of the state economy, a science that honors thought because it finds the laws that account for a mass of contingencies. It is an interesting spectacle to see how all the connections here have a retroactive effect, how the particular spheres group together, have an influence on the others and meet in them something which favors them or is an obstacle to them. This passage from one into the other, in which one does not believe at first because everything seems to be left to the arbitrariness of the singular individual, is especially remarkable and bears a resemblance to the planetary system, which never shows to the eye anything but irregular movements, but whose laws, however, can be known."

A remarkable passage that seems to come straight out of Adam Smith! The satisfaction of needs ("the maximization of utility" as economists would say today) acts in the manner of Newtonian universal gravitation; it is in a way the "Newton's law" of society. It spontaneously orders what seems to belong only to the arbitrary wills of individuals and to the contingency of circumstances. Order arises spontaneously from the freedom of individuals. An idea that Hayek will develop with the notion of *catallexy*. But the difference is that in Hegel, this spontaneity is never really spontaneous. The contingent expresses the necessary, and it is a dialectical movement that must be grasped here: what is narrowly limited must deny itself in order to become universal, and what is imposed (need) must deny itself in order for freedom to become in and for itself.

For the ancient philosophers, mainly the Stoics but not only, man had to free himself from need by learning to limit his desires, by learning to be satisfied with little - bread and fresh water are enough for pleasure, says Epicurus! With Hegel, on the contrary, there is no need to free oneself from needs, but rather to free oneself from need in the abundance of needs that allows man to choose and overcome his animal condition. Thus:

> "§ 190 - The animal has a limited circle of means and ways of satisfying his needs, which are themselves also limited; man, even in this dependence, proves at the same time that he comes out of it and exceeds it, first by the multiplication of needs and means, and then by the decomposition and differentiation of the concrete need into singular parts and sides, which become so many diverse particularized needs, and thereby more abstract."

To be human is therefore not, according to Hegel, to be obliged to limit the sphere of needs - which is the characteristic of the animal - but rather to multiply the needs. Here, Hegel exposes in a very condensed way this process of multiplication of needs, even by starting from the needs closest to the natural needs. Like any animal, man must feed himself - he is from this point of view in the same dependence as the animals. But he overcomes this dependence by the decomposition and differentiation of the concrete need: to feed himself, man needs instruments allowing him to kill the animal, to cut up the flesh; he also learns to prepare his food - by cooking it, a decisive step we now know in the process of hominization that leads to *homo sapiens*. He also learns table manners. The individual does not only need to eat or drink, he needs a chair, a tablecloth, a plate, dishes, forks, etc. The need is also differentiated: need for varied, refined foods, etc. This decomposition and this differentiation make precisely enter the world of the spirit.

> "Addendum to § 190 - [...] The need for shelter and clothing, the necessity of no longer leaving food in its raw state, but of making it adequate for himself and of destroying its natural immediacy, mean that man does not have it so easy as the animal; moreover, as a spirit, he is not permitted to have it so easy. The understanding, which grasps the differences, introduces multiplication into these needs, and, insofar as taste and utility become criteria of appreciation, the needs are also affected. In the end, it is no longer so much the need (real as lack) but the opinion that must be satisfied, and it is precisely culture that has to break down the concrete into its particularities. There is precisely in the multiplication of the needs a blocking of the desire, because, when the men consume much, the force which pushes them towards what would miss them is not very strong; it is a sign that misery is not at all so violent as that."

The need to be satisfied is not so much the "real need" as the "opinion". This is easily seen in fashion, but basically in all the development of consumption in modern societies. The distinction between natural and artificial needs is from this point of view almost empty. We have no real need for fast transportation, nor for telecommunications, nor for all that modern technology has brought: one can perfectly well live without all this technology, as the Amish do, but their sturdy wooden houses and their agriculture are no more natural. One can also live without books, without art, etc. But in the end, such a life would have nothing of a human life. It is thus well in the logic of the development (of the multiplication) of needs that culture is rooted, as Hegel still affirms. And culture in general is inseparable from refinement.

> "In the same way, the *means* corresponding to the particularized needs are *shared* and *multiplied,* as well as the ways of satisfying them, which in

turn become relative ends and abstract needs. This multiplication, which continues ad infinitum, is precisely in this proportion a *differentiation of* these determinations and an *appreciation of the* adequacy of the means to their ends: it is *refinement*."

And it is impossible to put a stop to this development of refinement.

> "Addendum to § 191 - What the English mean by *comfortable* is something absolutely inexhaustible which continues ad infinitum, since every comfort attained ends up proving its discomfort, so that these inventions have no end. This is why a need is produced not so much by those who experience it immediately as by those who seek to make a gain by creating it."

Here again, Hegel shows himself to be a faithful commentator of classical political economy. It is not the need that is primary, but the offer of novelties that create the need. What motivates this offer is the lure of gain, a motive that is in itself disreputable: no morality can be founded on this simple principle of the lure of gain, apart from the morality of the Mandeville of the bee fable. However, by a trick of reason, it is these bad inclinations of men that make them active agents of the process of development of culture, that is to say of the process of civilization.

Hegel, however, is not a blissful apologist for the new political economy. On the contrary, he clearly understands the limits of this logic of the development of needs.

> "§ 195 - This liberation is formal in that the particularity of goals remains the basic content. When the social situation is oriented toward the indeterminate multiplication and specification of needs, means, and enjoyments which, like the difference between natural needs and needs not formed by culture, have no limit, in short in luxury, there is an equally infinite increase of dependence and lack..."

The liberation from need is also an increase in dependence: this can be seen as the multiplication of social bonds and, from this point of view, an increase in freedom, but also as a limitation of this same freedom in the sense that there is also an infinite increase in lack. It is moreover a liberation that remains enclosed in particularity and is therefore only purely formal: the individual who satisfies his most refined needs is free from a certain point of view, but this freedom is not freedom in itself and for itself.

Real needs, false needs?

We dwelt for a moment on Hegel's analysis because it seems to us inescapable and will inspire Marx. Both of them consider that civilized man is the man "rich in needs". The criticism that it seems necessary to us to address to the "consumer society" will not thus relate to the fact that it would develop factitious needs, precisely because it seems impossible to us to separate the necessary from the superfluous or the real need from the artificial need. For the person who does not read, does not like to read, and finds reading a sterile occupation, the need for books is a perfectly superfluous need... The person who eats bread greased with minced meat considers that gastronomy is a luxury for snobs. If one thinks, like Pascal, that all the misfortune of man comes from the fact that he is incapable of resting in his room, the beginning of wisdom will be to renounce all travel - and besides, travel is tiring! If the need is first of all subjective, if it corresponds first of all to what the subject feels, one sees at once that it is impossible to form a common idea of these needs. And it is perfectly legitimate that each one in this field judges according to his own complexion. To want to decide socially which are the real needs and which are the fake needs, it is necessarily to establish a "dictatorship on the needs", formula which characterizes very precisely what was the "real socialism", according to the enlightening analyses of Ferenc Feher and Agnes Heller[110].

In a brief contribution, Agnes Heller makes a mockery of the distinction between "true" and "false" needs, a distinction that she believes is meaningless unless one imagines oneself to be a kind of god, overhanging society and capable of determining externally what the system of needs

---

110. See in particular, "The dictatorship on the needs" by Ferenc FEHER in HELLER (Agnes) and FEHER (Ferenc), *Marxism & democracy, beyond the real socialism*, Maspero, "Small Collection", 1981.

---

corresponding to that society should be. Those who decide which needs are true and which are false are merely reiterating a very classic figure, that of the alienated mass incapable of knowing what is good for it, opposed to a minority which, for mysterious reasons, is "disalienated" and therefore capable of having true knowledge. This distinction has always served as a justification for the churches as bearers of the truth and responsible for enlightening the vulgar. This includes the Leninist "church" which is based on the same kind of prejudice in favor of enlightened minorities.

This temptation to "dictate needs" is very clearly reflected in the policies advocated by environmentalists. Among the most noted is the French green deputy Yves Cochet, who has made various proposals, such as discouraging families from having a third child - an idea he took from the father of French political ecology, René Dumont - or eliminating meat products by proposing a compulsory vegetarian day in the National Assembly restaurant, a symbolic measure refused even by his own friends, no doubt frightened of what it revealed about the contempt for the most elementary individual freedoms. It is true that if one thinks, like Hans Jonas, the philosophical inspirer of the hardest ecology, that men must be treated like children in order to preserve future generations, it is quite coherent to dictate to them what they must or must not eat, whether or not they have the right to have children and so on.

Without going so far as to take the caricatured positions that have sometimes justified the label "green Khmers," even a reasonable attempt to limit consumption, for example on the basis of environmental imperatives, runs up against many difficulties. For a city dweller with a dense public transport network, condemnation of the private car is easy. But by generalizing it, it implies that the city lifestyle becomes the only "politically correct" one, because it is out of the question for obvious economic reasons to have a bus pass every ten minutes or even every hour in the smallest hamlet in the countryside. It is remarkable that environmentalists are often urbanites, supporters of the urban way of life, who only see the countryside as a relaxing place for vacations or as a nature reserve for biodiversity. If we want public transport to triumph over the individual car, we must complete the work of emptying the countryside that has been going on for several centuries. We know that this was one of the great ambitions of Ceausescu's regime... Undoubtedly, the transport crisis is a real crisis that requires radical solutions[111], but we must note the remarkable propensity of "social engineers" of all kinds to militate for solutions that inevitably lead to limiting the elementary freedom to choose one's own way of life.

Some proponents of degrowth, refusing authoritarianism, do not ask that consumption be limited by political intervention. They defend the idea of "voluntary frugality". In a tradition that could go back to Tolstoy, they advocate a call to individual consciousness and to action by example. *A priori*, one cannot object to this approach, except that it is not a policy.

There is a first obvious dimension. That each of us takes it upon ourselves not to waste non-renewable natural resources and, more generally, to take care of the world in which we live, is a step that should be part of the common *ethos*. Basically, it is the same as respecting the rules of politeness, carrying old ladies' bags up the stairs, or helping the blind to cross at the intersection. That we have to run political campaigns to promote these obvious things only illustrates one aspect of the "de-civilization" we mentioned earlier.

The second dimension is clearly more problematic. The notion of frugality is well documented in ancient or Christian ethics because it refers to a doctrine of the good life or of salvation. But disconnected from these contexts, it is difficult to see what it is about. There is no moral value, per se, in not taking a shower every morning, in taking the stairs and not the

---

111. The relocalization of the economy would drastically reduce transportation. If the "zero stock" rule had not become a sacred dogma, stock would not be circulating on trucks. If local commerce had not been deliberately destroyed for the benefit of a few oligopolistic hypermarket firms, people would not be forced to take their cars to go shopping in those hideous commercial zones, all identical, which disfigure the urban landscape. Without the perpetual relocations and a policy of social segregation through housing, workers in large cities would not have to spend several hours a day in transportation: everyone knows that workers and employees who work in Paris cannot find housing in Paris because of the prohibitive rents. These are some of the avenues that would make it possible to take serious action on the transport issue without making motorists feel guilty and without infringing on anyone's freedom - except perhaps the freedom of a few groups to impose their law on the entire population.

elevator, in not eating caviar at every meal, or in refusing to use dishwashers and disposable diapers. If we stick to ecological and not moral reasons, we can have fun pointing out the contradictions and endless discussions to which all this could give rise: the dishwasher is certainly a horrible symbol of the consumer society, but it saves water to a great extent. The real frugal person is not the one who washes the dishes by hand, but the one who does without dishes: we eat with our fingers and only one bowl for the whole family! As for the ecological balance of washing cloth diapers for babies, it would be worthwhile to do it...

No doubt, for reasons related to the capacity to feed 10 billion people before the end of the century, it would be necessary to discourage excess meat consumption and to revalue other modes of consumption. But then, we are no longer appealing to the moral conscience of each individual, but to public action. The State, citizens' groups, farmers' associations, etc., could take charge of such a socio-economic transformation. But then it is no longer a question of frugality and the will has become collective again. We are trying to trap citizens in a trapped debate: on the one hand, the fanatical technophiles think that technology can solve all the problems of humanity - and in particular those of food thanks to GMOs and the progress of chemistry[112] - on the other hand the technophobes who have no other solution to propose than to tighten our belts. More generally, it would seem that we are faced with the following alternative: either we admit that the infinite multiplication of needs is the only way that conforms to human nature and freedom, and we hope that technical and scientific progress will provide a solution to the serious questions raised by the ecological crisis; or we think that we need to organize a drastic self-limitation of humanity's needs and technical development, a kind of *global downsizing*, the consequences of which would undoubtedly be very far from the ideal of conviviality and happy simplicity that the defenders of this position would have us believe. But presented in this way, this debate

---

112. We are working on the artificial culture of muscle tissue which would allow us to eat steak (?) without having to raise cows...

is distorted because it is anhistorical and does not explore the real trends of contemporary society.

In the first place, while admitting that civilized man is man rich in needs, we shall observe that capitalism does not rest on the development of this wealth in needs, but on a kind of gluttony aimed at specific needs that correspond to the fields of accumulation of interesting capital. On this question, we find an interesting development in the *1844 Manuscripts*. Marx first notes that, in the capitalist mode of production, "each one applies himself to arousing in others a new need in order to compel them to a new sacrifice, to place them in a new dependence[113]." The drug market is, from this point of view, paradigmatic. *Dealers* start giving the drug, especially to young people, to create the addiction that will fill their coffers, or rather those of the wholesale supplier. But practically the entire market functions in this way, with advertising playing a fundamental role in its ability to manipulate the imagination and arouse desire. There is something strange about the throngs of "believers" who flock to specialty stores when the latest game console or cell phone that can do everything but sweep the room and toast the bread is announced. The same trance phenomena can be found in large religious events or, in a more secular way, among the groupies of singing stars, but this time it is for one thing. The fetishism of the commodity reaches its full extension here.

The mechanisms of this quasi-religious relationship to goods remain to be fully analyzed.

As we said above, in a society where social cooperation is expressed in the form of market exchange, individuals spontaneously perceive the relationships between themselves, between their concrete, living works, as relationships between the abstract qualities of things that are measured in each other. This general explanation must be refined. Needs are always socially conditioned and this is not peculiar to the capitalist mode of production. But capitalist society is the first in which men seem so radically subjugated to things. The master dominates his slaves in their own right, and the same

---

113. Marx (K.), *Manuscripts of 1844, op. cit.* p. 185.

is true of the relationship between lord and serf. In the capitalist mode of production, the boss is not there as a human individual with special qualities - like the nobles who claimed to be of a special race - but as the possessor of capital and dedicated to its use. If there is a certain kind of equality in the wage relationship (cf. previous chapter), it is only insofar as the owner of capital and the man with the money are equally subject to the need for money.

In the *Phenomenology of Spirit*, Hegel invents this original scene of recognition, which is the conflict between mastery and servitude (*Herrschaft und Knechschaft*), what is known as the dialectic of master and slave. It all begins with the struggle to the death:

> "The individual who has not put his life on the line can certainly be recognized as a *person*; but he has not attained the truth of this recognition, as that of an autonomous self-consciousness[114]."

The submission of the valet to the master is, in the fight, the submission of the one who prefers life. The valet is the incarnation of the non-autonomous consciousness, "the being for another". The desire of the master obtains its enjoyment by the intermediary of the jack. The valet is the intermediary between the master and the thing. Hegel shows the contradictory character and the development of this relation that must be overcome. But what is important to note here is that in the wage relation, there is nothing of the sort. The two contracting parties (who do not fight each other, but agree as free and equal abstract human beings) are equally subject to the need for the general equivalent. The capitalist, on the other hand, appears simply as capital that has come to life, and the worker is not the capitalist's means, but that of capital. This is why we do not find in the modern wage relation the master-worker relations that characterize earlier periods and still very often the old patrimonial and family capitalism. In Hegel's view, the master needs a valet because this valet is also a (non-autonomous) self-awareness. The representative of an investment fund does not need

---

114. HEGEL (GWF), *Phenomenology of Spirit*, IV, translation by J.-P. Lefebvre, Aubier, 1991.

non-autonomous consciousnesses, because he has no relation at all with the workers employed in what is not "his business", but an investment.

The totally abstract and completely dehumanized character of modern capitalism[115] explains this weight that things have taken in the phenomena of identification. Just as the abstract God of the Bible needs various figurations to make him accessible to sensibility, to the affects, so the god Money is too abstract to be the object as such of veneration. In the religious relation to the world of things, instead of money representing all equivalent wealth, that is to say, functioning as a general equivalent, as a representative of value, particular goods become representatives of their representative. From the point of view of political economy, a certain amount of money denominated in dollars is the equivalent of a fashionable electronic gadget. But from the point of view of the religion of our time, the gadget in question is not a commodity, nor even a use value, but the materialization of that dollar amount. The Apple Store is the temple where the theophany of the god Money is celebrated. The fact that we are in a religious world and no longer in the world of the ordinary market economy is proof enough of the fact that the basic rules of utility maximization do not apply. One buys the brand for the brand and not the commodity because it offers the best price-quality ratio. And the more useless the thing is, the more one becomes infatuated with it - the craze for game consoles, after which middle-aged men are now running around, should be enough to disprove the idea that people are rational beings acting by purpose.

Thus "the need for money is the true and only need created by the economy[116]." What capitalism develops, therefore, is not so much wealth in needs as a shortage of money.

> "Quantity is becoming more and more the sole and powerful property of money. Just as it reduces every being to an abstraction, so it reduces itself,

---

115. Long criticized - and rightly so - the old paternalistic capitalism now appears in almost more flattering colors. The boss was a man who met other men and eventually had to face at least their glances in times of conflict. There was still something of a man-to-man relationship, albeit an unequal and often perverse one.
116. MARX (K.), *op. cit.* p. 186.

in its own movement, to a quantitative being. Excess, excess becomes its true measure[117]."

The greed for novelties, the frantic search for things to buy, the piling up of things that are useless and end up in the "fairs of everything" - sacred places where the mysteries of the resurrection of fallen idols are practiced - all this is only the consequence of this submission of men to the social world they have created and reproduce with enthusiasm, the world where value dominates.

> "On the subjective level itself, this manifests itself on the one hand in that the extension of products and needs becomes the inventive and cunning slave of inhuman, unnatural and imaginary appetites[118]."

Here again the inversion of vital teleology is manifested. Products are no longer created to satisfy needs, but to produce imaginary needs, "to excite one's blunt faculties of enjoyment". One could discuss this distinction between imaginary needs and others since need is always subjectively felt as desire and desire is nothing other than the appetite linked to imagination. However, it is indeed the imaginary - the advertising image, for example - that organizes the need. But at the same time, the need is reduced to the need of material things that the capitalist mode of production can produce. The need for beauty cannot be satisfied by industry, which cannot produce masterpieces in series. But industry knows perfectly well how to produce reproductions on scarves, on diaries or key rings, of images of the masterpieces of universal art. Thus we have the invasion of the museums by the merchants of junk which end up submerging the works themselves. Man does not only live on bread, he also lives on ideals: as capitalism cannot produce ideals, it teaches that the only valid ideals are the goods (or services) that can be bought for money. Paradise is sold in travel agencies. Man needs love. Capital offers him mass-produced sex, industrial pornography. He needs community - relationships with others

---

117. *Ibid.*
118. *Ibid.*

are as vital as bread and water. Capital offers him communication tools that serve to talk to himself.

Even if the distinction between "real" and "false" needs is very problematic, it is possible to identify in what way the capitalist mode of production produces its own system of needs and in what way these needs are not needs that man would naturally develop in any type of society, but correspond only to a determined historical phase.

To this first aspect, we can add that capitalism, at the same time that it seems to develop needs in an unlimited way, restricts them on the other. Individuals as consumers must always desire more, but as workers, they must learn to restrain themselves. Marx, undertaking the critique of political economy, remarked:

> "According to his [the economist's] calculations, the most indigent life possible is the universal norm valid for the mass of men; the worker must therefore be a being devoid of sense and need, just as his activity must be purely abstract. The least luxury in the worker seems to him condemnable, and everything that goes beyond the most abstract need - even a passive enjoyment or any manifestation of activity - seems to him a luxury. Political economy, the science of wealth, is therefore, at the same time, the science of renunciation, of privation, of saving [...]. This science of marvelous industry is at the same time the science of asceticism, and its true ideal is the ascetic miser, but usurer, and the ascetic slave, but producer[119]."

To the man who walks through the supermarkets on Sunday, the advertisement says "let yourself be tempted", "give life to your desire", "buy: luxury, there is no such thing". But during the week, the capitalist, the same one who pays for these enticing advertisements, these tempting images, these standardized siren voices, says to his employee: "You are already costing me too much! Your salary is an unbearable burden for the company! Just live cheaply." The same government, at the same time,

---

119. Marx (K.), *Manuscripts of 1844, op. cit.* p. 188.

campaigns to encourage people to consume in order to boost the economy and to save for their retirement. Psychologists call this contradictory double *bind*, "double bond" or "double constraint", a situation that is frighteningly pathogenic. When children are educated under this double bind, they often become very aggressive and violent. This violation of the principle of identity drives them mad.

Finally, new needs are constantly appearing which are simply the needs to repair the damage caused by the satisfaction of other needs or by the modes of satisfaction of these needs. Certainly, distinctions must be made: the increase in the average life span - which simply corresponds to the effort of each being to persevere in his being - implies an increase in the need for care for the elderly. But since no one could reasonably want to make the choice to shorten life and renounce the efforts of medicine, we must accept this multiplication of needs which is part of the very process of civilization. On the other hand, the development of mass consumption within the capitalist framework does not aim at developing satisfaction, but rather habituation and addiction. These in turn give rise to new needs - the food industry develops, maintains and encourages obesity and in turn produces an anti-obesity industry and services. The overall behavior of wealthy societies resembles that of those drunks who make themselves vomit in order to continue ingesting their favorite alcohol. The logic of need that Hegel paints rather positively is here totally reversed. Things are not produced to satisfy human needs; on the contrary, human needs are conditioned and shaped to allow consumption and thus continuous production.

To try to understand the system without questioning the system of needs is to condemn oneself to understanding nothing. Needs are inserted in a system of which they form subsystems. To Henri Lefebvre, we owe some of the most relevant analyses of the way in which these subsystems program the daily behavior of individuals in the consumer society. Lefebvre defines a subsystem as a specialized social activity with objects and actors, organizations and institutions and texts. According to this definition, fashion forms a subsystem, but "from the perspective of programmed everydayness," it is, according to Lefebvre, the automobile that forms the best example of a subsystem. The Auto (the capitalization is necessary!) is indeed the king-object - this is perhaps a little less true today than when Lefebvre was writing, but it remains largely so. The car governs behavior, imposes its law on the city ("the city defends itself poorly" in the face of the "system," writes Lefebvre[120]). By imagining the constraints of the traffic carried to the absolute, he continues:

> "Space is conceived according to the constraints of the automobile. The Circulation replaces the Dwelling and this in the alleged technical rationality. It is true that for many people, their car is a piece of their "habitat", even the essential fragment. Perhaps it would be appropriate to insist on some curious facts. In car traffic, people and things accumulate, mingle without meeting. It is a surprising case of simultaneity without exchange, each element remaining in its box, well closed in its carapace. This also contributes to the degradation of urban life and to the creation of the psychology or rather the psychosis of the driver[121]."

The "Auto" object can be considered as a simple means for the satisfaction of a need (whether it is the need to move around, to impress girls or to show one's social success). In this sense, it could be considered as a tool for a greater freedom (without quibbling any more about the idea of freedom). Lefebvre's analysis shows us that this would be to blind ourselves. If the Auto is indeed a sub-system, this sub-system is part of the means by which individuals are disciplined to act in accordance with the needs of the system itself. Of course, the system and its subsystems are products of human activity. But we only find there, from another perspective, the classical problem of alienation.

What Lefebvre says about the Auto could without too much difficulty be extended to the subsystems that have developed since the 1960s. Much has been written about the object "cell phone" and its meanings. There is even

---

120. LEFEBVRE (H.), *Daily Life in the Modern World*, p. 191.
121. *Op. cit.* p. 192.

an "ontology of the cell phone[122]". The cell phone structures the mobile man. It is what makes universal mobility possible and what prescribes it. It gives the illusion of freedom - I am no longer stuck at home or in the office waiting for the phone to ring - but at the same time, it is the most radical form of enslavement of individuals that contemporary society has ever invented. I am always reachable! The cordless phone is a big drag.

We can extend this kind of analysis to all communication techniques based on the digital revolution. Perhaps it is really necessary to pay of a new servitude the advantages (real!) that these techniques bring us. Maybe we have to admit that there is no progress without loss. But it is better to know it: to know which chains we wear instead of taking these chains for the flowers of freedom, it is already to begin to free ourselves from them.

"Free time" or the ultimate alienation

Traditional societies justified the exploitation of the labor of slaves or peasants by the leisure that this exploitation offered to the upper classes, who, freed from the preoccupation with the needs of ordinary life, could devote themselves to the highest activities, those that require virtues that can only exist if they have been carefully cultivated. War does not only have the utilitarian function of protecting a territory or conquering others: it is the occasion for the nobles to show their value, their courage and their skill in the arts of combat. But leisure must also be devoted to the arts and to thought. Even political leaders who consider politics as a profession are careful not to spend all their time on it. For example, Louis XIV, penetrated by the burdens of his profession, never fails to reserve for himself large blocks of time devoted to leisure and to the protection of the arts and letters.

In the 15th century, the introduction of firearms made chivalric warfare obsolete. The bravery and individual qualities of heroes had to give way to the omnipotence of technology. Fighting was no longer a leisure activity,

---

122. FERRARIS (M.), *T'es où ? Ontologie du téléphone mobile*, Albin Michel, 2006, "Bibliothèque des idées", with an introduction by Umberto Eco.

worthy of the best men (the aristocrats), but a job like any other, usually a dirty job. What remained was culture, the prerogative of the clerics, which was soon to become the specialty of philosophers, literati, of this whole class of "intellectuals" before the letter. Protestantism theorized the changing world by devaluing leisure and valuing work[123]. In this respect, capitalism is egalitarian: no one is exempt from working, the capitalist as well as the worker must dedicate themselves to their trade.

Capitalism takes as its mission to put humanity to work, to controlled, rationalized, measured work. Peasants driven off their land often prefer to become beggars or bandits rather than wage earners. Never mind: we will make laws against beggars, we will arrest them and we will force them to work (cf. *above*). Capitalism hunts down leisure, as time wasted for production. Much has been written about the obsession of 18th and 19th century doctors and pedagogues with the question of masturbation in children and adolescents. The manuals of the famous Tissot have been extensively commented on - Tissot who had been influenced on this subject by Rousseau. However, it is impossible to avoid drawing a parallel between the transformation of masturbation into a central problem and the fight against laziness. Masturbation is an expenditure of time and energy which would be thus withdrawn from the requirement of work.

At the same time, the very dynamics of the capitalist mode of production implies the continuous growth of labor productivity, both through the division of labor, the rationalization of all labor activity - with what will become the OST (Scientific Organization of Labor) and Taylorism - and through mechanization and automation. The effect of this process is, from the point of view of capital, extremely paradoxical. In an oft-commented

---

123. In Protestant ethics, especially Calvinist ethics, which considers man from a radically pessimistic angle, work remains the only activity that can occupy man in the least bad way possible. See also WEBER (M.), *L'Éthique protestante...* Henri Lefebvre wrote: "The model of the over-repressive society is that which had *Protestantism* as its dominant ideology. Much finer and more rational than Catholicism as a theology and philosophy, much less repressive by the apparatus, the dogmas and the rites, the Protestant religion accomplishes more subtly the repressive functions of the religion. Each one carries within himself his God and his reason. Each one becomes his own priest. Each one is in charge of repressing desires, of containing needs. This gives an asceticism without ascetic dogma, without an authority that orders asceticism." (*Everyday Life in the Modern World*, p. 272).

passage from the 1857-1858 draft of *Capital*, Marx exposes the problem in all its acuteness:

> "Capital is a contradiction in act: it tends to reduce labor time to a minimum, while making it the sole source and measure of wealth. It also diminishes it in its necessary form in order to increase it in its useless form, making superfluous labor time the condition - a *matter of life and death* - of necessary labor time[124]."

But what is contained in this contradiction is that capital, in its own process, tends to abolish labor:

> "The *creation*, outside of the necessary working time, of *numerous leisure activities* for the benefit of society in general and of each individual in particular for the full development of his creative faculties, appears in the capitalist and pre-capitalist system as non-working time, as leisure for a few. What is new in capital is that it increases the time of surplus labor of the masses by all the means of art and science, since its *immediate goal is* not use value, but *value in itself*, which it cannot realize without the direct appropriation of surplus labor, which constitutes its wealth. Thus, reducing to its minimum the time of work, capital contributes in spite of itself to create social time available to the service of all for the fulfillment of each one[125]."

It is thus the contradiction that lies at the heart of the process of value formation ("value in itself"), as opposed to use value, that produces its own overcoming, and this overcoming is not the "liberation of labor", but its abolition or, at least, its reduction to the strict minimum. What capital makes possible is not leisure for the few, as in ancient or feudal societies, but leisure for all and the free creativity of each. That this society of leisure for all and free creativity for everyone is not realized is one thing: in the so-called socialist countries, on the contrary, it is work that is valued.

---

124. Marx (K.), *Draft of a Critique of Political Economy*, manuscripts of 1857-1858, in *Works II*, p. 306.
125. Marx (K.), *op. cit.* p. 307.

But the tendency analyzed by Marx is nevertheless manifested within the capitalist mode of production, and often in a contradictory way. Under the pressure of social conflicts, it has had to concede substantial reductions in working hours, paid vacations, the right to retirement, concessions most often made out of fear of losing everything, concessions often called into question (as in the period that began in the 1980s and continues today), but serious and real concessions all the same. For all that, this conceded leisure time is not strictly speaking free time. It is time that is also subject to the logic of the capitalist mode of production.

This submission takes place on different levels. The first, so important that it is too often forgotten, is that modern man almost never decides what will be his free time. He has to plan his work, his appointments; he is subject to the decisions and demands of the individuals with whom he has a professional relationship. If he is employed, he has to negotiate his hours, his vacations, etc. Even when schedules are flexible, there is a time clock to remind us that free time is only a complement to working time and that the latter has the last word. Again, we are so used to this that we don't pay attention. It is normal to ask your boss to leave an hour earlier to go to a doctor's appointment. Hardly anyone feels anymore how much this means that we have lost all sense of freedom. The farmer at the end of his field can stop whenever he likes to talk to a passer-by, to a neighbor; he can even, if he likes, go home and put off until tomorrow what he no longer has the courage to do that day. He doesn't owe anyone anything. The hairdresser, installed on the village square, still in the sixties, used to go out for a drink at the bistro with each new customer, leaving the customer he had started to shear... at the end of the day, the haircut was not always very straight, the customer could count on spending his morning at the hairdresser's, and the hairdresser did not die very old, but nobody counted his time, each one of them seemed to dispose of it according to his whim All this has become almost impossible. The principle of profitability has now established its tyranny even in this barber shop. If you want to have a drink with a friend, you have to check the diary, realize that you are *overbooked* and find, by chance, a small time slot that is not yet planned, scheduled and

176

definitely occupied. And, as we all know, under the Occupation regime, one is not free and the only freedom is to resist.

The programming of free time, that is, its transformation into occupation, begins in childhood. The educational model of the upper classes has spread to the middle classes and partly to the working classes: the child's time outside school must be occupied. One must attend the conservatory to try to play an instrument, play sports, go to dance classes, etc. The control of children's activities has probably never been so prevalent. Vacations are also highly programmed. The vacation club (paradigmatic example, the Club Med) is a vacation without a holiday, a turnkey vacation with no unexpected events - except, possibly, the weather.

Jean Chesneaux spoke of the "despotism of time" as one of the essential characteristics of modernity.

> "To program time is to posit that neither the productive order nor the social order can evolve other than along a univocal temporal axis. This unilinear vision of progress proceeds from a philosophy of the inescapable and the irreversible to which the partisans of the computer and the nuclear power constantly refer: "One does not stop the progress..." A discourse which, however, amounts to a docile submission to the fait accompli[126]."

This despotism of time invades all the space of the personal life until it closes it completely.

> "The traditional function of technical progress was to "save time": thus the washing machine. Today this progress multiplies the constraints of time and encumbers it to the point of congestion: thus the video recorder[127]."

Devices are sold to record programs and movies from the dozens of television channels that anyone can access. On computer hard drives, it's less cumbersome than the video tapes that used to pile up on the shelves and that we never had time to watch... until we realized that the VCR was an obsolete piece of equipment that we just had to throw those precious

---

126. CHESNEAUX (J.), *De la modernité*, p. 36.
127. CHESNEAUX (J.), *op. cit.* p. 40.

recordings in the trash. But the bottom line is the same: in order to make the purchase of all this electronic junk "profitable", we would have to have a machine to watch television in our place...

So-called free time is still subject to the principle of profitability and to the logic of the capitalist mode of production from another angle: leisure, which has given way to recreation, is in fact only a social organization of consumption necessary to keep the production machine running. Leisure is an integral part of the world of the commodity. Tourism is not about travelling, it is about moving around using transport that has to be booked in advance (plane, train) and using all sorts of service companies specialized in tourism. If advertising is the "language of merchandise", as Henri Lefebvre states[128], we must draw some conclusions:

> "In the second half of the 20th century, in Europe, in France, *nothing* (an object, an individual, a social group) *is worth anything* except its double, its publicity image that haloed it. This image *doubles* not only the sensible materiality of the object, but also the desire, the pleasure. At the same time, it makes the desire and the pleasure fictitious. It locates them in the imaginary. It is it which brings the "happiness", i.e. the satisfaction in the state of consumer[129]."

This is why "advertising acts as an ideology". It defines a normal happiness, the happiness consisting in consumption, the happiness identified with saturation. Excerpt from a conversation with a young girl: "You are going to Paris tomorrow, but it's Sunday, the stores are closed!" This is the cry of the heart: what could one do in Paris if the stores are closed? What can you do anywhere if the stores are closed? This is why it is necessary to open the stores on Sundays at all costs, in order to allow all the individuals reduced to the rank of anonymous consumers to commune in the aisles of hyper-markets and other shopping centers. But it is important to understand that advertising does not simply indicate goods offered for the enjoyment

---

128. LEFEBVRE (H.), *op. cit.* p. 198.
129. LEFEBVRE (H.), *op. cit.* p. 200.

of all. It is prescriptive. Just as religion promises eternal happiness only as a reward for observing its commandments and rituals, advertising orders the actions to be performed to reach the consumer's paradise. The imperative is its preferred mode (Buy! Sign up! Stay connected! Let your desires speak! etc.). It also provides models, ideals. Enough has been said about the image of women conveyed by advertising.

Finally, free time does not escape the extension of the process of technical rationalization and bureaucratization of society (to follow here again the analyses of Max Weber). The creation in 1981 of a "ministry of free time" was an unknowing reiteration of the *Opera Nazionale Dopolavoro* (OND) of fascist Italy... Free time is a serious matter! Created on May 1st, 1925 - precisely on the day of the workers' struggle decided by the International - the OND was part of the Mussolini policy aiming at forging a "new man". Article 1 of its statutes stated: "the aim of the after-work organization is to promote a healthy and profitable use of the workers' free time with institutions and initiatives directed towards the development of moral, intellectual and physical abilities in the spiritual climate of the Fascist Revolution." It was a matter of organizing all kinds of sports, cultural and artistic initiatives to supplant the spontaneous popular forms of celebration. In 1935, the regime instituted Fascist Saturdays: work was to stop at 3 p.m. to make room for sports activities oriented towards military training. The short-lived ministry of Michel Henry in 1981 had no similar ambitions; its essential function was to give a rattle to a trade union "bonze" of the PS that had just come to power. His initiatives in the field of leisure supervision remained very limited. But the idea that the festival should be linked to the state organization became well established. The Fête de la musique, the Nuit des musées, and others clearly express this state organization of free time. The popular balls have given way to gigantic commercial festive operations that mobilize large police forces, a bureaucratic organization and impressive sanitary devices: *gay pride, techno-parade, love-parade*, we are here in a domain co-managed by the State and private entrepreneurs in order to organize the leisure of the masses. Competitive sport is also clearly a kind of "state ideological apparatus", to use the language of the Althusserians. For all states, competitive sport is a considerable political and ideological stake. Taking up an old recipe that dates back to the Roman Empire (*panem et circenses*, "bread and circus games"), modern states have perfected and developed it with the means of the most sophisticated technology. On this point, we refer to the work of Jean-Marie Brohm. In 1968, with the number 43 of the review *Partisan* entitled "Sport, culture and repression", a radical criticism of the sport as a capitalist state system of embrigadement is engaged. Brohm affirms that "the political power leans everywhere on the *sports mobilization of mass*":

> "This sports mobilization - state sport, professional sport, amateur sport, mass sport, sport for all, school sport, working-class sport - is in turn based on a global policy of control and subjugation of bodies (incorporation of dominant habitus, regulation of drives and emotions, sexual repression, normalization of bodily techniques, imposition of a bodily order)[130]."

The opposition between submissive labor and free time is very confusing. In the *1844 Manuscripts*, Marx refuted this opposition by arguing that the worker cannot be free during non-working time since this time is devoted to "animal" activities, eating, sleeping, procreating, and that conversely, if during working time he devotes himself to human activities (producing), it is in an inhuman way. What we emphasize here is something else. We must admit that capitalism has created the conditions for the generalization of leisure and that it has allowed it in part, but under conditions and in forms that make it a time in which the control, the surveillance and the conformation of individuals to the needs of capital are extended. It is not a question of being the contemptuous of the greed of the masses, but rather of understanding the mechanisms of a domination that is not only violent coercion, but the fabrication of habits of consent to the capitalist order.

---

130. BROHM (J.-M.), "Corps et pouvoir : à propos du fascisme ordinaire" in revue *Mortibus*, 6/7, spring 2008. The quotation is taken from the author's introduction to a reprint of a 1976 text, published at the time by the journal *Quel corps?*

Repressive desublimation

In a famous work of his time, *The One-Dimensional Man*, Marcuse develops the concept of "repressive desublimation". The concept of sublimation is borrowed from Freud who designates by this term the process of "desexualization" of the sexual energy which then sets itself ideal goals. This process would allow, according to Freud, to account for human activities apparently unrelated to sexuality, but which would find their spring in the strength of the sexual drive, mainly artistic activity and intellectual investigation. "The drive is said to be sublimated insofar as it is diverted towards a new non-sexual goal and insofar as it aims at socially valued objects", say Laplanche and Pontalis[131]. More generally, according to the analytical theory, no civilization and, to say the least, no human society is possible without the repression/canalization of the sexual drive[132]. It could thus seem that the decrease of sexual repression and desublimation are two correlated processes. In the end, we would not have much choice: to renounce repression would be to renounce culture in its highest manifestations. Marcuse shows that the advanced society, that is to say ours, modifies considerably the data of the problem. After having shown that the increasing technological productivity and the conquest of man and nature have produced a political integration in the advanced society, he shows that there is an analogous phenomenon in the field of culture. There is a process of de-sublimation that prevails in certain sectors of society and that leads to the liquidation of many elements of the "great culture" or of what Marcuse calls "superior culture", not because the "great culture" would become vulgarized and degenerate, but simply because there is no longer a place for it in the advanced society.

---

131. Laplanche (J.) and Pontalis (J.-B.), *Vocabulaire de la psychanalyse*, PUF, coll. "Quadrige". The concept, however, predates Freud by a long way. The first sketches of it can be found in Plato (in *The Banquet*) and in Aristotle in his theory of genius.
132. This theme is extensively developed in two important essays by Freud, *The Future of an Illusion* and *Discontent in Civilization*.

> "The cult of personality, of autonomy, of humanism, of tragic and romantic love, is the ideal of a bygone era. [Today, man can do more than the heroes or demigods that his culture has honored; he has solved many problems that seemed insoluble. But he has also betrayed the hope and destroyed the truth that the sublimations of the superior culture protected[133]."

This does not mean that there is no more culture: books are being produced in unprecedented quantities, there are universities, there are students - and there are more of them than there ever were. But what Marcuse says is a little different: he argues that the culture that remains and thrives is *one-dimensional.* The "great culture", based on sublimation, supposes a distancing from daily interests, from immediate material realities. It thus constitutes another dimension of reality. The modern society brings down this second dimension on the first one. It does not destroy this second dimension of which it can make use in case of need - for example, during the cold war. It only takes away everything that manifests the process of sublimation, and this is one of the direct consequences of the extension of the domination of the commodity:

> "While mass communications seamlessly, and often surreptitiously, conflate art, politics, religion, philosophy, and commerce, they nonetheless reduce these cultural domains to a common denominator: the market form[134]."

Here, the content of works of art, the meaning of philosophical thought, is of little importance as long as they are reduced to commodities, marketable and all commensurable objects. The diagnosis that Marcuse made at the beginning of the sixties - his book was published in 1964 in the United States - has proved to be perfectly accurate and confirmed by the new developments that have taken place over the last half-century. Advertising films are considered equal to works of art and works of art themselves become advertising objects.

---

133. MARCUSE (H.), *The One-Dimensional Man,* p. 89.
134. MARCUSE (H.), *op. cit.* p. 90.

"Artistic distancing is sublimation. It creates images of situations that are irreconcilable with the established principle of reality; but as cultural images, they become tolerable, instructive even, and useful. This imagery has lost its effectiveness. The fact that it takes place in the kitchen, the office, the store, that it is put into circulation for commercial purposes, for leisure, is in a sense a desublimation - it replaces a mediated satisfaction with an immediate satisfaction. But this desublimation is done from a "position of strength" of the society that can afford to give more than before because its interests have been taken over by its citizens in the depths of their being and because the satisfactions it provides are elements of social cohesion and contentment[135]."

The "great culture" could not exist and did not exist except as a critique of the reign of the bourgeoisie. It was, of course, carried by the bourgeoisie, which made it its soul supplement and a factor of cohesion (respect for the masters, respect for knowledge, respect for that which goes beyond the ordinary man). But at the same time, it valued disinterestedness, criticized venality, exalted the highest values, it was spiritualist in essence - even if it recited Lucretius or the great materialist philosophers. The culture of the "advanced society" is no longer critical: it is inserted into the cultural industries and produces according to the norms of the industry. Where the "great culture" strove to institute hierarchies, the "desublimated" culture scorns these hierarchies. It is radically democratic. All is worth. Everyone has the right to be an artist and, to say it all, everyone is an artist and everything is art. With the desublimation, there is no more place for the sublime nor for the tragic. Make way for the party! Place to the fair! The "great culture" was the bad conscience of the bourgeoisie: from Balzac to Thomas Mann. Under the reign of desublimation, there is no more room for a bad conscience. Literature is normalized - the United States, always ahead of the game, leads the way with writing schools: one can become a good novelist as one became a good lathe operator. This desacralization of culture, this loss of the aura of the work of art of which Walter Benjamin

---

135. Marcuse (H.), *op. cit.* p. 105.

spoke, could be experienced as a liberation from the old disciplines - the entire modern art movement is presented as an effort to emancipate oneself from the tyranny of the rules of art. But it is also a consequence of the increasing weight of the techno-science in the everyday life, which participates of the "disenchantment of the world" and of the deepest tendencies of the "spirit of the capitalism", its equalizing tendencies as soon as the unique measure becomes the general equivalent, the money. But, at the same time, this equalizing tendency produces, as Tocqueville had already argued, a stifling conformism. Ironically and out of touch with his time, Régis Debray writes:

> "Today, the truth of personal feelings prevails over status and convenience, authenticity has pushed back pretense. So much the better. But one cannot be a non-conformist in everything; each era does its share of the fire. In the new era, originality of morals is recommended, originality of thoughts, artistic tastes and political choices is not recommended. The starch no longer encroaches on private life, it discolors the public space. It will take the form of a good Americanism, tempered by humanitarianism and diplomatically docile[136]."

Debray goes too quickly, however, about the originality of morals. At the heart of this process, we find the radical disruption of the relationship of the dominant social instances with sexuality. If "the principle of pleasure absorbs the principle of reality", it is possible not to liberate, but to liberalize sexuality under forms directly usable by the authorities in charge of producing consensus and submission to the domination. Fine analyst of this "sexual liberation" announced in the Sixties and which will explode after 1968, Marcuse sees there a "very effective desublimation", made possible by the development of the social controls of the technology which "generalize the freedom while intensifying the repression[137]". The liberation of sexual energy goes hand in hand with a de-eroticization of the

---

136. Debray (R.), *Dégagements*, Gallimard, NRF, 2010, p. 19.
137. Marcuse (H.), *op. cit.* p. 106.

world - for example of nature - and an increasing subjugation of sexuality to standardized technical devices. The pornographic industry, widely democratized by Internet, gives a first example. But, while we make a lot of noise around this phenomenon, we forget that the essential is played elsewhere. When "blossoming" sexuality appears in magazines between recipes of dietetic cooking and the apology of sports activity, it is well that sex has nothing to do with eroticism, but becomes one of the sub-disciplines of gymnastics. "Victorian" education repressed the manifestations of juvenile sexuality and confined the extras of fantasy to brothels. But it could well be that liberal education, which initiates young people to sexual affairs at an early age, by giving them advice on hygiene and prudence, finally has repressive effects that are just as devastating. The enjoyment transformed into an obligation to enjoy, into an orgastic imperative, creates new frustrations. We have pushed back the barriers of transgression much further than they have ever been, at least on a mass scale, and at the same time we make it more violent, more dangerous. The frontier between the fantasy (or its representation) and the real often becomes very thin. All the "psychologists" agree on this point: the difficulty of living of many young people (and in particular of the young boys) is largely related to the massive consumption of pornographic images which become the standard to affirm oneself as a "man", a "real".

Mass consumption is not content with ordinary consumer goods and usage: food, clothing, household appliances. It tends to invade all the fields of the life and singularly those which, formerly, were reserved for the intimacy. It is not only the media's treatment of sexuality or the sexuality of young people. In a very emblematic way, the "reality show", so named because it is the empire of the false, puts in scene the intimacy under the eye of the voyeur. The multiple "psych shows" invite stars and people to come and talk about what we were not talking about. One can ask a former minister what he thinks about fellatio. The overabundance of sexual discourse in the public space aims to regulate the intimate space, to submit it to the disciplines of the body required by the "advanced society". Up to the point where one asks for a state and legal sanction (or rather a sanctification) of the various sexual practices and orientations (cf. *above*).

Finally, while Hegel makes the dialectic of needs the principle of civilization through refinement, desublimation in the "consumer society" standardizes tastes and promotes coarseness as one of its important values. Is it necessary to give proof of this? Here again, we can see, and we must see, the collapse of social distinctions and the leveling effects of capitalism. A president in shorts, jogging in the streets of New York "like everybody else," is necessarily a democratic president. The abandonment, in the process of being generalized, of the wearing of a tie abolishes the social distances between executives, professionals and workers. The generalization of the use of the familiar, the standardization of language registers, the trivialization of "swear words" and vulgar expressions in public discourse, and the violation of syntax by the most senior members of the State are all part of this erasure of the marks of distinction that characterized the society of yesterday. We used to say: "He talks like a cartoonist"! But today's president speaks like yesterday's cart driver.

The marks of distinction are found elsewhere: in what the distinguished man can buy. You don't have to be a millionaire to use the imperfect subjunctive correctly or to construct negative sentences correctly... Correctness and civility, and even the wearing of a tie on Sundays or in gatherings and demonstrations[138] are within everyone's reach. On the other hand, big sedans and luxury watches are visible and directly measurable signs that social divisions remain. But they are expressed in ways that earlier generations would have found most vulgar.

There is no question of harboring regrets about the "good old days". The discipline by which the beauties of the "great culture" were inculcated in a few privileged people was appalling: refinement did not go without the

---

138. The workers' movement at its origins often tried to present itself as being as respectable as the bourgeois classes. In the workers' congresses, one put on one's "Sunday clothes" and the photos of the demonstrations never show us disheveled crowds. If the "you" of the comrades was imposed, the Bolsheviks insisted on the "vous", the "tutoiement" being considered as the mark of the brutality of the dominant classes towards the dominated.

worst forms of cruelty and barbarity and the great British schools with the practice of whipping and a total contempt for the suffering of the young people remained archetypes of what led to the revolt of the young generations against the old-fashioned education. It is not a question either of making the apology of the sexual repression on the Victorian model of which Freud showed sufficiently the pathogenic effects. It is only a question of lifting the veil on the alleged liberations of our time in order to wonder if, to the repressive desublimation, it would not be possible to oppose a non repressive sublimation.

More generally, contemporary society is not "post-capitalist". On the contrary, it deploys all that capitalism contains as potentialities. If the term "consumer society" is open to criticism, because consumer society is far from being so for everyone, the way in which capitalism extends its control in everyday life and through the elements of comfort it offers deserves to be analyzed. The works of a Marcuse or a Lefebvre contain a potential intelligibility of our present that deserves to be cultivated before falling into the dubious debate opposing the proponents of frugality to the apologists of consumption.

Chapter V
The factory of the post-human
or the end of a cumbersome freedom

This penultimate chapter brings us to questions that are both more distressing - because some of the great terrors of our time, born of human technological power, are concentrated there, with the procession of myths that are attached to them - and the most difficult to resolve because we are immediately drawn into metaphysics and we run the risk of sinking into rather abstruse developments. It will be a question of knowing if the technical progress and the evolution of societies at the beginning of the Third millennium do not lead to a radical questioning of the idea that we have of man and of human freedom.

Position of the question

Behind all the claims about freedom (political freedom, personal freedom, freedom to choose one's life, etc.), must we assume a metaphysical freedom? The question is one of those labyrinths of philosophy, in which reason regularly finds itself in contradiction with itself. The dilemma is quite simple: either man is free and then he escapes - at least partially - from the order of nature, or he is a natural being, a part of nature whose course he follows, and he is not free. But if man escapes from the natural order, then it is necessary to suppose a creator God transcending the natural order, which poses again, in another form, the question of freedom - a part of the theological quarrels concerns this. Without entering into this knot of difficulties, it is nevertheless possible to give a few minimal meanings of freedom:

- Man is free in the sense that his destiny is not written in advance, but depends to a greater or lesser extent on his own activity;
- Man is free because he is not the result of the project of another man or of a being, whoever he is, capable of making projects.

The first definition makes it possible to understand that one can both maintain that man is simply a natural being and that he is free. Thus, Spinoza denies human freedom in the sense of free will, but conceives of freedom as the unfolding of the human power to act, that is, to be the adequate cause of one's own actions. Spinoza's determinism is therefore not a fatalism, because it leaves the future open - nothing to do with the Augustinian and Protestant doctrine of predestination which makes man free while affirming that the damned are free from all eternity. But the Spinozist conception is also opposed to the scientist conceptions which make the individual a simple assembly of parts entirely subject to external laws: the Spinozist man is not a machine man.

The second definition apparently explains freedom by the contingency of human existence. It is compatible with existentialist conceptions, for example, but not only. In itself, the existence of a human individual is the result of several causal series. The parents are the cause of the children, since it was necessary for the parents to decide to sleep together and for this to happen on the right day, for the male gametes to seek out the female gamete, for the egg not to be rejected spontaneously, etc. We can assume a determinism in all this, and even we must assume it when we want to understand scientifically the mechanisms of procreation, but the child, in its essential characteristics, is not the result of a "parental project", that strange expression which makes the managerial vocabulary penetrate the meanders of human love. Parents may want to have a child, but the child is always beyond their control. "Making a child" has nothing to do with "making a chocolate cake", nor even with "growing radishes" and even less with "building a house". We will therefore define freedom negatively as the fact of not being essentially for another. Man is in himself like the things of nature, says Hegel, but he is also "for himself" and thus essentially free.

These two definitions of freedom are not contradictory to each other and are compatible with a large number of philosophical doctrines. They are, in any case, assumed at least in the other concepts of freedom whose fate in our time we have examined in the preceding chapters. Conversely, it is quite obvious that if neither of them is admitted, then the idea of human freedom simply does not exist anymore.

Real threats or irrational fears

Peter Sloterdijk caused a scandal a few years ago with a lecture that became a small book, *Rules for the Human Park*. He spoke - although this was not the focus of his talk - about biotechnology and tried to explore some of the anxious questions that arise for us from the new possibilities.

> "One of the characteristic features of the human condition," says Sloterdijk, "is that it places men in front of problems that are too heavy for them, without them being able to decide not to touch them because of their weight."

Sloterdijk evoked "a process of civilization in which a wave of unprecedented disinhibition is breaking, in a seemingly irreversible way". He added a question that is too poorly understood:

> "But will long-term evolution lead to a genetic reformation of species properties - will a future anthropo-technology reach the stage of explicit trait planning? Will humanity be able to accomplish, across its species, a shift from birth fatalism to optional birth and prenatal selection?"

There is something paradoxical about Sloterdijk's (and many other philosophers' and moralists') questions. Technical progress not only increases our control over nature, but even promises to leave the generation of humans no longer to the chance of encounters and the lottery of meiosis. It thus appears to be a progress of freedom, if freedom is the possibility of controlling one's own destiny, of being less subject to causes that do not depend on us. However, the biological mastery of the human being could soon appear as the prelude to a radical transformation of the human condition, in which the idea of freedom will no longer make sense.

Because, of course, environmental issues (greenhouse effect, preservation of biodiversity, GMOs, etc.) are, in themselves, only of relative importance, since they are questions posed in relation to the useful and the harmful. Humanity has survived profound climatic changes; GMOs can do important damage, but like other industrial nonsense, they will end up disappearing after having caused some sanitary ravages - like asbestos, in its time declared harmless by experts and scientific academies. But the application of genetic manipulation techniques to humans, the development of neural engineering with the possibility of grafting electronic prostheses onto the human neural apparatus, or the possibilities opened up by nano-technologies, all of this now places us on the brink of the abyss.

The new technologies that pose serious ethical problems can be roughly divided into three groups.

1. The processes that allow us to choose the humans to be born: this ranges from the use of IVF with selective sorting of embryos to work on genome modification. This is the question raised by Sloterdijk and it is also what Habermas tackles in his book on *The Future of Human Nature*;

2. Processes for taking control of human brains - in particular everything that revolves around brain chemistry;

3. Processes that allow direct modification of human nature itself, with the introduction of electronic prostheses as extensions of the brain and as means of controlling humans.

In any case, we have good reasons to develop these techniques and their advantages are difficult to contest. They are, moreover, in strict continuity with the conception of science which was outlined at the beginning of modern times and which is so clearly summarized by Descartes. No one would want to have a child suffering from a congenital handicap as long as the technical means to avoid it exist. The "selective sorting" of unborn children has existed for some time. Screening for Down's Syndrome results in abortion in 99% of cases... We have long since accepted that we can alter our brain and mental states by means of chemical molecules. Acetylsalicylic acid by thinning the blood can eliminate pain. Chemical medications for depression (Prozac, for example) or schizophrenia are in common and indisputable use. If one is unhappy, the stimulation of serotonin production will do the trick... In *Paradise for All* (1982) - the last film made by Patrick Dewaere - Alain Jessua invents a professor of medicine who has developed a process of "flashing the brain" to make the patient happy: in the end, the hero played by Dewaere ends up with a motor handicap, his wife is the doctor's mistress, but he is happy. We are perhaps not very far from fiction.

Prostheses have provided invaluable services to humans, victims of accidents, war or disease. No one thinks there is any ethical problem with wearing glasses or a hearing aid! If we can really develop a "chip" that would allow paraplegics to direct a robot by thought, where is the harm? After all, technology imitates nature or replaces it where it is not strong enough, as Aristotle said.

What leads us to accept and even to call for the unlimited progress of technical control over humans is the illusion of continuity. Basically, the classic argument is this: if you don't want programmed modifications of the human genome, you shouldn't have invented fire or the wheel! Go back to crawling. This was already Voltaire's answer to Rousseau. But this apparent "common sense" argument is fallacious. It simply forgets that, as the old Marxists who thought they had read this in Marx used to say, "quantity turns into quality."

There is a fundamental contradiction at the heart of modern science and it would be vain to deny it by simply denouncing the perversion of science by sorcerers' apprentices or by calling for a science with conscience. Since Descartes, to take a point of reference, we consider that there is no essential difference between the matter object of physics and chemistry and the living. The properties of living beings (capacity to maintain, relatively, the unity of the individual, capacity of reproduction and self-repair) are considered as properties which appear at a certain level of organization of matter, but which should be able to be fully accounted for by taking time. The development and success of molecular biology and genetics have validated this reductionist approach to a large extent.

One will easily agree that the question of human freedom has a close relationship with that of the nature of this particular science called psychology, whose scientific status remains very problematic. It is the same, more generally, for all these "concrete sciences of the mind" that we try to fit into the positivist scheme of the "sciences of facts". For Husserl, it is a question of subjecting to criticism the scientificity of all the sciences.

> "In the course of this task we will soon realize that the dubious character of psychology, this sort of illness from which it suffers not only today but already for centuries - in short the "crisis" that is proper to it - possesses a central significance for the uncovering of a certain number of enigmatic and unresolved obscurities in the modern sciences, including the mathematical sciences, and correlatively that it is also important for the bringing to light of a sort of enigma of the World unknown to previous eras. All these obscurities bring us back to *the enigma of subjectivity* and consequently form a whole with *the enigma of the thematic and method of psychology*[139]."

That the question of freedom has something to do, and even the essential, with the question of subjectivity, seems indisputable. If we study human activities externally, as a knowing subject is interested in an object, if we consider them as facts, they are obviously not free. We consider them as we consider all the phenomena of nature, as phenomena that are linked to each other according to regular chains of cause and effect. But if we consider our own activities, our decisions, our cogitations, we

---

139. Husserl (E.), *The Crisis of the European Sciences and Transcendental Phenomenology*, p. 9-10.

cannot do otherwise than presuppose this somewhat mysterious causality that Kant calls causality by freedom. We can ask the question, the same question, in another way: the constituted sciences, the sciences of nature, have nothing to say other than the observation that there are regular laws uniting the phenomena in an explicable whole. Consequently, they are neutral from the axiological point of view. Science can say why such and such a molecule can cure a patient of such and such a disease, but it is incapable of saying why this individual is called a patient and for what reasons he should be cured - when the doctor cures his patient instead of finishing him off, it is because he is obeying a moral imperative that the whole biology of the world is incapable of producing as one of its laws. Let's let Husserl speak again:

> "As regards the sciences of the spirit, which however in all their particular or general disciplines treat of the man in his spiritual existence, that is to say in the horizon of his historicity, it is said that their rigorous scientificity requires of the researcher that he puts scrupulously out of circuit any axiological position, any question on the reason or the unreason of humanity and of the forms of culture of this humanity which makes its topic. The scientific, objective truth is exclusively the observation of what the world - whether it is the physical world or the spiritual world - is, in fact. But is it possible for the world and the human being in it to have a real meaning if the sciences only allow as true what can be observed in an objectivity of this kind, if history has nothing more to teach us than the fact that all forms of the world of the spirit, all the rules of life, all the norms that give each epoch to men, are formed like fleeting waves and, like them, are again undone, that it has always been so and that it will always be so, that always again reason will change into unreason and benefits into plagues? Can we find our rest there? Can we live in this world whose historical event is nothing but an incessant chain of illusory impulses and bitter disappointments[140]?"

------

140. HUSSERL (E.), *op. cit.* p. 11.

Modern science is linked to a disenchanted world whose propensity to become a steel cage was already shown by Weber. As soon as science reigns (or at least what we call it), there is no longer any possibility of limiting its applications. This in turn feeds scepticism and relativism, i.e. nihilism with regard to reason.

A second difficulty stems from the very contradictions of Cartesianism: how to contain the mechanism to the living without touching, in one way or another, the mind? Descartes' entire work consists in trying to establish this delimitation between the immaterial thinking soul and the extended body subject to the conservation laws of physics. And yet, no one more than Descartes finally worked to break down this separation. We need only quote this astonishing passage from the *Discourse on Method to* understand this. The development of science and its technical applications

> "... is not only to be desired for the invention of an infinite number of artifices, which would make it possible to enjoy the fruits of the earth and all the conveniences found therein without any difficulty, but mainly also for the preservation of health, which is undoubtedly the first good and the foundation of all the other goods of this life; For even the mind depends so strongly on the temperament and disposition of the organs of the body, that if it is possible to find some means that will make men commonly wiser and more skilful than they have been up to now, I believe that it is in medicine that it must be sought."

In other words, medicine will not only cure diseases and prolong life, but also, by modifying the organization of the body, it will make man wiser! It is no longer possible to make the properties of the mind depend on the physical properties of the body. This astonishing passage is often left out by Descartes' commentators, but it is really at the origin of all modern ideas, which govern in their great majority contemporary researchers in neurophysiology. Let us be fair: this project is not only Descartes'. It can be found, a little earlier, in Francis Bacon, who sets out some of the objectives of the sciences as follows:

"Prolonging life; restoring youth; retarding aging; curing diseases deemed incurable; lessening pain; easier and less repulsive purges; increasing strength and activity; increasing the capacity to endure torture and pain; transforming temperament, stoutness, and leanness; increasing and elevating the cerebral; making new species; transplanting one species into another; making spirits cheerful and putting them in a good disposition, etc.[141]"

We notice the convergence. In both cases, it is not only a question of improving human life, of making it sweeter, but of improving man himself, of transforming him spiritually and making him a more efficient machine! Before modern times, it was thought that the only way to make man better was to educate him, i.e. to build on this "human nature" which seemed intangible. This is still the position of Rousseau or Kant: men are educable and it is the task of philosophy and/or politics to determine the right conditions for this education. But these two great philosophers of the Enlightenment did not notice that they were already "old-fashioned", overtaken by what a certain rationalist philosophy had posed. For if medicine can make man wiser or can "increase and elevate the cerebral", then philosophy is no longer of any use, nor is reflection on the art of governing men or on the most just constitution. It is necessary to make room for scientists and technicians. Auguste Comte will say it with audacity: it is necessary a social physics for the government to become truly a scientific government. But a scientific government needs laws that allow it to predict human behavior and technical means of action to force men to behave according to scientifically defined rules. From this point of view, the "counter-utopias" of which the last century has been not lacking clearly express, in their own way, the understanding of what is at stake in the scientific and technical domination of humanity, which is the most constant project of the last centuries. From Aldous Huxley to George Orwell, from Zamiatin to Ira Levin, they all say the same thing: what is being prepared, or what

---

141. BACON (F.), *The New Atlantis*, trans. by M. Le Dœuff and M. Llasera, GF-Flammarion, 1955, p. 133.

a certain number of circles of the ruling classes want to prepare, is what Günther Anders has called "the obsolescence of man[142]".

Fighting disease, suffering, healing wounds and prolonging life, these are all primary impulses found in all times and all societies. But today, it is about something else and we must ask ourselves why so much money is spent, so many hopes are put into research which, in the end, if it had any chance of succeeding, would teach us that human freedom is only an illusion, a painful illusion which it is good to get rid of because of the innumerable sufferings that it generates.

Does man produce himself?

One of the commonplaces of modern thought is to affirm that man is free because he makes himself. This may be true if we understand by "self-making" the capacity of man to transform his environment, to create a culture, to educate himself, in short to "be for himself". But if one understands "to make oneself" in the sense of "to make oneself", it is a completely different matter. We could schematize this distinction by bringing it back to the one that Aristotle makes between *praxis* and *poiesis*, between the action that is its own end and the production that is extinguished in a thing external to the agent. The domination of the "value form", that is, the transformation of all social relations into relations between the values of things, naturally tends to reduce all human activities to productions whose results can be measured and whose means can be rationally determined. In accordance with the general principles that govern social life under the capitalist mode of production, what concerns the birth, formation and development of a human being must fall under the general methods of production, and in particular under this technical application of the "science of facts", a science that is neutral as to values.

From this point of view, the process is well underway, and has been for a long time, which aims at rationalizing the production of human

---

142. See ANDERS G., *Obsolescence de l'homme*, Éditions de l'Encyclopédie des Nuisances-Ivrea, 2005, translated from German by Christophe David.

beings. As always, this rationalization is legitimized by good, "humanistic" reasons. The PMI (Prévention maternelle et infantile) aims to ensure the health conditions of the mother and the unborn child. But at the same time, technical control procedures are put in place, with compulsory steps, conformity tests that allow prediction and the organization of the health system that follows. To the point where it is the obstetric services that determine the date of delivery by artificial induction of labor, a technique that has the distinct advantage of allowing a rationalization of the practitioners' time. It is the same movement that leads to the birth of all children (except for "accidents") in maternity hospitals, that is to say in a technical environment subject to very detailed and supervised routines and procedures. All these procedures have played a decisive role in the radical reduction of infant mortality over the last century, and no one can regret the "good old days" when women died in childbirth and children in their first year. However, it is necessary to understand how, at the same time, the coming into the world of little men is radically transformed. Hannah Arendt, taking the opposite view of the Greeks who referred to man as "the mortal", made birth rate the fundamental characteristic of the human condition[143]. If we accept this idea, it follows that the very way in which newborns are welcomed into this already ancient world has a decisive importance, and cannot be reduced to the statement of techniques, supposedly neutral. The government of bodies begins at this moment and the "disciplines" of modern society are concentrated there. Even birth control, which was experienced by individuals as a tool of liberation, is also a tool of population control, and in particular of their numbers.

But here again, a qualitative step, made possible by all the previous developments, is underway, which engages humanity in a new way. The technology of the modern era was content to organize and channel a human being procreated still at random, according to the mysterious laws of *Deus seu Natura*. The technique remained in the Aristotelian scheme of

---

143. See in particular "The Crisis of Education", p. 237-239, in *The Crisis of Culture*, Gallimard, Folio, 1972, trans. Patrick Lévy.

accompaniment of the nature. Since the end of the seventies and the birth of the first "test-tube babies", man has begun to be conceived as a product of human production, and more precisely as a product of technoscience. The case of IVF (*in vitro* fertilization and embryo transfer) is exemplary. IVF aims to remedy certain cases of female infertility by proceeding with fertilization "in a test tube" and the reimplantation of the embryo thus produced into the maternal uterus. The first reason legitimizing the intervention of artificial means instead of the good old natural method can therefore be considered as a "good reason". However, it soon became apparent that the available technology allowed for many other things to be done that were not related to the initial objective. This is what motivated Jacques Testard's refusal to go any further in this direction. Here is for example what one can read in a major French daily newspaper:

> "Encino, an affluent suburb of Los Angeles. The *Fertility Institute* is located in a small, modern building on the city's main avenue. Inside, everything is new, comfortable and colorful: the treatment rooms, the operating room and, above all, the genetic diagnosis laboratory, equipped with ultra-sophisticated equipment. At first glance, this is a private in vitro fertilization (IVF) clinic, like the ones that exist in every major city in the United States.
>
> "In fact, under the leadership of its owner, Dr. Jeffrey Steinberg, the Fertility Institute has become a very special place: of the 800 women who underwent IVF here last year, 700 were perfectly healthy and could have had a child naturally. They decided to undergo this costly, time-consuming and possibly risky procedure for one purpose: to choose the sex of their baby.
>
> "In the United States, unlike most countries in the world, genetic diagnosis of embryos during IVF is legal regardless of the motivation of the prospective parents. Three days after the egg is fertilized, a cell is removed from the embryo to examine its genetic code.
>
> "Like many of his American colleagues, Dr. Steinberg routinely diagnoses embryos before they are implanted, in order to eliminate those that carry

an identifiable genetic disease. Then the lab performs a second type of test: sorting between male and female embryos[144]."

There are other, more frustrating techniques for choosing the sex of the child: in India, for example, ultrasound is used quite extensively to determine the sex for abortion of the female fetus. But this already scientific method is not very different from the very ancient infanticide: nature does its work and then we eliminate what does not correspond to the objectives. The choice of sex through IVF, on the other hand, implies programming practically from the moment of conception, but it is still necessary to sort the embryos. The ideal would be to be able to control meiosis... or to program the "genetic code" directly. That is to say, to do on human embryos what we do on seeds or on certain animals. After GMOs, HGMs, genetically modified humans?

We are still in the early stages of human manufacturing. The quality standards imposed in industrial production lines will apply. The choice of sex seems in itself a claim of no great consequence. Certainly, in countries like India where traditional norms make the birth of girls a calamity, the demographic imbalance between boys and girls is already quite strong in some states, with the annoying consequence that boys can no longer find wives and those from the upper castes are forced to marry into the lower castes - so the use of modern techniques in the service of the most backward traditions and prejudices leads to new contradictions. However, in societies where capitalism has swept away tradition, one can make the reasonable assumption that if parents could choose the sex of their children, in total, the distribution would not be very different from the distribution resulting from the vagaries of meiosis. However, even if the ratio remains unchanged (105 boys for 100 girls on average), the ontological situation of men would be radically different, since each one would be, at least by one important trait, the product of a parental project conceived in the mode of manufacture on demand, as when one orders a car by choosing the brand, the type and the paint!

---

144. *Le Monde*, 31/07/2010.

We are not there yet, but it is no longer science fiction. Since we can introduce genes for resistance to cold or pesticides into plants, since we can genetically modify pigs[145], there is nothing to prevent us from doing the same for humans in the near future. Of course, human genetic programming is a fantasy: we will not program in advance the characteristics of unborn babies as we choose our car. There is a major reason for this: the metaphor of programming and the "genetic code" is false and the relationship between genotype and phenotype is much more complex than the genetics of the late 20th century would have us believe. But the idea of modifying human DNA in order to obtain certain phenotypic properties is well anchored in people's minds and can obtain partial results that may be of interest to future parents, laboratories, biotechnology specialists or even health policy makers.

For a long time, it was claimed that this was a taboo that should never be violated. Cloning was presented as the height of techno-scientific barbarism - the Rael sect, advocates of reproduction by cloning, serve as a useful scarecrow for sparrows. Reproductive cloning in itself is of no interest - not only in humans, but also in animals - since it only allows an almost identical reproduction of the cloned being, whereas any serious breeder is constantly looking for the improvement of the races. But therapeutic or reproductive cloning serves as an experimental field for decisive interventions on animals and tomorrow on humans. For, as many observers note, all the barriers that were opposed to both reproductive cloning and human genome modification are falling. Jeremy Rifkin, Francis Fukuyama and many other successful essayists predict the production of genetically modified babies around 2030.

The next step was detailed in a small book by Henri Atlan dedicated to the "artificial womb[146]". In it, the author predicts that the technique for conceiving a child entirely outside the womb could be available within

---

145. Genetically modified pigs have been created whose saliva is rich in phytase, which allows them to digest phosphorus and thus reduce the level of phosphorus in pig manure, which is one of the major sources of pollution. Genetic engineering thus comes to the rescue of ecological concerns.
146. ATLAN (H.), *L'Utérus artificiel*, Seuil, 2005.

the next fifty years. Here again, as with cloning or human genetic transformation, it has become almost useless to protest: the reluctance would only be the result of retarded religious minds. We are invited to trust the "critical reason" that will determine the good use that can be made of these new techniques.

The problem, however, is not there. It is whether a being produced according to the methods of technical planning in industrial cultivation devices - analogous to off-farm cultivation - can still be called a "human being". We have no moral attitude towards the things produced by our industry. Things, as Kant said, have a price, but no value. We value them only insofar as they serve as a sign of the power of the human mind (e.g., works of art). Conversely, human beings are the object of respect because in each of them, in their very specificity, is embodied that mysterious thing that we continue to call humanity or human nature, which is not reducible to its observable physical characteristics. The products of human activity are in some way depthless: the fact that we have made them is enough to assure us that nothing in them escapes us, and their imperfections relative to our expectations can only be attributed to a defect in our technique or a design flaw that can be corrected. Nothing like that with humans in the sense that we give to this term, still today, but maybe not for a long time. The respect due to every human being is precisely because he is not ours, because we cannot appropriate him since he comes from God or from nature and because he faces us in an irreducible contingency. Anticlericals often despise religious tradition because they ignore its moral content: when Genesis says that God made man in his own image and likeness, one can take the expression literally and be clever by showing that Darwin's theory refuted biblical creationism, that the hypothesis of God is a hypothesis that we do not need. All this is indisputable in terms of "factual science". It is equally incontrovertible that all living things on earth are made of the same basic materials (the universality of DNA testifies to this) and that these materials themselves are not organized by a mysterious "vital principle", but according to physical-chemical processes which, in the end, follow the ordinary laws of physics and chemistry and do not require any divine assistance. Yet, important as these truths are - and they are important and deserve to be defended against obscurantism - they are still only half the truth. For the other half is contained in Genesis (and in all the "books", even the unwritten ones, on which civilizations are based): if it took a God to create the world and mankind, it is because mankind and its world have something sacred, something that must not be touched, something that must be respected absolutely. If man has inalienable rights by birth - as the French Declaration of 1789 (or its American counterpart) asserts - it is because he must be held sacred, or, to put it as Spinoza did, that "man is a god for man." He is a god because he proceeds from his own movement and not from my projects, my actions or my intentions. An industrially manufactured man would be the complete opposite.

Let us assume that such a being would come into being (as many scientists think); it could have the same cerebral equipment as that available to humans today; but subjectively, it would be fundamentally different, not for neurological reasons, but because subjectivity is formed in an intersubjective relationship, and this intersubjective relationship would be fundamentally different from what it is when it is formed between a mother and her child. Habermas identifies the problem by placing himself directly on the moral plane:

> "Through the irreversible decision that constitutes the intervention of a person in the "natural" equipment of another person, a hitherto unknown form of interpersonal relationship is born. This new type of relationship shocks our moral sensibility because it represents a foreign body in the legally institutionalized relations of recognition in modern societies. If one person makes an irreversible decision for another person, profoundly affecting the latter's organic apparatus, then the symmetry of responsibility that exists in principle between free and equal persons is necessarily limited[147]."

---

147. HABERMAS (J.), *The Future of Human Nature, Towards a Liberal Eugenics,* Gallimard, Nrf Essais, 2002, translated from the German by Christian Bouchindhomme. p. 27.

This could profoundly change the commonly accepted idea of what a person is and why we should consider him or her worthy of respect. To assert the contrary is to think that the mind has no connection with the processes of body formation, with the relationships between bodies, with what each person can perceive of the attitudes of others towards him or her.

The delirious project of man-made engineering is not simply - which would be reassuring - the work of a few deranged brains supported by specialists in advertising provocation. It is a serious project which could become a field of capital investment in the decades to come. It has many powerful supporters, and it is perfectly in the "zeitgeist". What is worrying is not its delirious side, but rather its "reasonable" side, in any case rational by purpose in a disenchanted world where only natural sciences have normative value. Even if the project in its maximum extension turns out to be unrealizable (but it begins to be realized in part today), the essential thing is the vision of man of which it is the bearer and the consequences that are already drawn from it. Starting simply from the current situation and without considering all the scenarios, Anne-Laure Boch notes that the techniques of medically assisted procreation occupy only a very restricted place and nevertheless provoke passionate debates. This is so because :

> "The important thing is the symbolic significance of these few cases, a significance that goes far beyond their small number. The attack on the idea of filiation, freedom, gratuity, determinism, chance, etc. does not wait for the generalization of these practices to penetrate the minds[148]."

The technoscience "desymbolizes" says again Anne-Laure Boch. But symbolization is the proper of subjectivity: I have something in front of me and this physical thing "means" another thing that is not present directly, in the sensible experience, but is nevertheless present in another way. The birth of a little man is not a physical process (even if it is also an extraordinarily complex set of physical processes), it is the production of a

---

148. BOCH (A.-L.), *Médecine technique, médecine tragique*, éditions Seli Arslan, 2009, p. 75.

meaning, of what essentially makes the human condition. Its reduction to a programmed chain of technical processes would mean the reduction of humanity to a manipulable and instrumentalizable object.

If such a project were to take shape definitively, then Hitler's project of improving the human species, of producing normalized humans and of exterminating or enslaving "sub-humans" would appear as a crude, costly, unnecessarily bloody version of the project of modern technoscience: the means were not good, but the ends perhaps not so bad as that! We are at the moment when a certain conception of science and technology functions as a supreme normative authority, an authority that is all the more dangerous because it denies itself as an authority by claiming to speak only the language of facts and of technical neutrality. The totalitarianisms of the last century legitimized themselves by the project of a new human race or the production of a new man. Biological technoscience could well want to accomplish this project, with its own means. The technical fabrication of humans would mean the destruction of the very idea of freedom.

Towards the disappearance of subjectivity?

Let's go one step further. We oppose freedom to constraint. How is constraint expressed? By suffering, by the inner feeling of oppression, by the dull resistance to this external power which is exerted on the subject. If we can chemically suppress this deaf resistance, if we can make the slave take pleasure in working, how can we say that this slave is still a slave? The use of drugs as a means of obtaining the consent of the dominated is an old business. During the First World War, hooch was often used as fuel to send soldiers to the front. In the aftermath of the Second World War, when it was necessary to "roll up your sleeves, produce first and claim later", according to Maurice Thorez's motto, certain categories of workers (for example the "ambulants" of the Post Office) received a ration of wine and cigarettes to keep them going. That one can temporarily modify the feelings of men by all kinds of *pharmaka*, it is a fundamental fact of any medical art since the highest antiquity. To be a *pharmakao is* simply to have one's mind clouded by a drink. Although, according to Descartes, the soul and the body are radically separated ontologically, the soul is closely united to the body, and this observation leads him, as mentioned above, to consider that one of the most important applications of medicine is to make men "wiser".

This idea opens the way to a new conception of the human mind, in conformity with the logic of positive sciences, which leads to its dismantling. The mind is considered as a thing (the brain, the neuronal system) or a way of speaking about the activity of this thing. And this thing is material, which makes thought a way of speaking about the movements that agitate this material thing. As early as the eighteenth century, a La Mettrie asserts that we must go to the end of Descartes' thought. Descartes had turned living bodies into machines, but for fear of confronting the religious authorities had preserved the idea of a soul separate from the body. We must have the audacity to say that it is the whole man who constitutes a "man-machine[149]". This idea is not, however, peculiar to a character who is ultimately rather secondary in the thought of the Enlightenment. Materialism in the theory of mind is already exposed without too many detours by Hobbes in *Leviathan*, Hobbes for whom thinking is calculating. The idea that rational thought can be reduced to calculation is defended by Leibniz, who is not a materialist, but who develops an ingenious calculating machine - much more sophisticated than Pascal's "pascaline" - and imagines the use that could be made of binary numeration or of a "language of characters" (the "universal characteristic") prefiguring the formal logical languages that are so important in the development of computing. Unquestionably, Leibniz is not only one of the precursors of computer science and artificial intelligence. He could also be the precursor of the Computational Theory of Mind (CTM) which has dominated the philosophy of mind even if its star has faded in recent years[150].

---

149. See OFFRAY DE LA METTRIE (Julien), *L'Homme-Machine*, Gallimard, "Folio Essais", 1999.
150. One of the founders of the TCE, Jerry Fodor, dealt him some hard blows in *L'esprit, ça marche pas comme ça*, éditions Odile Jacob, 2003.

Against the "strong materialism" of most of these theories, the TCE or the neuronal man of Jean-Pierre Changeux, we have outlined elsewhere the defense of a "weak materialism"[151]: if the mind does belong to nature and must therefore be thought of as something natural, for all that, the objectivist grasp of the natural sciences is incapable of really accounting for the mind because subjectivity, by definition, cannot be the object of natural sciences. It remains to be understood why neurosciences and researches in order to elaborate a scientific conception of the human mind are carried out with so much vigor.

The progress of neuroscience is undoubtedly a good thing: we know more about the brain, we know how it works and, consequently, we can better treat its disorders and lesions. We can even begin to consider prostheses for serious functional disorders. A lot of work is being done on devices that would allow us to decode thoughts (from an electroence-phalography) and transmit them to a computer. A subject deprived of all motor possibilities could thus, only by thought, control a robot. This is good news. But, as always, less good news follows. Experiments with "thought transmission" by computer are being worked on - recent experiments in this field seem to point the way forward. Computer advances could also take over from the good old lie detector. In short, we would be on the track of the "cerebroscope", the machine to read thoughts. If we can rigorously associate (*token identity*) a certain active configuration of neurons and a thought content, we will be able to have a complete semantic of the brain and, from then on, get rid of the notion of mind for good - as Jean-Pierre Changeux requested[152].

All this research is leading to the construction of human brain/computer interfaces, to the multiplication of electromechanical prostheses, in a word to the constitution of a man-machine continuum which leads to the "bionic man". The limit between science fiction and technoscience would thus be erasing itself. Welcome to the *cyborg*, the successor of man!

---

151. See COLLIN (D.), *La Matière et l'Esprit*, Armand Colin, 2004.
152. See CHANGEUX (J.-P.), *L'Homme neuronal*, Hachette Littérature, coll. "Pluriel", 1998.

But here again, the presentation of a continuity of the scientific mastery of man is misleading. From the prostheses of arms and legs to the heart batteries, why shouldn't we move on to a later phase, a greater integration of the individual and the artificial extensions that can be useful to him? Scientific psychology has never ceased to examine the functioning of the human mind and the pharmacopoeia of pills intended to regulate the functioning of the nervous system has never ceased to expand: sedatives, sleeping pills, antidepressants, mood regulators and other anxiolytics clutter the medicine cabinets of almost every home. However, what is at stake is something else: there is not a big difference between the absinthe of the poètes maudits, the alcohol of Zola's *L'Assommoir* and Prozac. We are in the domain of drugs that influence the functioning of the brain, disrupt thought and sensations, and eventually derail the imagination, like the delirium attacks suffered by the character played by Montand in *Le Cercle rouge*. But the alcoholic ravaged by alcohol remains a subject - just as Descartes' madmen continue to express outwardly that they have a soul, unlike automatons and parrots. The techno-scientific project that is taking shape today aims precisely at suppressing this subjectivity. The alcoholic may speak more than he would like to when he is sober, but in his speech the distinction between what is said and what he thinks inside remains. As soon as we have a "mind-reading machine", this distinction no longer exists, it is radically abolished, and if the individual's mind, his interiority, is exposed to the eyes and to understanding, then this interiority no longer exists and we are no longer dealing with a man, but with an android, analogous to those of Philip K. Dick in *Do Androids Dream of Electric Sheep*, the novel from which Ridley Scott's cult film *Blade Runner* is taken.

One may object to this: either this project of dismantling the mind according to the principles of nature is a pure chimera and then we don't have to be afraid of it any more than we are of Mary Shelley's story; or it is not science fiction, but science at all, and then it is stupid to refuse this scientific truth, which is very unpleasant for the backward humanists that we are.

The first part of this objection can be dismissed. Science fiction is... fiction. We are dealing with a serious project, on which many laboratories are working, mobilizing researchers from many disciplines - from computer science to philosophy, including neurobiology and psychology. We are not dealing with a free intellectual creation like the novels of Dick, Huxley or Orwell. Even if the techno-scientific program concerning the mind fails in its attempt to reduce subjectivity - and fundamentally, it can only fail - it produces effects, legitimizes practices and induces new relationships between individuals.

The second part of the objection is no more convincing. How could the techno-scientific program concerning the mind be true? It would imply that life itself would be discarded. I can always take Prozac to fight my depression, I will never experience depression as a simple problem of serotonin reuptake! I can know the mechanisms of pain, but that doesn't stop me from hurting, and "hurting" is not objectifiable. It is, simply, life apprehending itself. It is not at all by chance that the great "triumphs" of the technoscience of the mind have occurred in the techniques of simulation of thought reduced to calculating thought. Basically, when we make a calculating machine execute 2 + 2, we can safely dispense with the questioning of the effect it has on a human subject to think 2 + 2! Hobbes is right ("to think is to calculate") only as long as one suppresses from the operations of thought the thought itself, that is to say the thought that apprehends itself. By simulating the computational procedures of human thought, one does not build "machines to think", but rather "machines not to think". These philosophical refutations, it goes without saying, will never be able to convince a supporter of the program of the technoscience of the mind, since philosophical thought is precisely put out of play from the beginning.

This is because in reality, CTE, cognitive science and everything that revolves around the program of the technoscience of the mind do not have as their object to know the human soul, in the manner of Socrates or Descartes. Such knowledge is considered a meaningless enterprise. Instead, it is about developing techniques that allow one to act with predictable results on other minds. Neither truth nor care are the goals of this enterprise, but rather the pursuit of that "colonization of minds" of which Remo Bodei speaks. Bodei shows, through the study of authors characteristic of the 20th century mind and the profound turning points that mark it, how the idea of the soul, having progressively lost its strength, has begun the conscious construction of individuality by means of the artificial instruments of politics and scientific knowledge. By means of human engineering techniques, power, by becoming internalized, makes the individual more malleable, more flexible to govern; it invades his consciousness. The proper characteristic of the totalitarianisms, it is that they succeeded in "conquering and in profaning the interior citadel of the conscience[153]". Defending, in the manner of Adorno, the individual subject, the "I", as the only center of potential resistance and critical judgment, Bodei shows by what means, even in more or less "democratic" societies, this "colonization of consciousness" develops.

> "To the classical repressive means are added or substituted the means of seduction, to the fear of death as a permanent threat of power is joined the interest of politics for the life, health and well-being of citizens, as much as the availability of Paschalian mass *entertainment*[154]..."

To understand the transformation of the metaphysical situation of the man induced by the biotechnologies applied to the birth or to the control of the psyche is therefore possible only if we resituate them in the movement of the whole of the modernity, or rather in this involution of the modernity, born under the sign of the liberation of the man and the promotion of the individual, and that is transformed in generalized control and conformism of mass, even when it is about a narcissism of mass[155].

The process of liquidation of subjectivity as that to which any possibility of speaking about freedom is articulated has not yet come to an end and probably never will. But the meaning of the technoscience of the mind is unambiguous. It is for this reason that the question of philosophy, that is to say of the defense of what since at least Plato presents itself under this

---

153. Bodei (R.), *Destini personali, L'età della colonisazione delle coscienze*, Giangiacomo Fletrinelli éditore, 2002, p. 250.
154. Bodei (R.), *op. cit.* p. 267.
155. See Lasch (Christopher), *The Culture of Narcissism*, Climats, 2000, translated from the American by Michel L. Landa.

name, is an absolutely priority intellectual task, because philosophy - even materialist philosophy - is in its very existence an irreducible objection to the attempt to make man predictable and calculable.

Anders and the "Promethean shame

In his book, *Obsolescence of Man*, Günther Anders devotes the first essay to the "Promethean shame". Here is how he presents his first encounter with this "shame":

> "I visited a technical exhibition with T. that had just opened in the area. T. behaved in the strangest way, so strange that I ended up observing him rather than the machines on display. As soon as one of the most complex machines in the exhibit began to work, he looked down and was silent. I was even more struck when he hid his hands behind his back, as if he was ashamed to have introduced his own crude, clumsy, obsolete instruments into a high society of devices operating with such precision and *refinement*[156]."

This shame is that of the manant introduced by chance into the society of the great, with the difference that the society of the great was made up of humans and that the great in front of whom T. is ashamed are machines, things produced by humans. Anders continues:

> "If I try to deepen this "Promethean shame", it seems to me that its fundamental object, "the fundamental opprobrium" which gives to the man shame of himself, it is his *origin*. T. is ashamed to have *become* rather than to have been *made*. He is ashamed to owe his existence - unlike the products which, them, are irreproachable because they were calculated in the least details - to the blind, not calculated and ancestral process of the procreation and the birth[157]."

There is no better description of what drives the senseless desire to make humans, or the equally senseless desire to reduce one's mind to a simple,

---

156. ANDERS (G.), *Obsolescence of Man*, p. 38.
157. *Ibid.*

predictable mechanism. Augustine sees in the inversion of creator and creature the very manifestation of heresy. Anders notes that it is a similar process that characterizes man seized by "Promethean shame": the creature (the machine) becomes the object of admiration, it takes on a sacred character, and man (who is, however, the creator of the machine) becomes an object of contempt. Whether this has anything to do with the "commodity fetishism" mentioned above is absolutely certain. The manifestations of the cult of things are sufficiently numerous and sufficiently studied by sociologists that it is not useful to return to them. The most interesting thing is this aspiration to become a machine of man, that is to say, an aspiration to get rid simultaneously of the "I" and of the freedom that is inextricably linked to it. Anders summarizes the situation in a formula:

> "The subject of freedom and that of submission are interchanged: things are free, it is man who is not[158]."

This is why, as Anders notes again, man must devote himself to *human engineering*, that is to say to the attempt to make his body the equivalent of a machine, something as perfect as a machine. In the attention that individuals pay to their bodies, we too often see a simple manifestation of narcissism. If this were the case, it would not be too serious. But the truth is much worse: it is no longer the beauty of the gods of Greek statuary that sets the standards, because in it one can always recognize oneself, but the functional perfection of machines. A few years ago, a Citroën advertisement for its Picasso model showed the robots dedicated to painting on the assembly line. The robot would start painting the car following a graphic inspired by a Picasso painting. But the precision and speed of execution left no doubt as to the conclusion to be drawn: the machine is far superior to man and Picasso's genius must fade away in front of its machine-like perfection. Turning over in his grave, the painter must have been seized, too, like Günther Anders' T. by this Promethean shame.

---

158. Anders (G.), *op. cit.* p. 50.

Chapter VI
From the liberation

The time has come to identify some perspectives. The exercise is obligatory: the contemptor of modernity is asked for his proposals, otherwise he is disqualified. One could be satisfied with answering with all negative proposals, consisting in saying "no" to the spirit of the times. Today there is a refusal of progress which could well be the only truly progressive movement. Even if it seems desperate and hopeless. We cannot be satisfied with purely moral answers: when degrowth theorists like Paul Ariès advocate voluntary frugality, they may be right, but this proposal is only addressed to the individual in his search for the good life, and we can clearly see what could be sinister about voluntary frugality transformed into a political program. *A fortiori*, when it comes to the question of freedom, we are confronted with burning political questions that have often been debated in recent centuries.

The question is whether we simply want to lengthen the length of our chains or whether it is possible to break them and, like Sir Wolf, run wherever we want. This question immediately confronts us with another difficulty: since man is a "political animal", freedom cannot be confined to individual freedom, since the individual, too weak, would have only a very limited freedom. Spinoza starts from this point: each person naturally has the right to act as he pleases and nothing can limit him... except precisely his too weak forces which keep him in such a position that this "right of nature" of each person to dispose of himself and things as he wishes is in reality a null right. A true natural right of man begins to exist only where there are men united by common rights. But experience teaches us that these common rights are not simply means to increase individual power, but can be, and very often are, new chains that impose themselves on the individual. When the "we" takes precedence over the "I", it is then that individuals are subjected to the threat of tyranny and even of the most powerful of tyrannies. Is it possible to find a point of balance between the "I" and the "we" such that freedom is something other than a supervised freedom? Can the emancipation of individuals, which was at the center of Enlightenment thought, take another form than mass conformism and the submission of men to the omnipotence of their own creations?

On the proper use of liberalism

If, as we have seen in the first chapter, there is indeed a liberalism that conceives of itself as the absolute freedom of the powerful paid for by the submission of the immense cohort of the poor, a liberalism à la Callicles[159], there is, however, a good use of liberalism, a liberalism whose lineaments are to be found in Spinoza, Rousseau or Hegel, for example. Why defend liberalism, or at least a certain kind of liberalism, at the risk of being classified as a "social liberal", a category that is hated in radical circles? Behind this question, there are several oppositions that need to be clarified. The first, and most fundamental, is to know what the emancipation of humanity can mean. Marx's thought is placed under this sign: the proletarians are the most apt to lead the fight against capital, because they only have to lose their chains. It is therefore that this struggle against capital is a struggle that gives itself freedom as its primary objective. But traditional socialism, including and especially Marxist socialism or 20th century communism (in its Stalinist variant as in almost all the others), has changed this

---

159. A character in Plato's *Gorgias*, Callicles maintains that justice means that the strong dominate and use their strength to satisfy their desires as they see fit. To Socrates' moral prescriptions, he reproaches wanting to trim the claws of the lion cubs.

objective. It is no longer about freedom, but about equality. Capitalism is bad because of the inequalities it produces, and it is to this egalitarianism that the other political values must be subordinated. *Grobianisch* (crude) communism, which sets itself the goal of regulating the thickness of the wallet, or the socialism of resentment, leads to barrack socialism, which was the model of the collectivist utopias of the late 19th and early 20th centuries, utopias that were widespread in the social democratic parties and of which the Stalinist regime gave a fairly good illustration. From Marx's point of view, economic equality is nothing more than "bourgeois law". The question of equality is first of all the equality of exchanges, value for value. Men think of themselves under this category of equality only as long as their relations appear disguised under the relations between things. That the socialist parties have stuck to these egalitarian claims is simply the proof that the horizon of these parties has always been narrowly limited by capitalism[160] and that they never envisaged that men would no longer be subject to the blind power of their exchanges.

Does this mean that we should give up on equality? It all depends on what we mean by that. For example, when the right and the left agree in the cult of "equal opportunities" that the school is supposed to provide to all children, we are in the middle of ideology. It is claimed that with a few political efforts, all children would have the same chance to become poly-technicians, enarques, famous business lawyers or big bosses in a hospital. Since it is impossible for all of them to achieve their ambitions, and since the 600,000 or 700,000 baccalaureate graduates each year will not be transformed into polytechnicians or lawyers, "equality of opportunity" is nothing but a mystification that makes the organizational technology of the social hierarchy seem like an honest competition in which everyone has his or her chances and will be rewarded according to his or her talent and merit. At the same time, the purely "liberal" vision, in the sense of economic neo-liberalism, which presents society as the closed field of

---

160. When the French PS, at its 1991 congress in La Défense, officially admitted that "capitalism limits our horizon", it was simply acknowledging what has been true practically since the origins of socialism at the end of the 19th century.

rivalries between individuals, is renewed. And here we have a form of equality that legitimizes the perpetuation of domination. The question is therefore to know which equality should be defended.

A reading of Hegel can give some indications. In a very enlightening paragraph in the *Encyclopedia of Philosophical Sciences*, he writes:

> "*Liberty* and *equality* are the simple categories to which what should be the fundamental determination and the ultimate end and result of the Constitution have frequently been reduced. True as this is, these determinations have no less from the outset the defect of being entirely abstract; held firmly in this form of abstraction, it is they which prevent from being realized, or which destroy what is concrete, that is, an effected articulation of the State, that is, a Constitution and a government[161]."

Indeed, liberty and equality as presented in the declarations of rights, from the 18th century as well as in the UN declaration, are pure abstractions. Freedom as a political and legal principle only exists in a state and a constitution. Freedom, on this level, consists of rights (authorizations), protections and concrete possibilities of action. Hegel anticipates a criticism, sometimes debatable, but often useful, of the formal character of Human Rights. The rich and the poor are equal in the sense that they both have the right to sleep under a bridge... Equality is just as abstract and, to put it bluntly, it finds its full extension only in the domain of abstraction by extension that is commercial exchange. However, this abstract concept of equality has a real importance:

> "But the *concept of* freedom, in the way it exists from the beginning as such, without further determination or development, is abstract subjectivity as a *person* capable of ownership; this single abstract determination of personality constitutes the actual equality among men[162]."

The first moment of the concept of freedom is thus abstract freedom, that by which the subject is recognized as a person, that is to say as the bearer

---

161. HEGEL (GWF), *Encyclopedia of the Philosophical Sciences in abridged form*, § 539, p. 455.
162. *Op. cit.* at 456.

of the right of ownership, and the first equality is the equality of persons. It is even the only effective equality. In other words, equality, as Hegel thinks of it, is defined in a restrictive way as equality of rights in relation to property and first of all to the property of oneself - no one can be the property of another and respect for property is thus confused with respect for the person. There is no question of equal rights as a citizen or in all other manifestations of public life. There is thus something here that tends to absolutize the right to property, whatever the nature of the property in question - knowing that, for Hegel, the right to property covers very different things and that it is impossible to make it an absolute, as liberal theorists do. Let us note, however, that, for Hegel, this right of property is anything but a natural right:

> "But that this equality is present, that what is recognized as a person and has legal validity is *man*, and not, as in Greece, Rome, etc., only *a few* men, is so little a fact of *nature* that it is rather a product and a result of the consciousness of the deepest principle of the spirit and the universality and formation of this consciousness[163]."

Thinking about equality is therefore only possible from a certain stage of the development of human civilization. Equality is a historical result, not a natural fact. Naturally, men are not equal, they are rather unequal in all sorts of ways. Equality for Hegel is simply the equality of freedom, that is, the recognition of the human person in each individual. Hegel goes on to show that the very existence of social life necessarily entails all sorts of inequalities. Children do not have the same rights as adults, rulers have rights that ordinary citizens do not have, and even on the soccer field, the players are not equal to the referee. We can see that these are not natural inequalities, but socially constructed inequalities; a thought of law and freedom can only try to determine which inequalities are necessary and just, and in which domain the principle of equality is imposed - this is

---

163. *Op. cit.* p. 455.

properly the object of the research and discussions carried out under the banner of the "theory of justice."

But this seemingly narrow conception of equality can lead to the formation of a powerful concept of freedom whose critical significance cannot be underestimated. If men are equal as free persons, and equality is only that, then the first political and legal principle that must be followed is the principle of equal liberty for all, that is, the principle of political liberalism as defined by John Rawls. Let us be a little more precise: this equal freedom for all includes the refusal of all domination. It is therefore in line with the republican principle of freedom as non-domination. This concept of freedom is demanding: it presupposes that the political organization be designed in such a way as to protect citizens against all forms of domination - and not only the domination that could be directly exercised by political authorities, as in classical liberalism. As reformulated by Philip Pettit, republicanism is both a communitarian ideal and a radical claim to the protection of individual liberties. It pushes for social radicalism: the domination embodied in the submissive contract of labor (the social relation characteristic of capital's domination) is no more acceptable than other forms of domination. Cicero, an author often claimed by classical or contemporary republicans, already said it: freedom does not consist in having a good master, but in having no master at all. If, according to Rousseau's formula, freedom is obedience to the law that one has prescribed for oneself, this cannot apply only to certain aspects of life - life in the political space - but must necessarily be extended to all spheres of human life. This is not to displease our good Jean-Jacques who had conceived Sophie's education to make her a mother submissive to her husband and entirely devoted to domestic tasks.

Equality, in this context, is not the end, but the means to guarantee non-domination. That no one is rich enough to buy another man and that no one is poor enough to be forced to sell himself (to quote Rousseau again), does not make for an egalitarian society, but for a society in which inequalities of wealth cannot become means of domination by the richest over the poorest. This presupposes the widest possible distribution of property - the access of everyone to individual ownership of the means of production - at the same time as the disappearance (perhaps very gradual) of properly capitalist property. We have had the opportunity to develop elsewhere[164] some tracks that would allow us to envisage the effective realization of a society based on these principles. We could call this orientation "republican communism".

Is this an "anti-liberal" position? If liberalism is understood as "possessive individualism", no doubt. But liberalism cannot be reduced to the claim of property owners to be free from political power. Liberalism presents itself as a contradictory doctrine. Until recently, liberalism was classified as "left-wing" and opposed to "conservative". So-called liberals in the United States are often the left wing of the Democratic Party. Liberals are more likely to defend individual freedoms than conservatives, who are economically liberal but rather hostile to political freedoms and the liberalization of morals.

Classical political liberalism, that of Locke and Montesquieu, was first marked by the doctrine of the separation of powers, which is one of the major political principles claimed by republicans. Locke was also the one who theorized the right to insurrection against tyrannical power, a position that is not really in the arsenal of the conservative right. Although they do not agree on the definition of liberty (liberty as non-domination versus liberty as non-interference), republicans and classical political liberals can nevertheless agree on quite a number of concrete issues and often share similar views on constitutional matters. This again points to the theoretical debate: Philip Pettit's republicanism seeks to be an alternative to Rawls's theory of justice (political liberalism), but at the same time it strives to meet a "specification" that is not very different.

Carlo Rosselli's "liberal socialism" is a first attempt, unfortunately too little pursued, to overcome the sterilizing Marxism that reigned in the social-democratic and communist parties and to combine "revisionist neo-Marxism" and workers' praxis.

---

164. See *Revive la République !* and *Le Cauchemar de Marx.*

"Revisionist neo-Marxism and workers' praxis are the theoretical and practical face of a new liberal socialist conception in which the problems of social justice and life in society can and must be posed on the same plane as those of freedom and individual life[165]."

It is, for Rosselli, a renewed liberalism, which has overcome the opposition between bourgeois enlightenment and proletarian socialism. Rosselli acknowledges that the expression "liberal socialism" may seem strange, since the word *liberalism* has been used to smuggle a wide variety of goods! But Rosselli, like other authors before him, clearly separates liberalism (economic liberalism, i.e., the affirmation of the central role of the market economy) and liberalism (political). He thus gives this definition of liberalism:

"In its simplest expression, liberalism can be defined as that political theory which, starting from the presupposition of the freedom of the human spirit, declares freedom the supreme end, the supreme means, the supreme rule of human social life. End, in so far as it proposes to reach a regime of social life that assures to all men the possibility of a full development of their personality. Means, insofar as it considers that this freedom cannot be granted or imposed, but must be conquered by hard personal work in the perpetual flow of generations. This one conceives freedom not as a given of nature but as becoming, development. One is not born but becomes free. And one can only keep oneself free by maintaining active and vigilant awareness of one's own autonomy and by exercising one's own freedoms.
"Faith in freedom is at the same time a declaration of faith in man, in his infinite perfectibility, in his capacity for self-determination, in his innate sense of justice[166]."

It only remains for Rosselli to define socialism as the accomplishment of the liberal ideals. The transformation of the relations of property and exchange allows to make effective and for all the liberties which are reserved only to some in the societies dominated by the capitalist mode of production.

---

165. ROSSELLI (C.), *Socialismo liberale*, p. 88.
166. ROSSELLI (C.), *op. cit.* pp. 89-90.

"The socialist movement is thus the concrete heir of liberalism, the carrier of this dynamic idea of freedom which is actualized in the dramatic movement of the history. Liberalism and socialism, far from being opposed according to what a hackneyed polemic would like, are linked by an intimate relationship of connection. Liberalism is the ideal inspiring force, socialism is the practical realizing force[167]."

Between the "republican communism" that we mentioned above and this liberal socialism, the distance is not very great; in both cases, it is a question of taking as a principle that the social movement can only develop insofar as it poses the question of emancipation from all domination, the question of freedom as a central question. This is why anti-liberalism is really not the political program that the social movement needs. As if our societies were threatened by an excess of freedom when, as we have had ample opportunity to point out in this book, the automatic evolution of capitalism, and at the same time the evolution of governments, leads to the drastic reduction of freedom in all its senses! We are undoubtedly suffering from the weakening of collective structures for the protection of individuals, but we are not suffering from a lack of State, which is, on the contrary, more insistent, more insinuating, more surveillant, more repressive than ever.

Individual, common and community freedom

In the ranks of French-style republicans, communitarianism gets a bad press. Since 1793, they have held that "the republic is one and indivisible" and that particular communities are potential enemies of the republic. This is one of the Rousseauist aspects of French republicanism: only individuals are recognized and all forms of "brigades" or partial coalitions pervert the expression of the general will.

"If, when the people are sufficiently informed and deliberate, the citizens had no communication with each other, the general will would always

---

167. ROSSELLI (C.), *op. cit*, pp. 91-92.

result from the great number of small differences, and the deliberation would always be good. But when brigades are formed, partial associations at the expense of the great one, the will of each of these associations becomes general with respect to its members, and particular with respect to the State; one can then say that there are no longer as many voters as men, but only as many associations. The differences become less numerous and give a less general result. Finally, when one of these associations is so great that it prevails over all the others, you no longer have as a result a sum of small differences, but a single difference; then there is no longer a general will, and the opinion that prevails is only a particular opinion[168]."

The condemnation of "partial associations" is linked in Rousseau to his refusal of the separation of powers and to the defense of direct democracy (the general will cannot be represented). Applied to a political regime of representative democracy based on the separation of powers and admitting the representation of the bodies of "bourgeois civil society" (such as the trade unions), this vestige of Rousseauism seems quite out of place. Similarly, the desperate attempt to revive Jacobinism is not inspiring. Revolutionary Jacobinism had set itself the task of unifying the nation and finally completing the work of administrative centralization that the absolute monarchy had largely begun. But Jacobinism ended up giving birth to Napoleon's centralization, which imposed a rigid straitjacket on the French nation. While the revolution conceived centralization essentially as the unity of laws, based on local self-government, napoleonic centralization subjected all local powers to the supervision of the central power. The prefectural corps, a typically Bonapartist institution, is a wart grafted onto the body of the republic. And there are many others of the same kind. The first Clemenceau, the radical Clemenceau of the 1880s, entered the political battle with a radical democratic political program, which included the abolition of the prefects, the autonomy of government of the communes and a reduction in the power of the central administrations. He proposed, in short, to take a step towards

---

168. Rousseau (J.-J.), *The Social Contract*, book II, chap. III, "If the general will can err".

this "cheap government" of the type of the Paris Commune, which was the first social republic.

In other words, the republican ideal is not inevitably linked to a "Third Republic" conception of the indivisibility of the nation, nor to the cult of the State, nor to "Jacobin centralism. The Third Republic had its merits, and sometimes one begins to dream of politicians who would have the reforming courage of the old rad-socs who have now disappeared. But the Third Republic was also an "empire without an emperor", according to Engels' formula: "the French empire" colored the maps of elementary school pink. If the republican theorists deserve to come out of oblivion[169], the spirits of Jaurès and Briand can no longer inspire the younger generations. It is said that the republic recognizes only individuals: indeed, the most radical individualism inspired the revolutionaries of 1789 who, by the Le Chapelier law, organized the dissolution of corporations, but at the same time forbade unions and even mutual aid societies, which were most often born in hiding. But this particular form of the republic and of political liberty should not be taken as its essence. Jacobinism is also a political expression of the new dominant class, the bourgeoisie and the intellectual petty-bourgeoisie, for whom individualism is second nature. The individual, moreover, has no place in it unless he is an owner - the limitations placed on the right to vote by the democratic constitution of the second year show this without the least ambiguity.

The vision of the ideal political body, Rousseau confesses, may be suitable for gods, but not for men. Aristotle, to whom it is always good to return, defines the city, that is to say the political unit properly speaking (the *polis*), as a unit of communities: men form with women natural communities which naturally become households, which regroup into villages and the villages finally into a city, which is the completed term of human communities. Let us remember that the political community, the republic, is a community of communities. Therefore, we must admit that each community, within its own perimeter, has a large autonomy,

---

169. See Spitz J.-F., *Le Moment républicain en France*, NrF, Galiimard, 2005.

exercised within the framework of the general laws of the republic which protect individual liberties.

Anarchists - at least Proudhonian anarchists - believed that the state could be advantageously replaced by a federation of free communes, with all other forms of social organization giving way to mutualism and cooperatives. If one wanted to dogmatically implement such a plan, one would certainly not succeed without plunging the country into chaos - let alone extending it internationally. But utopias often have their merits, provided they are made reasonable by integrating them into a more realistic perspective. Proudhon's idea, far from being, as he believed, the theory of the abolition of the State, can be perfectly integrated into a republicanist political conception (a word that would have horrified a Proudhonian) in the sense that we give here to this term. The freedom of communes, that is to say communal autonomy, is a powerful factor in the development of civic spirit and the sense of liberty.

The disadvantage of local autonomy is twofold. First, the communes that are better off by nature or by history will tend to take advantage of their advantages, while the others will accumulate difficulties, thus creating unjust inequalities. It should be noted, however, that inequalities of this kind have developed considerably in Jacobin France: the supervision of the central State is therefore not a guarantee of equality, but it can play its role in the equalization of resources and the mutualization of risks. Secondly, it is possible to think that small political communities exert greater pressure on individuals and lead to conformism and the spontaneous restriction of individual freedoms. The example of the United States supports these fears. We see a much larger local democracy there than in France, but also a much stronger weight of the community on individuals. Conformism and the "gentle tyranny of the majority" of which Tocqueville spoke could then appear as the unpleasant consequences of greater political freedom at the local level. Reading Rousseau sheds light on this:

> "If I had had to choose the place of my birth, I would have chosen a
> society of a size limited by the extent of human faculties, that is to say by

the possibility of being well governed, and where each one was sufficient for his job, no one would have been forced to entrust to others the duties with which he was charged: a state where all individuals knew each other, the *obscure* maneuvers of vice nor the modesty of virtue could have escaped the public gaze and judgment, and where this sweet habit of seeing and knowing each other, made the love of the fatherland the love of the citizens rather than that of the land[170]."

The Rousseauist republic is a small republic - all citizens must be able to know each other! - which allows everyone to participate in the political functions without being obliged to delegate them to others. We have a bureaucratic apparatus reduced to the strict minimum. But it is also a political body where citizens watch each other and where virtue is thus ensured by the force of the common opinion. Freedom is the freedom to be virtuous and thus this capacity of the community to thwart the "obscure maneuvers of vice" is not perceived by our Genevan citizen as an obstacle to freedom, since:

> "So that the social pact is not a vain form, it tacitly contains this commitment which alone can give force to the others, that whoever refuses to obey the general will will be forced to do so by the whole body: which means nothing else but that he will be forced to be free[171] [...]."

A proposal in which one has often read the expression of that "despotism of freedom" that Hegel spoke of in connection with the revolutionary Terror in France. Could we have the advantages of local democracy and of this self-government of small communities without having the disadvantages?

This brings us back to the old question of protecting the individual against the tyranny of the majority. Philip Pettit rightly argues that freedom in a nation must be defended by recourse to a supranational institution. Similarly, it can be argued that individuals can be protected from the effects of conformism in small communities as long as their individual

---

170. Rousseau (J.-J.), *Discourse on the origin and foundations of inequality among men*, Dedication.
171. Rousseau (J.-J.), *Social Contract*, book I, chap. VII, "Of the sovereign".

rights and freedoms are protected by a justice system that is independent of the community in question.

Certainly, small political communities have an almost natural tendency to seek consensus, with dissenters being seen as "bad sleepers". Yet, again following Philip Pettit, it makes more sense to conceive of democracy as a system that operates by contestation rather than consensus. The model of a republic from below, operating from local communities that delegate to the higher level only what is necessary for the prosperity of all and for the protection of rights and freedoms, is precisely a model that leaves room for contestation because each community is limited in the exercise of its sovereignty and finds itself in relationship with its neighbors, whose orientations may be contradictory to its own.

In sum, then, a democratic republic, that is, a republic based on the principle of freedom as non-domination and not on the principle of absolute sovereignty of the majority, would be a highly decentralized republic, offering everyone the opportunity to participate widely in public affairs and to develop a sense of initiative and responsibility, whereas centralized states are more favourable to "big machines", which have all the public offices filled by political professionals and encourage the development of a welfare mentality among citizens, which has become a powerful brake on any serious movement to challenge the established order.

We have dealt here only with institutional communities based on territorial divisions. But it is also necessary to deal with the case of other communities, those based on emotional or elective ties, or those based on national or ethnic origins. In France, at least, this type of community is the object of often unreasonable polemics in which conflicts unrelated to the precise object are reinvested. The same politicians who would not miss the annual CRIF lunch for anything in the world then denounce Muslim communitarianism... Instead of a hasty condemnation of "communitarianism", we should rather ask ourselves if the return in force of small communities, religious, regionalist or other, does not first of all express the refusal of a society of individuals separated from each other. Faced with the decomposition of the "great community" that is the nation absorbed

228

into the great world market, faced with the progressive destruction of work communities (the unions) or mass political parties, the return to more archaic communities such as the religious community or the ethnic community is "reactionary" only in the first sense, reactionary rather: it expresses a reaction to a future perceived as unbearable.

Without doubt, we must exclude *a priori* the "reasonable arrangements" in the Canadian style, which went so far as to admit Islamic jurisdictions in certain civil law matters (notably divorce). The reason is simple: no one should be subject to the power of his community, he should be able to leave freely without being ostracized and even less threatened as an apostate. Freedom as non-domination includes protection against domination within the family as well as within the various communities to which one belongs and, for this reason, the law must remain equal for all. Likewise, all policies that lead, in one way or another, to separate development, which in other places was called *apartheid,* must be fought. And it is in public places, community facilities, health or school that the principles of equality and the refusal of discrimination, not only ethnic or racial, but also sexual, must be firmly maintained. The proposals (sometimes implemented) to open swimming pools at times reserved for women are part of a segregation approach against women that reproduces the most backward features of Islam, perhaps not so much as the Bedouin societies of the century in which it was born. If school canteens must offer dishes acceptable to the various religious convictions, they cannot forbid themselves to offer pork or meat at the same time on Fridays: no one can impose his own whims on others. After all, a Muslim could very well have the desire to eat pig, considering that in truth God has other things to do than to deal with diets. The republican state, if it grants parents a "natural" authority over children, must at the same time protect children from domination:

> "Parents and teachers are under such constraints and exposed to such possible sanctions that they should ideally be able to ensure two things: on the one hand, they will seek to serve the relevant interests of the children; on the other, they will seek to do so in a non-idiosyncratic way.

From the liberation

They will, in other words, be able to exercise considerable power to interfere in children's lives, but this power to interfere will take into account children's interests as they are usually represented, and will not constitute a form of domination[172]."

This being said, the demands for cultural autonomy are perfectly legitimate, as are the demands concerning religious freedom, which is moreover very well guaranteed by the law of separation of 1905 which institutes religious associations. The will of political powers to interfere in the affairs of believers - in particular the interventions of French public authorities in the organization of Islam in France - must be firmly rejected. Believers organize themselves as they see fit and impose on themselves the disciplines they deem fit as long as they respect republican laws and individual liberties. In any case, multiculturalism (i.e., the defense of minority rights) should be integrated into the Republican ideal, as Philip Pettit argues. It could even go so far as to grant a minority culture a certain degree of political autonomy within its territory, when the problem arises in practice - Pettit cites the case of the Amish in the United States.

If one must renounce the anarchist idea of the suppression of the State as well as the Marxist theory of the withering State, it remains that the dispersion of authority in "partial associations", provided that it is judiciously organized, is favourable to individual freedom and can largely contribute to the development of the autonomy of people and to their blossoming.

The common and the individual: the question of morality (or ethics)

The fundamental articulation of modern political philosophy was that of civil society and the state. Liberalism had tried to establish as complete a separation as possible between the state, public, political sphere in the restricted sense of the term, and the sphere where the private interests of individuals could come into play. This separation justified the fact that the social contract was only valid for public life, while civil society remained

---

172. PETTIT (P.), *op. cit.* p. 159.

the place of the economy, i.e., of the management of private affairs. This distinction was obviously untenable and, in fact, never had any effective reality. The "economic policy" expresses this impossible separation. In capitalist society, the function of the state is to organize economic life - which, curiously and paradoxically for the dominant dogmas today, does not manage to organize itself by its own spontaneous, "natural" movement. At the same time, it is known that the strength of a state lies primarily in its economic power. Economic policy is so pervasive that it has devoured the best part of politics itself.

The separation between civil society and the state, which overlaps with the separation between public and private, is neither the most necessary nor the most durable. Suffice it to say that the family belongs to the private sphere, but that the education of children is ultimately the responsibility of the public authorities, who must ensure that parents give their children a proper education. Otherwise important is the dichotomy between the intimate, the individual in his or her own immediate sphere of existence, and the common. The common designates quite simply our social relations, the whole of the series by which we are attached to the others, short series, those of the family, longer series, those of work, studies, public life. In his 6th thesis on Feuerbach, Marx writes that "the essence of man is not an abstraction inherent in the isolated individual. In its reality, it is the totality of social relations." Once again, we notice that these brief and enigmatic notes on Feuerbach open up abysses of thought. The essence of man as "generic being" is not an abstraction, something whose meaning could be exhausted by saying that "man is a social animal". The effectiveness of this essence exists in the social, concrete, specific relations that each individual ties. The universality of gender has no other reality than this infinite ramification of the links that the individuals weave and that make that its being is always at the same time something common with others. But to stop there would be one-sided. The development of the social relations, of the bonds of community, produces also the development of the individual specificity, of a zone of the life which is only to him. The existence of an intimate life seems to take importance only by the development of the bonds of community.

Freedom finds its place in this tension. On the one hand, community ties (in the broad sense) are both constraints and open possibilities. There is strength in numbers! and therefore sociability allows the development of effective power to act. But on the other hand, this increased power to act gives more existence to this ego which is oriented only according to its "own natural". But this tension which can function as a positive reciprocal reinforcement can be transformed into its opposite. One is wary of the encroachment of the community on individual life, which is still very prevalent in traditional societies or in certain groups of immigrant origin. One might think that the difficulties of integration explain the withdrawal into community traditions, but it is often because integration is in the process of being achieved that traditionalism makes a comeback. As important as these problems are, they may appear to be residual, destined to dissolve in "modernity." In reality, it is not in the excessive weight of the community, but in its weakening, that the most serious threats to the individual now lie. Even the manifestations of reactionary communitarianism are largely explained by the collapse of the national community of reception.

In capitalism, which has rid itself of traditional forms, all that remains is the naked individual, in competition with other individuals. Community ties break down: the satisfaction of one's desires set up as a categorical imperative, the imperative of mobility ("bougism"), competition ("free and undistorted") transformed into a rule of life are rigorously contradictory to the existence of stable community ties. But this disintegration of the community does not correspond to a promotion of the individual, but on the contrary to its weakening. The exposure of the self, which is so loudly demanded by the media system - from reality shows to personal data on the Internet - simply completes the increasingly systematic listing, spying and violation of everything that is most personal.

The defense of privacy requires legal protections - first and foremost, the outright destruction of everything that has been built up over decades in terms of personal records and spying on individuals. But it also presupposes the reconstruction of a community *ethos* based on the search for a decent life, which, in turn, requires individual commitment. And here we fall back, inevitably, on questions of morality, because we fall back on the dispositions acquired by individuals and their orientations in relations with others. If freedom cannot reside in the rarefied atmosphere of a society of individuals leading separate existences - according to Robert Nozick's excellent formula -, it cannot exist in the relations of the individual with other individuals, social and interindividual relations. That is to say, there must be a shared morality, a public morality that guarantees that each individual can benefit from the respect and solicitude of others and that he or she shows the same respect and solicitude towards all others. Speaking of the conditions for social revolution, Gramsci did not hesitate to speak of the need for "moral reform," an expression that is quite inaudible today. Yet this is what is at stake if we want to talk seriously and not just draw plans on the comet.

It might seem that morality, and a public morality at that, is opposed to freedom. This is why some "liberal" thinkers believe that morality must be minimal; it must be imposed only to force the individual to remain within the limits already defined by the Declaration of 1789: freedom consists in being able to do everything that does not harm others. The "minimal ethics" proposed by Ruwen Ogien sticks to three principles which, according to their author, derive from the acceptance of the principles of political liberalism: the principle of neutrality with regard to substantial conceptions of the good (this is a principle that Rawls supports, but in another context); the principle of non-neglect; and the principle of equality, which consists of giving the same value to the voices or interests of everyone. Ogien first applies these principles to thorny issues such as pornography, surrogacy or sadomasochistic practices. But the test of a moral theory on these very particular cases - which should rather be the subject of casuistry - is by no means comprehensive enough.

As for the idea that one could construct an ethics that is neutral with respect to substantial conceptions of the good, it is highly problematic. We have had the opportunity to show[173] the contradictions of the claims to

---

173. See COLLIN (D.), *Morale and Social Justice.*

From the liberation

neutrality of Rawls' theory of justice, which is presented as a political and not a moral theory. *A fortiori*, it is difficult to see how an ethical theory could be neutral as to the substantial conceptions of the good. The only possibility (itself dubious) is to reduce morality to the conditions of contractuality - as in the "morality by agreement" defended by David Gauthier. We would thus be led back to one of those attempts made since Mandeville and Adam Smith to replace morality by the calculation of utility maximization, according to the principles of bourgeois political economy.

In truth, we keep deep inside us the idea that there is a ban, that not everything can be negotiated, that not everything obeys the deductive modes of instrumental rationality. The question that we intuitively perceive is that of the limit, a question from which we cannot free ourselves and which makes sudden and devastating returns regularly in the chronicle of the news or in the judicial chronicle. In a world submitted to the empire of desire (and to the tyranny of pleasure, to take up a formula dear to Plato and of which it would be necessary to explain all the ins and outs), everything becomes possible. The desire of the desiring subject is, by definition, unlimited (a limited desire is only a need easy to satisfy, like the need to drink a big glass of fresh water when one is thirsty). Perhaps this is the source of the ethics mania (3,000 business ethics professionals in the United States), the muted need to find that limit somewhere, without which we risk pure and simple madness. This explains the increasingly difficult to control swerves in the field of morals where contradictory injunctions are multiplying.

If freedom is not a capital to be made profitable as a good capitalist, but fundamentally a dynamic of life, an effort to free oneself from the multiple alienations in which the individual continually loses himself, it is then a question of constructing an ethic that can be shared by the greatest number. The lineaments of such an ethic are exposed with the greatest clarity in the work of Spinoza. We will only give a few glimpses of it here.

In propositions 29 to 38 of the fourth part of the *Ethics*, Spinoza develops the rational principles on which politics is based: he shows that "proper utility", i.e. the life that is good for the individual, leads to the common utility by following reason, and, consequently, there can be no antagonism between the freedom of the individual to lead his life as he wishes and community membership. Spinoza first states the principle of sociability in an abstract form. Let us summarize the reasoning:

1. can only be good or bad that which has a certain relationship with us, that which has something in common with our own nature;
2. to the extent that something has something in common with us, it cannot be bad;
3. therefore, a thing is good for us insofar as it is consistent with our nature.

The central point of this demonstration is the idea **of agreement in kind**. Men agree in kind. However, Proposition 32 states:

> "Insofar as men are subject to the passions, they cannot be said to agree by nature[174]."

Spinoza justifies this assertion by an argument that concentrates his whole philosophy: the nature of a thing is its power, and the passions are man's powerlessness, so to agree in powerlessness cannot be to agree in nature. An agreement cannot be made on purely negative criteria: we cannot say that black and white agree because they are not red. Hence this conclusion:

> "things that agree in negation alone, that is, in what they do not have, do not in fact agree in anything." (Scolia of Proposition 32.)

Besides the logical value of this proposition, we must immediately grasp what it means in concrete terms: passions are not a source of union, but a source of division between men. It is obvious for the passions which lead to an exclusive possession, sexual love, wealth or power are at the origin of incessant conflicts. But not only do men differ from each other in their passions, but they are divided within themselves by their own inconstancy. This is why "anti-something" gatherings lead nowhere and, moreover,

---

174. We quote the *Ethics* in the Pléiade edition, translation by Roland Caillois.

disintegrate very quickly. Communities based on resentment or hatred of the other are necessarily enemies of the freedom of their members. There are many examples of this. And this is the main obstacle to the development of a powerful and sustainable social movement today. All the social movements that make demands are defensive movements, movements against this or that law, this or that government, this or that regression. There is no question of contesting their legitimacy: when you are at war, you have to defend yourself. But what characterizes the impotence of our time is the near impossibility of transforming reaction into action, of opening a new way, in short, to repeat it here, of doing anything other than disputing the length of the chain.

The process of this division, which Spinoza analyzes with subtlety, must be specified. Thus the love that two men have for the same woman cannot in itself be a source of hatred. It is even, according to Spinoza, an agreement in nature and "these two men are not unwelcome to each other insofar as they agree by nature, that is, insofar as they both love the same thing." If hatred intervenes between one, it is because the possession by one of the object loved is the loss of this same object for the other and therefore it is indeed in this that they differ. This situation comes from the fact that the object of love is a finite object. We see again how for Spinoza love and possession not only do not go together, but even contradict each other in their effects. Here again, we can draw some consequences. To strive to direct desires towards goods that can be shared is to increase sociability, whereas to channel desire towards goods that are the exclusive property of one - all consumer goods - is to excite rivalries that make individuals vindictive, hateful and finally divide the community into as many enemies.

Proposition 35 seems to provide a solution:

> "Insofar only as men live under the guidance of Reason, they always necessarily agree by nature."

By acting according to Reason, men do what is good for human nature and consequently "for every man." This is because to act according to reason is to act according to man's own nature, whereas to suffer is not to be the adequate cause of one's own acts, it is to undergo the action of forces outside oneself. But the scolie of this same proposition specifies what is to be understood by this. If men repeat that "man is a god for man", practical experience shows that these are only words. For:

> "Yet it is rare that men live under the guidance of reason; but that is how it is: most of them are jealous of each other and unbearable to each other."

The only thing that limits the outbursts is not that man lives under the guidance of reason - in fact no man always lives under the guidance of reason - but that he is a "social animal." Even if evil passions divide men, social tendencies are spontaneous. Spinoza takes the opposite view of Hobbes' thesis that man is a wolf to man. Hence the resumption of the polemic, recurrent in Spinoza, against the Theologians and the Melancholics who depreciate man and praise the beasts. These two propositions, and especially the scolies that follow the last one, state again that following virtue is acting for the good of all men. One cannot desire the good for oneself alone if one lives under the guidance of reason.

> "The sovereign good of those who practice virtue is common to all and all can equally find their joy in it." (Proposition 36.)

The good of a wise man does no harm to anyone! That is why it is perfectly possible to live free in the midst of men, in any case much freer than the hermit or the misanthrope who shuns company. And so:

> "The good that anyone who practices virtue desires for himself, he will also desire for other men, and all the more so because he has a greater knowledge of God." (Proposition 37.)

In the scolie I of proposition 37, Spinoza defines three terms to which we will return later:

- **Religion**: all the desires and all the actions of which we are causes as we have the idea of God;

- **Morality**: the desire to do good which originates from what we live under the guidance of reason;
- and **Honesty**: to be attached to others by the bonds of friendship.

This definition of virtue and of acting under the guidance of Reason allows Spinoza to settle a number of practical problems (for example, the relationship between man and animals). Scholia II lays out the foundations of morality, law and politics (which we find in the *Political Treatise*). It defines the rules of value judgments (praise and blame, merit and fault, just and unjust). But these rules cannot be abstract. They only make sense if we consider man in the state in which he lives in society. Man is a "social animal", but he must be considered in two ways: as a natural being, i.e. as an individual; and as a person bound by social ties to other men. For Spinoza, the individual dimension is just as essential as the social dimension. He thus defines the **Law of Nature** as the supreme right, expressed in terms almost identical to those of Hobbes.

> "Each one exists by the sovereign right of nature, and consequently each one by the sovereign right of Nature does what follows from the necessity of his nature; thus by the sovereign right of Nature each one judges what is good, what is bad, and thinks of his own utility according to his own naturalness." (Proposition 37 Schist II.)

But since men cannot all live under the guidance of reason, they must, in order to live together, renounce this natural right (in part) and unite with each other in order to increase their power. This is precisely the meaning of the constitution of the city and of political power. Each one then submits his own naturalness to the requirements of this political body (formed of the individual bodies of the subjects), but it is not an "unnatural" operation (besides, reason does not command anything that is unnatural), but the logical extension of the requirements of the preservation of the own nature of each individual. If the operation by which the political body is constituted suppressed the natural freedom of the individual, it would at the same time suppress all his own power, which cannot be and would lead the individual to annihilation or to revolt. A society made up of annihilated individuals, of formatted bodies all mechanically repeating the same gestures and the same words, a society completely subjected to capitalist logic, to put things in terms that Spinoza could not use, would be a dead society or one ready to collapse at the slightest shock.

From then on, we will be able to talk about fault and merit, that is to say, to find the basic rules of all morality. Spinoza makes fault derive, not from man's natural state (in the state of nature, it cannot be conceived), but from his civil state.

> "Therefore, the fault is nothing other than disobedience, which for this reason is punished under the sole right of the State."

Therefore:

> "It is clear that right and wrong, fault and merit are extrinsic notions, not attributes that explain the nature of the Spirit."

The role of **the institution** in the practical life of men is thus decisive. The political institution appears indeed as the means which makes it possible to make coexist the requirements of the Reason and the weakness of the men subjected to the passions.

So let us summarize. If we want to define what guarantees both individual freedom and social harmony, these are moral precepts (or ethics, if you like). The religious precept is to be understood here in Spinoza's sense: "all the desires and actions of which we are the cause insofar as we have the idea of God" are those that follow from our adequate ideas. For example, the desire for knowledge, but also all the precepts Spinoza expounds at the beginning of the fifth part of the *Ethics*, proceed from the "idea of God". Let us leave aside this aspect, which is very specific to Spinoza's thought and perhaps less easy to share than the others.

On the other hand, as far as morality is concerned, there is no difficulty: "the desire to do good which originates from what we live under the guidance of reason" is easy to share. Since no one seriously defends the absurd post-Sixties slogans such as "unfettered enjoyment" or "everything, right now", everyone will agree that the free life cannot be a life subject to destructive passions and that, consequently, the minimal social life supposes that one lives according to reason[175]. But morality for Spinoza does not consist only in wanting to live according to reason, but in doing good. We can take "doing good" in its most immediate sense. To do good is to be charitable, that is, to love one's neighbor, to come to his aid when he is in misery, to respect his physical and moral integrity. In short, all the basic prescriptions of a decent life that simple common sense knows. But a simple common sense that leads us far from "minimal ethics" and brings us closer to an ethics that a believer would not deny.

Finally, honesty, which consists in "attaching oneself to others through the bonds of friendship", makes it a virtue, according to a tradition that goes back to Aristotle and Cicero, two thinkers in the pantheon of republicanism. For his part, Rawls, a thinker of political liberalism, identifies the meaning of the principle of difference[176] as a principle of fraternity or civic friendship.

If we follow the path indicated by Spinoza, we have a strong ethic which is nevertheless compatible with a good part of the requirements of classical liberal thought (freedom of conscience, freedom to govern one's life, one's professional or sexual choices as one wishes, political freedoms), but an ethic which, unlike classical liberalism, positively articulates the link between individual and community.

The possibility of emancipation

The right political constitution, morality and honesty as Spinoza defines them, are conditions for the safeguarding of freedom. These conditions are not very difficult to achieve, if one states them simply, although, on

---

175. Rawls, to take an author from a rather different tradition from Spinoza, defines reasonableness as "the capacity of persons to have a sense of justice" (in *Justice and Democracy*, p. 172).

176. Rawls' theory of justice is based on two principles: the first is the principle of equal liberty for all and the second is the principle of difference, which states that "the basic structure of society is organized in such a way that it maximizes the primary goods available to the less advantaged, so that they use the basic freedoms available to all" (in *Justice and Democracy*, p. 184)

reflection, they require a radical rethinking of the fundamental tendencies of the era of unrestricted capitalism into which we have entered. The question therefore inevitably arises: are not these formulations (republicanism, a morality of freedom and community) moralistic abstractions with no relation to actual reality, condemned to remain pious wishes that may console the beautiful souls, but have no real effect?

To answer this question, one could scrutinize the slightest tremors of society to spot the swarming of movements that express the excess of life over scientific and technocratic representations, the regular overflowing of the borders drawn by the bureaucrats and managers of the State and the economy. The word "alternative" has become, to the point of being overused, a "magic" word. To win the minds of people, it is necessary to be in an alternative to the existing order. Even if the alternative merchant is only a charlatan, the use of this word as a means of capturing desires is revealing of a certain reality. Advertising is the ideology of our time, as Henri Lefebvre said. But the ideology, this upside down world, under certain aspects also expresses the real. And from this point of view, there is not only the recovery, to turn them in derision, of the old revolutionary slogans. In order to direct the desire of the client-consumer towards the merchandise to be sold, it is necessary that the image of the merchandise be associated with other things that have nothing to do with the world of the merchandise.

This "negative" argument could be complemented by a positive one that would expose the multiple, sometimes clumsy, attempts to escape the machinery of capitalism that are born from below. But the essential is elsewhere. As Marx argued, with arguments whose validity is finally completely assured only in our time, the very development of production contains within itself not the necessity, but at least the possibility of a historical bifurcation where the very destiny of humanity could be played out - "socialism or barbarism", said Rosa Luxemburg. In other words, capitalism can only survive by destroying the civilization from which it originated. It has created the possibilities for its own overthrow: the development of machinery, of science and technology, of the productivity of labor through national and then global cooperation, has made a comfortable life possible on the basis of a radical decrease in the necessary working time - that is, the working time imposed on any society to ensure the reproduction of humanity. But at the same time, these immense technical advances are threats to capitalist profit. Dead capital (the wealth accumulated in the form of the means of labor) suffocates living capital, i.e. the part of capital that reproduces capital on a larger scale, i.e. the capital that is exchanged for labor power.

The further accumulation of capital is only possible through the massive destruction of existing wealth and the impoverishment of the working classes. As a rule, the theory of absolute impoverishment wrongly attributed to Marx is false. But circumstances are proving it in some of the old advanced capitalist countries. It seems hard to understand that a country like France, whose wealth doubles about every thirty years, can no longer afford a system of social protection and pensions that it invented when it was broke and its inhabitants were eating on ration coupons. It is difficult to understand what logic is at work when on the one hand productivity increases by 2 to 3% every year (at least) and on the other hand political leaders and their masters repeat that we must "work more". The need for repressive laws (like HADOPI) is another example: potentially, the law of value is dying in a whole series of sectors where technical means make the value of goods fall to practically zero, but if goods fall to zero, capitalist profit also annihilates itself, and the law of value, a supposedly natural law, survives only under police and judicial surveillance.

The orthodox Marxists believed - and this was a religious belief - that capitalism would necessarily bring about its own demise, and their narrow conception of what they wanted to understand about Marx led them to see the overcoming of capitalism in the generalization of wage labor (often called "collectivism"). But this erroneous belief does not invalidate the analysis that shows the possibilities of which capitalism is full, possibilities that can only be realized if sufficiently strong and sufficiently numerous individuals appear to implement these potentialities.

Moishe Postone, after a rigorous reconstruction/reinterpretation of Marx's thought, comes to this conclusion:

> "The Marxian concept of the fundamental contradiction of capitalism is ultimately that of a contradiction between the *potential* of the general capacities of the species that have accumulated and their *alienated form existing* as constituted by the dialectic of the two dimensions of labor and time. The relation between the existing and its determined potential is at the heart of the Marxian conception of the possible overcoming of capitalism[177]."

It may be that no active social force will succeed in realizing these possibilities, because they do not depend on an "objective" dynamic but require action, that is, individuals acting in view of goals they have decided to set for themselves. Experience has shown in a century and a half that the only reaction of workers to the degradation of their working conditions leads at best to the "humanization" of capitalism (which is neither negligible nor despicable) and not to the overthrow of the system of domination that is wage labor.

All this would require development: separating society from its capitalist form is exactly what Marx called communism. Marx refused to cook in the pots of the future, but to draw the guidelines of a non-utopian communism and the means to achieve it, these are tasks that are necessary as soon as one maintains the perspective of human liberation as a political perspective[178].

The life of free men

Let us retrace the path we have taken. Freedom, the key word of modernity, is threatened on the political level, on the level of individual rights, on the very level of the metaphysical definition of man. Nevertheless, the capitalist mode of production contains in itself the possibility of its overcoming, and one could find evidence of this in the analysis of social

---

177. Postone (M.), *Time, work and social domination*, Mille et une nuits, 2009, p. 527.
178. We have given some milestones on this path both in *Le Cauchemar de Marx* and in *Revive la République!*

movements. But it remains to determine what we could expect from this social emancipation, which would also be a liberation of individuals. We have spoken enough about the political regime that would be the most favorable to freedom. But freedom is not limited to politics. It is perhaps even one of the great illusions of anti-Stalinist revolutionary Marxism: to have believed that "the masses" could permanently be mobilized to ensure the direction of society through workers' councils or "soviets". While classical civic humanism saw public life as the realization of man and at the same time a duty for each citizen, republicanism is conceived by admitting that citizens can be only remotely interested in public affairs.

Starting with the simplest, if we accept the definition of freedom as non-domination, freedom begins with the end of wage labor. Not the end of labor in general, a perspective that is both utopian and certainly catastrophic, but the end of wage labor, that is to say, of labor in its capitalist form, which is not labor in general to which we have unwisely added wage labor, but a system of domination of individuals. Marx gives a description of what is a social organization freed from wage labor. Thus:

> "Let us represent at last, for a change, an association of free men working with collective means of production and consciously expending their many individual labor forces as one social labor force[179]."

This association of free men, these associated producers who cooperate voluntarily and consciously, could be a workers' cooperative... but on condition that cooperation extends to the major part of the production system. For competing cooperatives selling their products on a market would be a disguised form of wage labor, with the most efficient cooperatives exploiting, without having sought it out, the cooperators of the least efficient. The ideal would therefore be a union of cooperatives planning production. Assuming a very utopian solution where the whole world would become communist, we would have a worldwide network of cooperatives planning production on a global scale. In reality, central

---

179. Marx (K.), book I, chap. I, 4.

planning would automatically generate a gigantic bureaucracy that would simply expropriate the producers and turn them back into de facto wage earners. Planning was the social foundation of the bureaucratic caste in the USSR; this is forgotten by those who sacrifice, even negatively, to the cult of personality and blame everything on the broad back of Koba the Terrible[180]. In the organization of the production of material life, one must be just as wary of constructivism as in political theory.

Let us add that the dogma of central planning simply neglects the fact that it is not only a question of planning production, but also of producing to satisfy needs, and thus of planning production in relation to consumption. But the social validation of a product intended to satisfy a need always occurs *ex post*, as economists say. And the producers themselves do not necessarily have the same interests or the same vision of things when they consider themselves as producers and when they consider themselves as consumers.

All this leads us to think that it is necessary to maintain the market, a market that would no longer be capitalist and whose scope could be much more limited than it is today. We will not develop this question any further: we have developed elsewhere a few leads in this field and above all we refer to the work of Tony Andréani on models of socialism, important work, but too little known and too little discussed[181]. In any case, Marx's general formula, that of the associated producers, can only come to life through the experience that men will make of it - even if we already have partial experiences, within the very heart of capitalist society, which indicate both the difficulties and the open possibilities.

But in the end, the freedom we have just been talking about is only a freedom framed by the necessity of reproducing the conditions of material life. It remains within the framework of a work that is absolutely not optional. This is why Marx adds that this new organization of production goes hand in hand with a radical reduction of the working day. This

---

180. Koba was the other pseudonym of Stalin during the underground period of Lenin's party.
181. See bibliography.

reduction is entirely possible both through technical progress that allows for an increase in labor productivity, through the reduction of production linked to the durability of products whose accelerated obsolescence is now programmed by capital, and through the elimination of waste and of the colossal costs of communication, advertising and everything else that is necessary to ensure the domination of capital over labor. There is no reason to believe that material needs will increase indefinitely: if men find in social and intellectual life higher satisfactions than those of consumption, they will no longer feel the need to buy the latest useless gadget. But while the theorists of "degrowth" advocate "voluntary frugality" and lecture individuals who buy flat screens (sic), we consider on the contrary, like Spinoza, that the limitation of desires fixed on things will come from human liberation. Proposition 42 of the fifth part of the *Ethics* states this excellent principle:

> "Beatitude is not the reward of virtue but virtue itself; and we do not experience joy because we repress our inclinations; on the contrary, it is because we experience joy that we can repress our inclinations."

As we can see, Spinozist frugality has nothing to do with the vows of poverty of the mendicant orders - all the more so since Spinoza considers that a comfortable life, allowing for the reasonable enjoyment of bodily pleasures, is one of the preconditions of virtue.

It remains to examine the essential. Beyond the eternal constraints linked to the necessity of reproducing the material conditions of human life, the field of a true freedom opens up, the one in which man is to himself his own end[182]. The young Marx, at the same time as he states *"the categorical imperative* to overthrow all social conditions in which man is a lowered, enslaved, abandoned, despicable being", defines the goal of the critique:

> "The criticism of religion disillusions man, so that he thinks, acts, forms his reality as a disillusioned man, who has become reasonable, so that he moves around himself and therefore around his true sun. Religion is only

---

182. See *above*.

the illusory sun that moves around man, as long as he does not move around himself[183]."

When man is not subjected to something external, but when he manifests in his activity his own human essence, this is precisely what is called praxis. The activities of manufacture (*poiêsis*) die out in the work (the work is more important than the implementation). On the contrary, in what concerns the praxis, it is the activity itself which is important. In praxis, man tends only to the perfection of his capacities to act, to his own perfection. A central concept in Marx's *Theses on Feuerbach* - which refers materialism and idealism back to back -, praxis is found in Italian philosophers and thinkers such as Labriola, Gentile or Gramsci who define Marx's philosophy as "philosophy of praxis". We can also stick to the Aristotelian definition that makes praxis the action guided by a thoughtful choice, that is to say by prudence (*phronêsis*). But this characterization is also that of happiness in the *Nicomachean Ethics*. In other words, man finds his true realization, he is really himself, that is to say really free, only in action guided by a reflective choice. Free action and activity subject to the necessity or domination of another person are thus opposed. The typical free action is the political activity, that is to say the activity by which each one participates in the collective deliberation in view of the common good.

If we are content to define by praxis all the activities in which the activity is as important, or even more important, than the result, in a life where man has a large amount of time to himself (leisure in the sense of the Ancients, *skholê* among the Greeks or *otium* among the Latins), many activities which would ordinarily be work or manufacture become in some way praxis. The amateur gardener or the Sunday tinkerer are generally not so much interested in the result as in an activity in which they can find themselves, recognize themselves. Hegel thus analyzes the processes of self-consciousness in artistic activity: man, by imposing his mark on external nature, removes its "fiercely foreign" character and recognizes

---

183. Marx (K.), *For a Critique of Hegel's Philosophy of Right*, in *Works III*, p. 383.

himself as a free spirit. When Marx sees the true freedom in the open possibility for each one to become a creator, he undoubtedly does not want to limit this creation to the fine arts!

Thus, gradually, the boundary between work and leisure becomes more permeable. Between work imposed by necessity - but over which one can acquire a large degree of control - and pleasure, there is a whole part of life that can be that of "free work", an expression that might seem an oxymoron as long as capital dominates. However, the idea that people can work and be useful to others freely, by choice, as a manifestation of their human essence, is so little utopian that even in societies where capital dominates, where everything is bought and sold, there are many who work voluntarily and find in it a worthy manifestation of their humanity. We could talk about the voluntary work that keeps alive all sorts of sports, cultural and humanitarian associations, etc., or about those computer scientists who dreamed of free Internet and make their software available to everyone[184], or about all those cultural activists who work to make culture accessible to all. Here again, we can measure the gap between the possible and the miserable reality imposed by the world of merchandise.

This is enough to know what a free life in a free republic could mean. What remains refers more directly to man's relationship with himself, to what lies beyond "the present life", as Spinoza says in the fifth part of the *Ethics*, where human liberation is identified with "the intellectual love of God". It was not our intention to lead the reader down this very steep path. Let us stick to the program we had set ourselves: to make a kind of inventory of the situation of freedom, under its different figures, at a time when a so-called liberalism seems to have triumphed everywhere. To think about this question lucidly, however, requires that we avoid two symmetrical errors. The first, well known, consists in putting flowers on the chains, in painting life in pink and in praising the comfortable and sweet servitude to the point of disgust in which a part of the privileged middle classes have lazily wallowed. The sophists and rhetors employed for this task are finally

---

184. Even if the free software is finally recovered by the capitalist machinery.

easy to unmask. The other flaw consists in painting life in black on black. Literally, this can be successful: pessimists are often more interesting than optimists. But there is a whole literature that is anti-capitalist, anti-imperialist, anti-liberal, willingly ready to see everywhere the plotting hands of diabolical dominators rather than to understand objective processes, and this literature that teaches us that we are fighting with our backs to the wall, that tomorrow will be even worse than yesterday, cultivates a despair as vain as the hopes of the fools who still believe in the progress willed by divine providence. Criticism is only worthwhile if it opens a new way. Let's leave once again, and to finish, the word to Marx:

> "Criticism has stripped away the imaginary flowers that covered the chain, not so that man would wear the prosaic and desolate chain, but so that he would shake off the chain and pluck the living flower[185]."

---

185. MARX (K.), *ibid.*

Bibliographic references

ANDERS (Günther), *L'Obsolescence de l'homme*, Éditions de l'Encyclopédie des Nuisances-Ivrea, 2005, translated from the German by Christophe David.

ANDRÉANI (Tony), *Le socialisme est (à) venir. 1. L'inventaire*, Syllepse, 2001, collection "Utopie Critique".

ANDRÉANI (Tony), *Le socialisme est (à) venir. 2. Les possibles*, Syllepse, 2004, collection "Utopie Critique".

ANDRÉANI (Tony) (ed.), *Le Socialisme de marché à la croisée des chemins*, éditions Le Temps des Cerises, 2003.

ANDRÉANI (Tony), *Un être de raison. Critique de l'homo œconomicus*, Syllepse, 2000.

ANGENOT (Marc), *L'Utopie collectiviste. Le grand récit socialiste sous la deuxième internationale*, PUF, 1993.

ARENDT (Hannah), *The Crisis of Culture*, Gallimard, Folio, 1972, trans. Patrick Lévy.

ARENDT (Hannah), *Condition of Modern Man*, Calmann-Lévy, 1961, 1983, reprinted in "Pocket", translated by Georges Fradier.

ATLAN (Henri), *L'Utérus artificiel*, Seuil, 2005.

BERLIN (Isaiah), *In Praise of Freedom*, Calmann-Levy, 1988.

BOCH (Anne-Laure), *Médecine technique, médecine tragique*, éditions Seli Arslan, 2009, with a preface by Pierre Magnard.

BODEI (Remo), *Destini personali. L'età della colonisazione delle coscienze*, Giangiacomo Fletrinelli éditore, 2002.

CHESNEAUX (Jean), *De la modernité*, La Découverte-Maspero, 1983.

COLLIN (Denis), *Le Cauchemar de Marx*, Max Milo, 2009.

COLLIN (Denis), *Comprendre Marx*, Armand Colin, 2006-2009.

COLLIN (Denis), *Lire et comprendre Machiavel*, Armand Colin, 2008.

COLLIN (Denis), *Revive la République*, Armand Colin, 2005.

COLLIN (Denis), *Morale et Justice sociale*, Seuil, 2001, collection "La couleur des idées".

COLLIN (Denis), *La Fin du travail et la Mondialisation, Idéologie et réalité sociale*, l'Harmattan, 1997, collection "L'ouverture philosophique".

COLLIN (Denis), *La Théorie de la connaissance chez Marx*, L'Harmattan, 1996.

FRASER (Nancy), *What is Social Justice? Reconnaissance et redistribution*, translated from English by Estelle Ferrarese, éditions La Découverte, 2005.

GRAMSCI (Antonio), *Quaderni del carcere*, Einaudi, edition in four volumes.

HABERMAS (Jürgen), *The Future of Human Nature. Vers un eugénisme libéral*, Gallimard, collection "Nrf Essais", 2002, translated from the German by Christian Bouchindhomme.

HARRINGTON (James), *Oceana*, preceded by *L'Œuvre politique d'Harrington* by POCOCK (JGA), translated from English by Claude Lefort and Didier Chauvaux, Belin, 1995.

HEGEL (GWF), *Principles of the Philosophy of Law*, translation by Jean Kervadec, PUF, collection "Quadrige".

HEGEL (GWF), *Encyclopédie des sciences philosophiques en abrégé*, translation by Maurice de Gandillac, Gallimard, Nrf, 1970.

HEGEL (GWF), *Phenomenology of Spirit*, Aubier, 1991, translated from the German by J.-P. Lefebvre.

HELLER (Agnes), *La Théorie des besoins chez Marx*, UGE, 1978, translated from the German by Martine Morales, preface by Jean-Michel Palmier.

HELLER (Agnes) & FEHER (Ferenc), *Marxism and Democracy. Beyond Real Socialism*, Maspero, 1981, translated from English by Anna Libera, introduction by Michael Löwy.

HOBBES (Th.), *Leviathan*, Sirey edition, 1971, trans. F. Tricaud.

Husserl (Edmund), *La Crise des sciences européennes et la Phénoménologie transcendantale*, Gallimard, reprinted in the collection "Tel", 1976, translated by Gérard Granel. Gérard Granel.

Lasch (Christopher), *La Culture du narcissisme*, Climats, 2000, translated from the American by Michel L. Landa, preceded by *Pour en finir avec le XXIe siècle* by Jean-Claude Michéa.

Lasch (Christopher), *La Révolte des élites et la trahison de la démocratie*, preface by Jean-Claude Michéa, translation by Christian Fournier, éditions Climats, 2003.

Lefebvre (Henri), *La Vie quotidienne dans le monde moderne*, Gallimard, Nrf "Idées", 1968.

Machiavelli (N.), *Œuvres complètes*, Robert Laffont, collection "Bouquins", 1996, translated from Italian by Christian Bec.

Marcuse (Herbert), *L'Homme unidimensionnel*, Le Seuil, 1970, translated from English by Monique Wittig (first French edition: 1968, éditions de Minuit).

Marx (Karl), *Œuvres*, edited by Maximilien Rubel, "La Pléiade", Gallimard, 4 volumes.

Marx (Karl), *Manuscripts of 1844*, translation and notes by Goujon, GF-Flammarion.

Nozick (R.), *Anarchy, State, Utopia*, PUF, 1988, collection "Libre échange", trans. Évelyne d'Auzac de Lamartine.

Pettit (Philip), *Républicanisme, une théorie de la liberté et du gouvernement*, translated from English by J.-F. Spitz and P. Savidan, Gallimard, 2004.

Postone (Moshe), *Time, Work and Social Domination*, Mille et une nuits, 2009, translated from English by Olivier Galtier and Luc Mercier.

Rawls (John), *Theory of Justice*, éditions du Seuil, 1987, translated from English by Catherine Audard.

Rawls (John), *Justice and Democracy*, éditions du Seuil, 1993, reprinted in the collection "Points", 2000. Introduction, presentation and glossary by Catherine Audard, translated from English by C. Audard, P. de Lara, F. Piron and A. Tchoudnowsky.

Rosselli (Carlo), *Socialismo liberale*, Introduzione e saggi critici di Norberto Bobbio, a cura di John Rosselli, Einaudi, Piccola biblioteca, 1973-2009.

Rousseau (Jean-Jacques), *The Social Contract*.

Simmel (Georg), *Philosophie de l'argent*, PUF, 1987, collection "Quadrige", 1999, translated from the German by S. Cornille and P. Ivernel.

Sklair (Leslie), *The transnational capitalist class*, Blackwell Publishing Ltd, 2001.

Spinoza, *Œuvres*, Pléiade edition, Gallimard.

Spitz (Jean-Fabien), *Le Moment républicain en France*, Nrf, Gallimard, 2005.

Stirner (Max), *The Unique and its Property*, SLIM editions, 1948.

Vico (G.), *La Science nouvelle*, Fayard, 2001, translated by Alain Pons.

Weber (Max), *Protestant Ethics and the Spirit of Capitalism*, Gallimard, collection "Tel", 2003, trans. Jean-Pierre Grossein.

Table of contents

Best sellers Max Milo Editions

Hitler's banker, Jean-François Bouchard

Confessions of a forger, Éric Piedoie Le Tiec

The Koran and the flesh, Ludovic-Mohamed Zahed

Governing by fake news, Jacques Baud

Governing by chaos, Collectif

A political history of food, Paul Ariès

Mad in U.S.A.: The ravages of the "American model",
Michel Desmurget

Mondial soccer club geopolitics, Kévin Veyssière

Putin: Game master?, Jacques Braud

Treatise on the three impostors: Moses, Jesus, Muhammad,
The Spirit of Spinoza

TV Lobotomy, Michel Desmurget